MW01000362

Children at Play

Howard P. Chudacoff

Children at Play

An American History

New York University Press • *New York and London*

NEW YORK UNIVERSITY PRESS
New York and London
www.nyupress.org

Library of Congress Cataloging-in-Publication Data
Chudacoff, Howard P.
Children at play : an American history / Howard P. Chudacoff.
p.   cm.
Includes bibliographical references and index.
ISBN-13: 978-0-8147-1664-9 (cloth : alk. paper)
ISBN-10: 0-8147-1664-4 (cloth : alk. paper)
1. Children—United States—History. 2. Play—United States—History.
3. Children—United States—Social life and customs.   I. Title.
HQ792.U5C46 2007
305.2310973—dc22   2007007865

*To Naomi, Aliya,
Goldie, and Sari.
Children I love.*

Contents

Acknowledgments

Researching and writing a book about children's play has enabled me to interact with a number of fascinating people and places, and I have benefited from their assistance. I especially acknowledge the support I received from the Kate L. Peterson Fellowship at the American Antiquarian Society of Worcester, Massachusetts, as well as the library staff, especially Carol Sandler, at the Strong National Museum of Play of Rochester, New York, which houses the Doll Oral History Collection. The John D. Rockefeller Library at Brown University, especially its librarians Michael Jackson and Steven Thompson, provided valuable aid, as did the special collections at Brown's John Hay Library. Pembroke Herbert and PRC Picture Research Consultants have made this book far more appealing than it otherwise would have been, and I am deeply appreciative of the encouragement and faith shown me by Eric Zinner and New York University Press.

I benefited from the research assistance of some very capable individuals, namely, Anna Galland, Sarah Blum-Smith, Danielle Slevens, and Hannah Copperman. Colleagues Steven Mintz, Gary Cross, and Paula Fass were especially generous in their support and comments on my work. Also, James T. Patterson, Judith E. Smith, Richard Meckel, Carolyn Dean, and Frederic Reamer provided valuable comments. Though I am exclusively responsible for any errors and misinterpretations, their contributions have strengthened the analysis.

When it came time to think and write about children's activities in the present era, I received valuable insights by observing and talking to children themselves. Leah Siegal-Reamer, Naomi Raznick, Aliya Thaler, Goldie Raznick, and Sari Thaler may not have constituted a representative sample, but their actions and insights proved worthwhile. Finally, as always, the support, editorial skill, and love of my wife, Nancy Fisher Chudacoff, has left a mark on everything I say and do, and I am forever grateful.

Preface

When I was a kid, I broke the child labor laws. Or, rather, my Uncle Jack did. At the age of twelve, I began working twenty hours a week during school vacations in the warehouse of Uncle Jack's business, Mutual Distributing Company, located in Omaha, Nebraska. By the time I was fourteen, I illegally worked full-time, forty-four hours a week, and I continued to do so every summer and at Christmas time through high school and college. Saturday mornings, too, eight o'clock until twelve.

Besides providing a nice income for a teenager, the job had two key effects on me. First, loading and unloading freight, packing and unpacking boxes alongside workingmen who at most had graduated from high school but who had a kind of commonsense wisdom, drew me to the lives of ordinary folk like them and sparked my eventual interest in social history. Second, the experience got me intrigued by the concept of play. Mutual Distributing, you see, was a toy wholesaling business. Uncle Jack bought toys (no bicycles or sporting goods) from manufacturers and sold them to small stores in eastern Nebraska and western Iowa, places such as drugstores and corner groceries that kept a limited inventory and had no space to store goods. Big-box establishments, e-trade, and the disappearance of independent retail enterprises have made wholesalers such as Mutual Distributing outmoded today, but in the 1950s and 1960s, Uncle Jack did a good business.

My job in a toy warehouse enabled me to be "present at the creation" of such now-classic playthings as the hula hoop, Frisbee, Barbie, whiffle ball, and more. It was an era before electronics came to dominate toy operations, so most commercial playthings were not complicated or expensive. Unconnected to a story line and unrestricted by inflexible rules or software, most of the toys could be used in both intended and unintended ways. Monopoly money was a necessity to the Parker Brothers game, but it also could serve countless purposes unrelated to the board game. A cap gun could enable its owner to play a specific role as, say, Hopalong Cassidy, but that owner also could use it for other roles such as a soldier or a space explorer. A teddy bear could be a pet, a friend, or a guest at a tea party. The point is that many formal toys promoted improvisation and stretched a child's imagination in a manner that, unlike today's electronic toys, was not ruled by a media backstory.

Before I began working in earnest for Mutual Distributing, I spent most of my out-of-school time with three other boys in my urban neighborhood. When weather permitted—and sometimes when it was inclement—we gathered outdoors, abjuring games and other indoor amusements, to engage in our own kinds of play. We roamed nearby vacant lots, taking roles for ourselves as soldiers, jungle explorers, or visitors to another planet. Often we embellished these pastimes with self-fashioned accoutrements: sticks serving as rifles, piled-up rocks serving as a fort, or discarded planks serving as a river raft. We also invented special rules for shooting baskets and a competition involving kicking a football. Mostly, however, we played "scrub," a bat-and-ball game with baseball equipment and a backyard ball field but playable with as few as three or four participants. I once joined a Little League baseball team, and I played in a Sunday morning basketball league to comply with my parents' desire to enrich my boyhood with some adult-guided structured play, but I much preferred the informal competitions of our neighborhood gang.

With these stimuli swirling around me—the toys of Mutual Distributing Company; the fascination with the social history of ordinary people; the recollections of playing with Tim, Tom, and Bob (note the all-male retinue)—I decided to write a history of children's play in America. But from the beginning, I wanted the project to be different. Most historical inquiries into the nature of children's play—and by "play" I mean amusing activities that have behavioral, social, intellectual, and physical rewards—have examined activities and objects constructed by adults for the benefit of children. As a result, formal games, mass-produced toys, organized sports, and the like have been identified as the principal components of girls' and boys' diversions. Yet, as anthropologists and psychologists know, children have always cultivated their own underground of unstructured and self-structured play, which they did not often talk about with adults. This book attempts to peek into that underground; it focuses as much on what children did as on what adults thought and wanted children to be doing.

I argue in the following pages that from a child's perspective, play serves as a means of asserting autonomy, and I examine the ways that this process ebbed and flowed over different eras of American history. I believe that generally, and in a complex way, children's ability to play independently has eroded over time and that in the modern era this shrinkage has had unfortunate, if not perilous, consequences. My analysis treads a hazard-strewn path because every reader will have lived a childhood and will have read about and observed children at play. Each reader may already have preconceived attitudes about play, some of which may correspond with my evidence and interpretations; others might dispute them. I do not wish to use historical analysis as the basis for a plea that children should run completely free, nor do I intend the book as an indictment that holds adult obsession with structuring every hour of children's lives responsible for current problems such as childhood obesity, drug use, delinquency, and the like. Nevertheless, I hope to provide historical depth to these and related issues and illuminate in a nuanced way a vital but overlooked dimension of American culture.

In constructing my analysis, I have tried to listen to what historian Harvey Graff has called "voices of the past."[1] Thus my major resources consist of several dozens of children's diaries and several hundred autobiographical recollections of childhood. These first-person accounts are complemented by primary-source surveys of children's use of time collected by educators, psychologists, anthropologists, journalists, and market researchers. I also synthesize from secondary works published by a wide range of social scientists, journalists, and others who have studied children and play. And I attempt to reconstruct the larger context affecting children in each chronological period by applying census data, along with information from child-rearing manuals and secondary studies, to delineate pertinent demographic, technological, social, and economic patterns.

First-person accounts and reminiscences offer extremely useful insights into children's behavior and culture, but, like all retrospective sources, they also can be fraught with biases and limitations. Memory, even of recent events, can contort actuality, cracking the barrier between truth and fiction. Post-structuralist critics have challenged the genre of recollection, arguing that memoirs and autobiographies are really acts of inventing a life, a form of storytelling that is mediated by the ways that their writers wish to interpret their lives to others and to themselves.[2] There is no doubt that many of the autobiographies that I have read during research for this book were written by individuals who were attempting to create a persona. Moreover, I recognize that the experiences that diarists and, especially, autobiographers chose to write about, especially those of childhood, were most frequently blissful; the unhappy childhood recollections they related usually involved the death of a dear one or a tragedy such as a house fire. Nevertheless, I agree with Graff's argument that, if read carefully, personal accounts can provide direct insights into how people grew up and how they acted as agents in their own history.[3] No other source offers so many insights into the experiences of childhood. An individual account, if taken alone, can be misleading. But in the aggregate, patterns do emerge, and from these patterns one can perceive consistencies and varieties of behavior, as well as change over time.[4]

Personal accounts also contain class biases: most of them have been written by the most literate, the most introspective, and often the most successful people. Yet I also have been able to draw from testimonies left by "nonelite" people, as well as by those who became famous. Accounts by working-class men and women, narratives collected in the 1930s from former slaves by the Works Progress Administration (WPA), Indian autobiographies, and immigrant memoirs have been consulted, along with observations of children written by explorers, clergymen, and politicians. Moreover, most writers of autobiographical accounts were "ordinary" as children, and most had common childhood experiences; only in adulthood did they become cultural or social elites.

Cognizant that first-person accounts and professional surveys cannot be used alone, I have incorporated observations and theories from other social sciences, as well as findings from important historical works by scholars such as Bernard Mergen, Gary Cross, Steven Mintz, Stephen Kline, Joseph Ilick, Harvey Graff, and Karin Calvert. The scholarship of Brian Sutton-Smith, probably the most prolific and iconoclastic analyst of children's play of the past half century, has provided valuable insights, as have the writings of anthropologist Helen Schwartzman and the market and media studies of Stephen Kline. Also, though mine is not a study of toys and games, I have researched some particular material aspects of children's play culture that have not garnered much scholarly attention but have had important roles in both reflecting and restricting play. These include the chapbooks and ephemera of the nineteenth century, the alternative ways children used commercial products in the early twentieth century, the Doll Oral History Collection at the Strong National Museum of Play, Rochester, New York, and more recent play features such as double Dutch (the jump-rope games of African American girls), the American Girl phenomenon, and internet game sites.

What I mean by "children" is the age group between about six and twelve. These years mark the period that Freud identified as characterized by "latency," when children direct their energies toward nonsexual activities such as forming friendships, athletics, and hobbies.[5] In Erik Erikson's scheme of personality development, this stage involves a crisis of competence and transition from the world of home to the world of peers.[6] It is a time when children learn that their world is structured by gender and age.[7] Some pediatricians have labeled this period "real" childhood, separated from infancy and early childhood on one side and adolescence on the other. Marketers call it the age of "tweens."[8] And probably most colorful—and accurate—is Linda Perlstein's definition of children at this age as "a species that hungers for freedom as it lives on reliance."[9] Whatever its qualities, this life stage is from a historical perspective the least-studied cohort of childhood but one in which play has had significant meaning.

After a brief discussion of definitions and contexts in chapter 1, I follow a chronological path from colonial times to the present. Though specific years bound each succeeding chapter, the periods represented are not intended to be discrete; rather, I consider them as approximate and, in some respects, overlapping. Much of the text, however, focuses on the twentieth century because I believe that it is during this period that the most important and contrasting developments in the history of children's play occurred.

The scope of this book is intentionally broad, making it unfeasible to provide a focused examination of every population subgroup in every context and at every point in time. But when possible, I do attempt to be sensitive to differences related to race, class, ethnicity, place (urban-rural-suburban), and, especially, gender. For the most part, however, children who were and are exceptional because of circumstantial and physical qualities—that is, kids who have been institutionalized, who had and have disabilities, who belonged and belong to criminal street gangs—have not received attention. I recognize also that for much of the American past, boys' and girls' daily schedules

were filled with higher priorities than play—chiefly, family responsibilities, work, and school—and that they often lacked time for nonutilitarian diversions. Nonetheless, play has been and remains a central
element of children's culture, an institution that youngsters jealously
claim for their domain.

Introduction

"WORK CONSISTS OF whatever a body is *obliged* to do," Tom Sawyer lectured to his friends, and "Play consists of whatever a body is not obliged to do."[1] Mark Twain's definition of play seems so simple, so clear. Yet those who have observed and thought about the play of children have embellished the concept with a dizzying array of variations and qualifications. Articulating a single acceptable definition of play is almost impossible. In fact, the *International Encyclopedia of the Social and Behavioral Sciences* admits that "No one definition of play is necessary or sufficient" and that it is "a controversial and unresolved topic."[2] An anthropologist's concept differs from a sociologist's, whose concept differs from a psychologist's, and so on. Most agree that a child's play has a purposeless quality—Tom's view that it is not work —but they also agree that play does have a function that is immediate in its behavioral, social, intellectual, and physical rewards and in the development of the child into an adult.

For the most part, the theorists—all of them, of course, adults— link the play of children to another simultaneously simple and complex concept that probably would have satisfied Tom Sawyer: fun, meaning the feeling of bliss and amusement. Play, in this regard, is the spontaneous, joyous activity of children. But the experts also conclude that play has functional, utilitarian qualities related to a child's development and learning. An individual, according to a common school of thought among educators, psychologists, and philosophers, acquires vital social, emotional, physical, and cognitive skills through play, thereby learning how to prepare for a future role as a productive adult. At the same time, play is said to ease a child's adjustment to the present and make life meaningful. Play, say the experts, inspires imagination and invention, helping children attain positive emotions and control negative ones.[3]

The dynamic factors that characterize play are legion. They traverse a spectrum from elation and freedom to tension, conflict, and destructiveness. Along this path lie various intensities of behavior: fantasy, competition, risk, and mimicry.[4] Some kinds of play, including such competitive sports as Little League baseball and youth soccer, or the activities sponsored by commercial play spaces, such as Kids Sports Network and Discovery Zone, fall under adult supervision; they are formal and bound by rules, and they take place in predetermined environments. Other play activities—interactive experiments occurring in children's museums, for example—are semiformal; adults facilitate play activity but do not directly control it. Still other kinds of play are completely informal, improvised, and "childish," involving what some psychologists believe to be children's innate biological impulses to investigate and engage with their world and to amuse themselves in unstructured ways.[5] Thus, daydreaming and exploring have been considered playful activities. But so, too, are child-instigated games and sports, such as playing "house" or pick-up baseball, that require memory, strategy, and dramatizing but transpire away from adult scrutiny.

Equally important, different children play in vastly different ways. Age, sex, social class, access to time, and other characteristics affect the preferences, style, and quality of play. And what might be deemed as "fun" play to one child might not be so to another, and what a particular child might consider as play one day may not seem so the next.[6] A condition of innocent joy is not the sole factor present in play, for what passes as playful activity may also be dangerous, cruel, destructive, or unpleasant. French philosopher Roger Caillois, for example, noted that play could involve "endlessly cutting up paper with a pair of scissors, pulling cloth into threads, breaking up a gathering, . . . [and] disturbing the play or work of others."[7] Children who may be deficient in certain social, physical, or intellectual capabilities, whether from lack of maturity or from permanent developmental incapacity, may find no delight in a particular game or activity that is beyond their faculties. Physical or psychic injury can result from even innocent play, such as might ensue from climbing a tree, bicycling on a rough surface, or being the target of snowballs, and some activities that a child might enjoy, such as capturing insects or bullying other kids, could also be malicious and sadistic. Thus, as much as the concept of children's play invokes positive reactions, it can have a darker side.[8]

As soon as childhood became a subject of serious social scientific study at the end of the nineteenth century, children's play came under close scientific scrutiny. Adopting a developmental model of child-hood as a rehearsal for adulthood, many observers designated play as the "child's work" and the "principal business of childhood."[9] To these experts, play was not the opposite of work but, rather, another form of it, an activity so vital as to demand adult supervision.[10] But then and now, if asked, a child would probably offer a definition of play that is more akin to Tom Sawyer's than to the serious qualities that are important to parents and scholars, for to a child play always has meant freely experiencing joy, independence, and, above all, as Tom avowed, not working.

Tom's definition of play as something a person is not obliged to do has particular relevance when it is considered from a child's per-spective—which is what Mark Twain, from his own view of child-hood, was trying to express. A child's viewpoint—and here I mean specifically a child from the age group six to twelve that is the focus of this book—might fit the model of psychologist Catherine Garvey, who split the concept of children's play into four components. In her scheme, play first of all is pleasurable, and thus it has positive effects. Second, play has no extrinsic value, no large objectives; it is inherently unproductive. Third, play is voluntary; as Tom Sawyer noted, it is freely chosen, not obligatory. Fourth, play involves active engagement on the part of the player.[11] Mostly, as Brian Sutton-Smith, the most prolific and insightful play scholar, has pointed out, children consider play as "valued personal experience," but otherwise it is "inexplica-ble." Thus, he adds, "we don't know why children play, even if they can't help doing it."[12]

My consideration of play as a component of children's culture in-volves four contexts. First is the environment: the setting(s) where play activity takes place. Second involves the materials: the instru-ments (or absence thereof) that facilitate play activity. Third is the dramatis personae: how many and who is or are playing, as well as the relationships among those playing, including solo players. Fourth is freedom: how much control a child or children have over their play activity and what risk(s) that autonomy might entail. These contexts frame the analyses presented in the following chapters.

Environment

The site of their play activity has always served as the most basic factor in children's abilities to assert their own culture. Though play theoretically can take place anywhere, the three main play settings for children have been and remain: nature (woods, fields, parks, etc.), public spaces (chiefly the street and the playground), and the home (including the yard and indoor space). As dependents and partially developed beings, children grow up in a world they have not constructed, a world ruled by their elders. Yet children have always sought to create spaces for themselves both within and outside the environment circumscribed by adult regulations. As they sought, co-opted, and sometimes were granted play spaces, children became connoisseurs of rural fields and woods; city byways and buildings; and indoor bedrooms, attics, and basements—places where they could keep adults at a distance.[13]

As the United States became increasingly urbanized, protecting that distance posed a special challenge for city youngsters, who of necessity had to incorporate and transform objects and settings of the cityscape into their play. Rural children often had more opportunities to claim unused spaces as their own; they could take over a hillside or enter the woods and engage in what both Silas Felton, growing up in Massachusetts in the 1780s, and R. L. Duffus, growing up in rural Vermont in the 1890s, called "roving" or "roaming."[14] Urban youngsters, however, more than counterparts in the countryside, had to negotiate and share their play areas with other kids and with adults. Both rural and urban children had to define and recognize safe zones and danger zones, marking or adjusting boundaries, but youngsters in cities had to do so as they confronted the changing dynamics of buildings, sidewalks, streets, and vacant lots.[15] Autobiographers frequently recalled using city streets as play environments. Bellamy Partridge, raised in upstate New York in the 1880s, labeled a nearby street a "family playground" for himself and his siblings. Sarah Bixby Smith, who spent her childhood in Los Angeles in the late nineteenth century, referred to a street corner as "our neighborhood playground." And Henry May cherished memories of converting public spaces in Berkeley, California, in the 1920s into "inexhaustible playgrounds."[16] To youngsters like these, the urban counterpart to rural children's "roaming" was simply "hanging out," inhabiting and exploring the environment for their own purposes.

The environment, whether in a city, town, farm, or forest, functioned as more than just an imposed backdrop for play. Children interacted with and transformed the play setting in myriad ways. In the countryside, kids cleared brush and rocks to create campsites, collected and cut branches to build forts and playhouses, and dammed streams to create waterways for miniature boats. City kids scavenged and appropriated objects from streets and alleys, and they transformed the built environment into an active player for their games. Two girls wishing to play jump rope, for example, could tie one end of a line to a lamppost or protrusion from a building so that only one had to swing the rope while the other jumped. Boys used brick walls and stoops as inanimate competitors as well as boundaries in ball games, and their play often altered the environment drastically, as when an errant ball shattered a window or when some other destruction resulted from their active play.[17]

By transforming and incorporating the environment into their play, children also experienced the landscape as a battleground. While uninhabited nature might have lacked adult occupancy, plant and animal life sometimes got in the way and required forceful removal. Vegetation, insects, and small creatures not only acted as nuisances but also could be victims of kids' destructive behavior. Several autobiographers, for example, recalled hunting and capturing an insect, tying a thread around it or removing one of its legs, and using it for sadistic play. The contest over space was more intense in crowded cities, where, aside from playgrounds—which adults officially designated as children's spaces, though kids challenged adults for control of these sites[18]—territory had multiple users and multiple claimants. Occasionally, children could annex unoccupied urban sites such as a vacant lot or an unused alley, laying out boundaries by consent or formally with chalk, boards, or some other marker. More frequently, children had to struggle against adults and against each other over public spaces. On a given city block, urban folklorists Amanda Dargan and Steven Zeitlin have observed, "children, the elderly, automobile drivers, parents, store owners, strangers, the fire department, sanitation workers, and city authorities [have had to] negotiate use of spaces."[19] When the young competed with each other (sometimes violently) or with adults (such as with shopkeepers or police officers), disputes often arose over control of turf, and those children who succeeded in the contest won a sense of ownership and a right to free play. Youngsters, according to one observer, "seize the opportunity to play as the opportunity arises, inserting the game into the interstices of the city's grid and schedule."[20]

Material Culture

In the modern era, the concept of play has connoted doing something with toys, and the concept of toys usually implies mass-produced, commercially marketed objects and games. But historically, both play itself and the meaning of a toy have been more complex than this assumption implies. The term "toy" as an artifact of childhood is of recent vintage. In premodern societies, literature on children rarely mentioned toys, and only a few depictions of children in artwork included toys. Many of the objects that today might be considered children's toys—dolls and miniatures of various sorts—were often the decorative possessions of adults, especially of adults with means, as much as of children. Games also were as much an adult as a young people's pastime. Some historians even maintain that before the modern era the most common form of children's play occurred not with toys but with other children—siblings, cousins, and peers.[21]

Thus, at least until recently, adults have valued manufactured toys more than children have—with the exception of a few items that youngsters seem to have cherished, such as dolls, sleds, bicycles, and skates. Most formal toys owned by children traditionally were received as gifts given by adults, ostensibly as a means to provide happiness but also to promote education (blocks), comfort (stuffed animals), stimulus to the imagination (crayons), companionship (dolls), simulation of adult activity (miniature tools and tea sets), and more. Adults also have used toys as bribes, instruments for bonding and affection, and diversions to keep youngsters from interfering with grown-ups' activities.[22] Modern consumer society has placed such high value on formal toys that anything else that children collect and play with often is labeled as "junk."[23]

But the "junk" of childhood has always carried more significance than most parents and child-study experts assumed. Indeed, the term "plaything" is perhaps more applicable than "toy" to the material culture of childhood: not only could play take place anywhere, but also a child could use practically anything as a plaything.[24] Thus, children have transformed space to enhance their play, and they have transformed objects as well. For example, historian Bruce Catton, recollecting his humble boyhood in Benzonia, Michigan, in the early 1900s, wrote about fashioning a "Kentucky rifle" from a broomstick. Growing up in Oklahoma in the 1930s, Estha Brisco Stowe "improvised with whatever became available." African American youngsters on the lowest end of both the socioeconomic and the social scales needed to be especially inventive. Ruby Berkley Goodwin, born in 1903 and raised in DuQuoin, Illinois, remembered how her friends "salvaged rubber-tired wheels from broken Christmas wagons and made bullet-headed expresses that raced with incredible speed." And, lacking a wagon or bicycle to transport her, Elizabeth Laura Adams, a black girl growing up in Santa Barbara, California, transformed her living-room carpet into a "magic rug" that could carry her to the moon.[25] In many ways these informal artifacts, which children had to purposefully seek out rather than receive as gifts, and their imaginative uses reveal more about children's culture than do manufactured toys, because the formal toys—dolls, vehicles, board games—as goods purchased mostly by adults, more accurately have reflected adult culture, at least until the onset of the television era in the latter half of the twentieth century.[26] Thus, like the meaning of "play site," the meanings of "toy" and "plaything" have been contested between children and adults.[27]

The differences of meaning often have revolved around the perceived function of toys. Parents, educators, and psychologists have generally favored toys that they believe promote their version of children's creativity and knowledge, scorning toys that, to them, appear as nonutilitarian indulgences. For much of the twentieth century, and into the twenty-first as well, so-called educational toys—sturdy objects and games designed explicitly to expand intellectual, motor, or adaptive skills—were seen as the most suitable for children, and companies such as Playskool (founded in 1928) and Fisher Price (founded in 1930) profited heavily by marketing wooden[28] pull toys, blocks, puzzles, and games that won applause from educational and child-safety experts. The goal was to extend the function of schools into children's free time and impose parental control of play as a bulwark against crass consumerism. The ideology of educational play and toys resulted in play being labeled the "child's work" and toys as children's "tools."[29]

From a child's perspective, of course, "work" and "tools" rarely exist on the conceptual horizon. As the Swedish sociologist Birgitta Almqvist has noted,

> Children do not say "Now I'll improve my thinking by means of constructional play." Or "Now I'll play something that can develop my creativity." They just play, and usually they do not do one instead of the other. Rather, they say, "Let's take all the blocks and pretend we build the highest house in the world."[30]

Even though mass popular culture and the media have, to a considerable extent, overtaken parents as arbiters of children's toy tastes, the experts overestimated the importance of toys. Research has demonstrated that kids usually play with most commercial toys for only a short time, and, when not relegating a toy to the back of the closet, they rebel against adult intentions in various ways by creating their own styles of amusement. They assert independence, for example, by inventing their own rules for a board game or by taking miniature people out of a dollhouse and stuffing them into a toy vehicle that was never intended to be used in conjunction with the dollhouse or its figures.[31] Moreover, as suggested by the testimonies above, the most popular playthings have been those informal objects that children fashion or discover themselves. It is within this form of children's material culture that the imagination is stimulated to productive (and destructive) ends, and where, as Sutton-Smith has argued, "toys are meant for the empowerment of play rather than as teaching machines that can replace what parents want their children to learn."[32]

Individual and cultural variations strongly affect choices and uses of toys. According to child psychologists, young children, below age six, seem to need more structured, realistic toys to assist their pretend play, while preteen youngsters more easily transform ordinary objects into playthings. In addition, children from disadvantaged socioeconomic groups usually own fewer and less elaborate toys than those of more affluent groups. In the eighteenth and early nineteenth centuries, American Indian and African American slave children, as well as white children on subsistence farms, owned almost no formal toys; they or their family members made most of what they played with. By

INDIAN BOYS AT PLAY. This sixteenth-century engraving reveals Indian youths grouped together away from adults, amusing themselves while also practicing hunting and warrior skills they would need as adults. *Library of Congress*

the twentieth century, expanding consumer culture enabled children of all socioeconomic groups to have access to at least some commercially produced toys, though, of course, family means limited the quantities and quality of products.

Above all, gender has enveloped age differences and has had numerous consequences in play. For example, toys can control children's play culture differently according to gender: a Barbie doll, whose "story line" revolves around fashion, governs how girls talk about their object of play, while the once-popular *Transformers* television show, with its specific heroes and villains, determined how boys related to and played with Transformer toys. Alternatively, gender can influence attitudes about a toy: a boy would have different kinds of interaction with Barbie than a girl would. Diverse studies by psychologists have shown that at young ages, girls are more likely to play pretend games with toys, especially dolls, than boys do, while after about age seven the pattern reverses as boys, who by the time they are preteens possess vehicles, machines, and military toys that girls generally do not receive, have more paraphernalia around which to structure their play.[33] Though some research argues, debatably, that, at least in part, biological factors of gender determine toy preferences, there is no doubt that social and cultural influences create gender differences in choices as early as age two. Parents and same-sex peers have traditionally established whether a toy is appropriate for a boy or girl, and in the modern consumer age advertisements portray girls and boys much differently in their relationship to toys. Girls are often shown interacting with—that is, adopting an identity separate from their toy—while boys are shown identifying with their toys: that is, assuming the character of the toy as their own.[34]

Whatever the variations, there is strong belief that toys have some kind of effect on children. But just exactly what that effect is has provoked extensive debate. Some writers decry the power of certain toys to reinforce sex stereotypes (dolls and action figures, for example), teach violence (guns and video games), promote sexual promiscuity (physiological realism in dolls), stifle imagination, suppress creativity, and serve as opiates for purposes of social control. Others see toys as promoting socialization, building confidence (as a youngster masters a skill), and abetting autonomy. To adults, the "best" toys are those that stimulate "healthy" imaginative thought and simulation of an ordered society. But, as I suggest in the following chapters, to a child, toys are mostly objects of fun, vehicles to fantasy, and objects that need not be taken too seriously. For example, as Elizabeth Laura Adams proved as she sat on a carpet and pretended to be carried to the moon, children do not need toys to imagine.[35] And, as Sutton-Smith has written, "It is not so much what the toy does by itself, but in what way it gives the child an instrument with which to express and manipulate the cultural forces that bear upon him or her."[36]

Dramatis Personae

Parents and other child specialists have long believed that children learn special skills of socialization by playing with other youngsters. In addition to the ways that these abilities serve the needs of adult society by making kids adults-in-training, children acquire "play skills" that enable them to interact more pleasurably with each other and to cultivate friendships. Though over the past two centuries children seem to have spent increasing amounts of time in solitary play,[37] they have always fostered their own culture within communities of those who share their same values and activities. Through their play, children form what sociologists Schlomo Ariel and Irene Sever have called a "mini society," usually determined by similarity of age, residential proximity, and social interaction of parents. (Similarity of gender must be included as well.) Within these societies, which are often spontaneously created, children follow a system of unwritten convention regarding the sharing of playthings, the boundaries of play territory, and the qualifications for membership in the playgroup. Though Ariel and Sever observed Arab Bedouin children, they concluded that there are customs and languages to social play that are universal, a finding that has been supported by other social scientific studies. Thus, as anthropologist Douglas Newton has asserted, "The world-wide fraternity of children is the greatest of savage tribes, and the only one which shows no signs of dying out."[38]

In their text on the psychology of childhood and adolescence, L. Joseph Stone and Joseph Church have validated the power of a preteen (or, as it is currently known, "tween") children's culture in America:

> Among his friends, the middle-years child lives in a special culture with its own traditional games, rhymes, riddles, tricks, superstitions, factual and mythical lore, and skills, transmitted virtually intact from one childhood generation to the next, sometimes over a period of centuries with no help from adults and often in spite of them.[39]

The peer culture of children, however, is far from homogeneous. How a child plays depends on what qualities he or she brings to the play situation. As with toy choices, playgroup associations are heavily influenced by age (intellectual and emotional age, as well as biological age), sex, race, ethnicity, socioeconomic status, and location (urban, suburban, or rural).[40] Perhaps even more than with toy choices, gender has proven to be the most important factor in determining play partners. Though exceptions have existed and continue to exist, such as when a brother might be enlisted to play house with his sister and her friends or when a "tomboy" girl engages in sports contests with some neighbor boys, most kids have adhered to a strictly sex-segregated play world. Whether in Indian villages, plantation slave quarters, small-town America, urban ethnic neighborhoods, public playgrounds, or suburban yards, preadolescent boys and girls very seldom have played jointly.

Playmates have powerful influence over the kinds of roles children assume, even beyond those related to gender. Child psychologist Fritz Redl pithily made the point—to which many parents would subscribe—when he suggested that preadolescence was the time in which "the nicest children begin to behave in the most awful way."[41] He was referring to the "split personality" of school-age children: their "nice" behavior in front of and with adults (usually not in front of their parents, however), and their "awful" behavior with friends and away from adult attention. Though Redl and other observers applied the distinction mostly to preadolescent boys, girls could and do fit the model, too. For example, Louise Dickinson Rich, raised in rural Massachusetts, recalled following her parents' restrictions on where she could play one hour and breaking into her town's stables and horsing around on the wagons and snowplows the next; Caryl Rivers reminisced from her suburban Baltimore childhood that she did the expected "girl" things some of the time but also was "daring and resourceful" when she accompanied her girlfriends on invasions of her town's sewer pipes.[42]

In a larger sense, the assumption has always been that adults—mainly parents but also teachers and helping professionals—were, and are, the only people capable of molding children into proper (well-behaved), productive citizens. Left to their own devices and in the company of peers, children supposedly pursued "childish" instincts and behaved badly, if not evilly. To be sure, the dramatis personae of play sometimes did engage in acts that were inappropriate, dangerous, and destructive. But adults who observed or theorized about children at play often overlooked the ways that kids, alone and with peers, might have used their seemingly aimless play to achieve a positive result by different means. Humorist Robert Paul Smith expressed this point succinctly: "When I was a kid, there was a lot of loose talk . . . about how a father was supposed to be a pal to his boy. This was just another of those stupid things grownups said. It was our theory that the grownup was the natural enemy of the child. . . . What we learned we learned from another kid."[43]

Freedom

For much of the time, adults have used their superiority in age and status to prevail in the conflict over what the younger generation should do and how they should act, and children have peacefully acquiesced. It is their nature to obey and want to please. For purposes of safety, education, socialization, and family mutuality, children have always needed adult supervision. Yet, there is a powerful tradition that maintains that the pleasure derived from play is the basic freedom of childhood.[44] Children have always strived to gain control over their play, while adults have endeavored to define the "right way" and "wrong way" for playing.[45] In some circumstances, adults used guilt and sin as means to regulate children's playful behavior; at other times, they applied physical punishment or the threat of such punishment; and at still other times, they used instruction, persuasion, or material inducement. In general, the older generation has always wanted play to be rational so that it will lead a child to some beneficial end such as wisdom and proficiency.

But often youngsters have employed their guile to cultivate an underground of self-structured and informal play that they did not care to talk about and that the older generation undervalued or did not approve. Preadolescent children, especially, were and are often willing to defiantly accept risk and to "offend against their status."[46] What youngsters tried to do on their own did not always result in fun in an idealized sense; as mentioned previously, it may have been irrational, hazardous, or antisocial. And, what to a child might have appeared to be free choice may actually have been manipulated by educators, television programming, advertisement, and the constraints of a computer program.[47] Regardless, preadolescent youths have always used their play as a means of seeking and asserting independence from adult constraints.

As they grow up, children participate in what one historian has called "the dialectical dance of generations," an exercise that involves stepping in, out, and around a whirl of authority, morality, and tradition. Whether it takes place inside or outside the family, that dance has contained inherent intergenerational conflicts, and children have confronted those conflicts in diverse ways. Their expressions of their own culture—whether in games, songs, jokes, or hobbies—are tied tightly to values and behaviors that have been transmitted from an older generation. In premodern America, religion and the family sanctioned (and in many places still sanction) games, books, music, and general playtime. In more recent eras, schools, public agencies, private organizations, and marketers have joined (and sometimes replaced) parents in infusing children's culture with seemingly contradictory themes of social purpose and meaningless fantasy. In modern American society, teeming with experts, adults impose on children forms of play to achieve therapeutic, academic, and economic goals. And at all times, the cultural orientation of parents has guided what children say and do.[48]

The influential Swiss child psychologist and philosopher Jean Piaget once suggested that children's culture consists of "complementary" interactions with adults and "reciprocal" interactions with peers. The former relationship involves a one-way imposition of authority on children. How free children are in this relationship became a matter of debate. Piaget believed that interactions only with adults, because of their unilateral nature, could inhibit emotional growth, especially in areas such as moral development. Sociologist Erving Goffman took this conclusion further, likening children to prisoners and mental patients, whose playtime (Goffman focused on what he called "game time") was completely constrained by adult authorities. While not wishing to remove the "complementary" role of adults from children's lives, Piaget reasoned that the reciprocal and negotiated behavior that characterize the freer qualities of peer interaction encourage children to assume more varied roles and to use more varied language that, in turn, would aid their adjustment to society.

Russian psychologist L. S. Vygotsky, in contrast, believed that child-adult interactions are critical in enabling the young to develop intellectually and morally. To Vygotsky, problem solving should be mediated by adult help, and freeing children to act in isolation of that supervision hinders their ability to acquire new skills. To be sure, Piaget and his followers understood that not all peer relationships are reciprocal; at times, one child can teach, lead, or bully another in a unilateral, complementary way. At other times, such as when a son and father compete in playing a video game, a child and parent can enter a reciprocal or even reverse complementary (son teaching father how to play) relationship. Thus age, materials, and situation can affect how peers and adults interact.[49]

The debates over children's interactions illuminate the bifurcated culture of childhood and play: adult-structured in one dimension, peer-structured in the other. And while never isolated from myriad external, generational, and gender influences, preadolescents by themselves and with peers operate in a separate society: one that is not anarchic but is freer than the society that includes their elders as arbiters in children's lives. As anthropologist Gary Alan Fine has observed, "Children, particularly with their peers, behave more in accord with the world as they observe it than with the world as professed by adults."[50] Thus, in this autonomous world, kids resist adult pressures while at the same time, in the presence of adults, they are willing to buy into, or at least accept, the rewards of attempts to convert—read: socialize—them to the moral verities of the older generation.

This is not to say that children deliberately exploit their status (though they sometimes do); while kids profess a desire for freedom, they often simultaneously complain about lack of adult guidance. In his analysis of preadolescent boys playing Little League baseball, Fine found that coaches who failed to apply some measure of discipline and allowed team members only to have "a good time" were blamed by those same players for not giving them that good time.[51] Still, the inventiveness of youngsters when they are released from an enforced adult regimen can be not just vital but astonishing. Educator William Wells Newell, who was one of the first Americans to apply scientific method to the study of children's play in the late nineteenth century, was also one of the few to realize how parents and other adults overlooked the importance of free play. One of his observations is worth quoting at length:

> Observe a little girl who has attended her mother for an airing in some city park. The older person, quietly seated beside the footpath, is half absorbed in reverie; takes little notice of passers-by, or of neighboring sights or sounds, further than to cast an occasional glance which may inform her of the child's security. The other, left to her own devices, wanders contented within the limited scope, incessantly prattling to herself; now climbing an adjoining rock, now flitting like a bird from one side of the pathway to the other. Listen to her monologue, flowing as incessantly and musically as the bubbling of a spring; if you can catch enough to follow her thought, you will

find a perpetual romance unfolding itself in her mind. Imaginary personages accompany her footsteps; the properties of a childish theatre exist in her fantasy; she sustains a conversation in three or four characters. The roughness of the ground, the hasty passage of a squirrel, the chirping of a sparrow are occasions sufficient to suggest an exchange of impressions between the unreal figures with which her world is peopled. If she ascends, not without a stumble, the artificial rockwork, it is with the expressed solitude of a mother who guides an infant by the edge of a precipice; if she raises her glance to the waving green overhead, it is with the cry of pleasure exchanged by playmates who trip from home on a sunshiny day. *The older person is confined within the barriers of memory and experience; the younger breathes the free air of creative fancy.*[52]

Not only alone but also when with each other, out of adult sight and out of adult mind, children have always displayed remarkable capacity to create their own pleasure, sometimes in conspiratorial ways. Beyond the instrumental play that is defined and governed by adults, children engage in two kids of unsupervised play: "real" or self-directed activities that are adult sanctioned but carried out without adult intervention; and illicit, unauthorized play that defies adult rules and that kids are careful to conceal. Slave children became particularly adroit at eluding supervision, pilfering objects for their games or slipping away, as Mississippi slave Prince Johnson did, to play in orchards and fields. But white children also practiced what immigrant daughter Kate Simon called the "hypocrisies" of being a good child while at the same time indulging in taboo acts of fun and excitement on her neighborhood's rooftops.[53]

Beyond simple hypocrisy and deviltry, illicit sorts of play like those of Johnson and Simon have provided preadolescents with ways to extend their sense of autonomy and power. Whether creating a secret language, exploring forbidden sites, or engaging in dangerous games, children reveled in freedom. Thus Frances Parkinson Keyes, describing how she and her friends challenged each other to navigate along the top rail of a cemetery fence or how they explored an underground cavern, recalled that in these and other similar activities, "We did not seek . . . advice from any of our elders; however, in fact, none of us felt it necessary to inform them of our decision."[54]

British folklorists Ilona and Peter Opie, whose studies resulted in

. Severall young men playing at foote-ball
. on the Jce upon the LORDS-DAY are all Drownd

DANGERS OF PLAYING FOOTBALL. Defaming the Lord's Day by
engaging in a frivolous and dangerous game, these boys were
depicted as falling through the ice and drowning, a severe re-
minder of Puritan proscriptions against idle play. *Picture Research
Consultants and Archives*

the most extensive catalog of child-structured games in the twentieth
century, concluded that the games most in decline over time were
those that adults knew about and were most inclined to endorse.
Those games that continuously flourished or increased in popularity
were those that adults either did not understand or disapproved. And
when parents and child-study professionals have lamented, as they
have been doing for decades, that without adult guidance children are
unable to develop creativity, kids have retreated into their autonomous peer society and have proved them wrong. Thus, as anthropologist Helen Schwartzman has remarked, "Often when children are followed out of their houses or schools and into the streets, backlots, and
alleys of their lives, their behavior is observed to be highly creative,

self-sufficient, active, and resourceful." Herein lies the true autonomy of childhood.[55]

The fact remains: There has never been a time of carefree childhood in American history. In spite of the belief that childhood was every person's birthright, in every era children have been deprived of that legacy by necessities of the family economy, tragedies of parental death and desertion, and the evil of predatory and brutal adults. The uninvited intrusions of poverty, disease, injury, bondage, and bigotry have robbed kids of essential opportunities, including those for play. As I argue in subsequent chapters, adults increasingly tried to restrict and control children's pleasure by obliging them to follow adult rules, presumably for reasons of rationality and safety. The result was a constriction of autonomous, unstructured, or self-structured play.

In many non-Western cultures, parents have considered children competent at an earlier age than Western children, permitting play to take place without strict supervision or organization; "free" play is considered and tolerated as "natural." The play of American youngsters, growing up in a technology-dominated, competitive, future-oriented culture, has required both adult guidance and adult protection lest children's, and society's, healthy development be jeopardized. This nexus between generations, and the resulting contest over the site, materials, participants, and autonomy of children's play, has resulted in both benefits and costs.[56]

I

Childhood and Play in Early America, 1600–1800

LOOKING BACK ON his own childhood in the late eighteenth century, Silas Felton harbored regrets that he wished to convey to parents of his generation. The son of a Marlborough, Massachusetts, farmer and later a common (public) school teacher, Felton spent most of his youth under the strict auspices of his father and his schoolmaster. Though he occasionally enjoyed some free time, he so chafed under the restrictions placed on him that once he became an adult he wanted his contemporaries to appreciate a child's need for autonomous activity. "People do not pay attention enough to the Inclinations of their children," he complained in his autobiography, "but commonly put them to the same kind of business, which they themselves follow, and when they find them [children] not attentive to those particular occupations accuse them of being idle." Such chastisement, Felton continued, "often damps [children's] spirits, which . . . sometimes leads to looseness of manners, whereas if the leading inclinations of the children were sought after, and when found, permitted to follow them, [such inclinations] might prove highly advantageous to themselves, their parents and society."[1] Felton's advice for his fellow adults, voiced at a time when general attitudes about childhood were beginning to shift, reflected a rarely recognized appreciation for the natural play instincts—"inclinations"—of early American children.

The view of children varied across regions of the American colonies. The belief of New England Puritans—that children were born evil, the products of Adam's sin—has tinged common assumptions about the childhood of European colonists with hues of austerity and piety. According to this exaggerated perspective, any kind of frivolity, play or otherwise, took place in the devil's workshop. An American child's life certainly brimmed with such qualities in the seventeenth and eighteenth centuries. But, in fact, different groups of early Americans—the Quakers of the mid-Atlantic states, for example—tolerated youthful indulgences, and virtually all groups, including the Puritans, lavished affection on their children, disciplined them gently, and rationally tried to shield them from the adult world's corruptions. When it came to playful pursuits, many groups openly accepted at least a limited measure of childhood precocity while also expecting youngsters to control their passions.

For most colonists regardless of region, play was to have a purpose, whether it served God, the community, or the family; otherwise, it was considered to be "idleness." To children, however, what their elders considered idleness meant amusement and recreation—in a word, their own brand of play. Limited in the time that they could devote exclusively to diversions and short on formal objects to play with, colonial youngsters nevertheless contested with adults over what was "idleness" and what was not. And in defining their play, they created spaces and activities in which to amuse themselves independent of the domestic and social worlds created by parents and other adults.

The Colonial Context of Childhood

American society in the colonial era was triracial—consisting of white, African, and Indian peoples—and in each racial society, children were numerous and valued. White children were especially abundant. Indeed, at no time in American history were there more white children, relative to the number of white adults, than in the colonial era. But also, at no time in American history were white children more seriously involved in adult society than in that same period.

Variations existed across regions and classes, but high birthrates, the result of young marriage age[2] and generally healthier environmental conditions than in Europe, meant that in spite of widespread and frequent infant mortality, most free families had numerous offspring. Families of white indentured servants, residing mainly in Pennsylvania, Maryland, and Virginia, tended to be smaller than free families because indentured parents were less healthy and more transient than free parents. But, generally, white women's fertility in the colonies was greater than it was in those areas of the colonists' origins in England and the European continent. In New England, for example, women typically gave birth to seven to nine children; further south, by the eighteenth century women were having five or more children. Often, only about two-thirds or fewer survived to age twenty-one, compared with 99 percent reaching that age today. Most revealing, though regional differences were significant, the median age of the white American population in 1700 was under sixteen years, meaning that over half of the colonists were what today would be considered children. In the child-centered American society of the early twenty-first century, the median age is over thirty-five, which is more than twice the colonial figure, and only around one-eighth of the population is under age sixteen.

Though most of the first colonists in the New World claimed European origins, by the eighteenth century, Africans were the most numerous migrant group, involuntary though their immigration had been. Enslaved women married, formally or informally, at even younger ages than white women—often in their teens—and therefore bore more children than white women did. Slaveowners of Chesapeake Bay–area plantations discovered a profitable resource in female slaves, whose offspring could increase the labor force at relatively little cost or could be sold as a commodity. Consequently, in spite of a high ratio of slave males to slave females and the vulnerability of black children to infectious diseases, white masters encouraged slave births so that the number of African American children per adult female was quite high. As well, by the late 1700s, West African slave traders, who previously had captured mainly young adults, were kidnapping children and selling them to western planters, further increasing the number of black colonial children.[3]

Little is known about exact birthrates and age structures among North American Indians, the original inhabitants when Europeans and Africans arrived in the seventeenth and eighteenth centuries. Before their populations were decimated by imported diseases and killing by whites, an estimated half million Woodland natives lived in groups and villages in eastern North America in the era immediately preceding contact with European colonists. Unlike white children, who tended to live in two-generation families, Indian children, such as among the Iroquois, which was the largest native nation, often lived with a grandmother as well as with parents present in the household. Because Woodland Indian women nursed their children longer than white women did—sometimes up to four years—they had fewer births, usually three or four per mother. Once contact with European invaders ensued, pathogens from smallpox, chicken pox, measles, syphilis, and other infectious diseases carried by the colonists ravaged Indian peoples at staggering rates, killing up to 90 percent of native children and nearly as many adults. Thus, Indian families suffered child illnesses, deaths, orphanage, and overall loss at significantly higher rates than did white and African families.[4]

Due to white invaders

The demography, economies, and social structures of colonial America (excluding Indians) affected childhood and, relatedly, children's play in several important ways. First, mortality framed black and white children's lives more starkly than would be the case in future times. With 10 percent or more infants dying before they reached age one, and many more failing to live beyond their teen years, surviving kids experienced the death of siblings as a fact of life. Clergy such as Cotton Mather frequently warned children that they could be called before God at any time, but youngsters did not have to be reminded; parents had no qualms about exposing them to corpses and dying relatives, young and old. Moreover, with life expectancies in the forties, many children had to cope with the loss of one or both of their parents. Consequently, there were many orphans who were raised by an older sibling or by grandparents, aunts and uncles, or other kin. If no relative was present or capable, an orphaned child could be assigned or apprenticed to someone in the community. A widowed parent often remarried, meaning there was a good chance that a child would share a household with stepsisters and stepbrothers. As well, a large proportion of colonial children, even with two surviving natural parents, were indentured or in permanent bondage and therefore in the custody of masters and mistresses.[5]

As a result of these factors, distinctions between economic roles, communal experiences, and social spaces of older and younger generations in colonial communities were blurred. In a society that fused private life with public supervision, and where both domestic architecture and family responsibilities seldom allowed personal privacy, children mingled with adults and assumed important duties early in life. Until recently, historians commonly concluded from these patterns and from artistic representations of the period that colonists, especially in New England, considered and treated children as "miniature adults." But such a characterization misrepresents kids' status. Even though children everywhere mingled with the older generation in the fields, in the household, in the shop, and in the community, Puritans in the North, Quakers and Catholics in the Middle Colonies, and Anglican planter families in the South all recognized that children differed from adults, not just physically but also morally, emotionally, and legally. The most varied patterns occurred in how families and communities handled youthful natures. In the Chesapeake Bay and Virginia area, parents took a relaxed stance toward discipline, while in the Puritan Northeast, a constant preoccupation with making offspring aware and fearful of sin dominated child raising.[6]

Within white families and their communities, the years before 1770 marked a time when children operated under strict pressures to be obedient to parents and to God. Clerical warnings against disobedience and willfulness have long been used to illustrate the severity of adult-child relationships during this period. For example, Pilgrim pastor John Robinson sermonized, "And surely, there is in all children . . . a stubbornness, and stoutness of mind arising from natural pride, which must, in the first place, be broken and beaten down; that so the foundation of their education being laid in humility and tractableness, other virtues may, in their time, be built thereon."[7] But methods of child-rearing and attitudes toward children were more diverse and compassionate than historians previously have believed.[8] The style in Puritan New England was not uniformly "stern," nor was parenting in the middle colonies and the South commonly "lenient." Sources suggest that in all regions children were genuinely loved and even pampered by their parents. Nevertheless, the historical record also makes it clear that during childhood, a young white person learned how to "earn" adulthood in ways that were delimited by family, church, and community.[9] Thus children's culture and adult culture intertwined, extending from daytime labor into nighttime and Sunday leisure-time pastimes when parents and children jointly engaged in community activities outside the home. At home, they partook of Bible reading and games, such as puzzles and cards, that were intended to teach moral lessons.

In contrast to whites, Indian parents harbored less severe attitudes toward authority and child rearing. As historian Gloria Main and others have discovered, seventeenth- and eighteenth-century observers such as Baptist renegade Roger Williams in New England, Catholic missionary and ethnographer Father Gabriel Sagard, and Jesuit priest Pierre de Charlevoix (the latter two in the Great Lakes region) noted that native peoples gave their children considerable independence as well as affection. David Zeisberger, a Moravian missionary who worked among several eastern Indian communities in the eighteenth century, recorded in his diary how Indian parents seldom disciplined their children, who were allowed to "follow their own inclinations" and "do what they like and no one prevents them." Native kids, wrote Zeisberger, unlike white youngsters were spared the rod—"reproved by gentle words" rather than suffering physical punishment. Among many native peoples, gender separation usually occurred once the early years had passed. Girls, who at quite young ages joined the company of women in undertaking household tasks, likely experienced more regimented lives than boys, whose outdoor activities, at least until adolescence, generally took place outside of adult male presence.[10]

Enslaved African and African American children endured the hardest childhoods. Forced into taxing labor at early ages, they confronted capricious family disruption when one or both of their parents were sold to another owner—assuming, that is, that their parents survived the high slave mortality rates. Still, black children received similar kinds of affection as other youngsters did. Studies of farms and plantations in various colonial southern communities have revealed that around three-quarters of slave children lived in families with at least one parent present and that black children received loving attention from their elders. When parents were absent in the fields, died, or were sold away, other adults in the slave community, often referred to as "aunt" or "uncle" even when unrelated, served as surrogate mothers and fathers. When possible, the older black generation bought, made, and gave gifts to slave children, and the bond between slave children and their parents was so strong that some newspaper ads seeking runaways mentioned children who had fled the plantation in search of a parent who had been sold away.[11]

Adults thus employed a variety of ways to raise—or in social scientific terms, to socialize—children in American colonial society. Few if any parents, whether Anglo, Euro, Indian, or African, spoiled their children or were permissive in the modern sense of the term, and some historians have long believed that white colonists, especially New England Puritans, disdained children as innately evil beings in need of immediate, strict, and frequent moral tutelage. The oft-quoted Cotton Mather characterized even babies as sinners, asserting that "the *Devil* has been with them already. . . . They go astray as soon as they are born." Yet more recently, scholars have uncovered convincing evidence that most parents felt and expressed deep fondness for their young. They grieved openly when an offspring died—as happened frequently—and took tender care to protect the young physically and emotionally. To be sure, not all parents exercised restraint; a study of early British and American diaries by historian Linda Pollock has revealed that cruelty and beatings were regular occurrences in some children's lives, as they have always been. Nevertheless, references to gentle and forgiving treatment are evident throughout the colonial period. Whatever the method of discipline, adults of all races firmly believed that they could and needed to guide their children's rehearsal for adulthood in very specific ways, and they worked hard to implant their own and their communities' norms of behavior in the young.[12]

Children, on their part, shouldered family responsibilities, caring for younger siblings and working in the family economy. Except for the wealthiest white youngsters, these duties characterized the preadolescent years of all racial groups, though male Indian offspring appear to have had the fewest responsibilities. In all groups, gender divisions arose early in life, as girls stayed close to home to help mothers or otherwise occupy themselves in the home while boys ventured farther away, either to aid fathers in the fields or, in the case of Indians, to learn hunting skills. Mostly, kids adapted to their roles, but even when pressed hard to accommodate adult needs, they did not unconditionally accept a daily routine of relentless labor. Innovative by nature, children developed their own culture, one that sometimes challenged their assigned place in society and diminished parents' confidence about governing the lives of their offspring. That culture, if not one of play in the modern sense, certainly involved playful behavior.

"Devil's Workshop" or "Gamesome Humour"?

Devereux Jarratt experienced a childhood that in many ways typified the patterns of the colonial era described above. Born in 1733 to a relatively poor Virginia family, Jarratt lost his mother to disease when he was six, and his father, a carpenter, died less than ten years later. With one parent gone and the other struggling to support the family, young Devereux was left mostly in the care of his oldest brother. Looking back on his youth, Jarratt, who had become a "New Light" Presbyterian minister, recognized some waywardness in his behavior and his brother's neglect of him, but his reflection contained elements of both confession and pride, when he wrote that his brother permitted him "all the indulgences a depraved nature and an evil heart could desire." Knowing the shortcoming of a "depraved nature" and his possible congress with the devil, Jarratt nevertheless engaged in a kind of mischievousness that characterized independent childish behavior that today would be considered as independent, unstructured play.[13]

In the minds of the pious, play as a pastime of a colonial white child was considered "the devil's workshop," leading to sin and dissipation. New England Puritans seemingly had the strictest attitude toward childish recreation. Seventeenth-century Massachusetts preachers such as Thomas Shepard and John Cotton regularly sermonized that at least some forms of play wastefully diverted both children and adults from their serious responsibility of serving God. Pennsylvania Quakers, though less harsh, also emphasized a person's godly duties and urged their youngsters to spend more of their time at prayer than at play. Southern aristocratic parents were more tolerant of play, as long as the games being played taught decorum and discipline.[14]

Still, as late as 1792, the Methodist Church of America, worried that the serious mission of life was threatened, warned that children "shall be indulged with nothing which the world calls *play*. Let this rule be observed with the strictest nicety; for those who play when they are young, will play when they are old."[15] Even the accoutrements of play lacked value. Unlike the present, in most regions of the colonies, the term "toy" meant something frivolous or inconsequential —an object that could amuse an adult or a child but which was not exclusively reserved for children. What existed then and might today be considered as formal toys, such as dolls (usually imported from Europe), carved soldiers, animal figurines, and miniature houses, were mostly intended for ornamental purposes and belonged to families of means.[16]

As inheritors of the Protestant Reformation and its work ethic, however, American colonists in all regions recognized that children needed to be put under special control, not just to serve God but also to be educated in a way that would prepare them for adult industriousness. Historians credit philosopher John Locke, especially his work *Some Thoughts Concerning Education* (1698), with implanting new ideas about children in the minds of parents and educators. Believing children to be inherently innocent with minds that were blank slates rather than demons whose will had to be broken because it was tainted by original sin, Locke asserted that a child's "gamesome humour" was natural and could be used to shape character and self-control. Thus, he posited, play should not simply be tolerated but encouraged. Though he never counseled parents to surrender to their children's desires, Locke gave new tolerance to childish joys:

structured, that is Recreation is as necessary as Labour, or Food. But because there can be no *Recreation* without Delight, which depends not always on Reason, but often on Fancy, it must be permitted [to] Children not only to divert themselves, but to do it after their own fashion. . . . Gamesome humour which is wisely adapted by nature to their age and Temper, should rather be encouraged to keep up their spirits and improve their strength and health, than curbed and restrained.[17]

Locke was no modernist; his aim was to inculcate self-control, denial, and order in children's behavior, and the play that he most favored was the kind that a child could undertake under a teacher's careful supervision. Unstructured play, to him, was not appropriate.[18]

It is unlikely that many ordinary colonials read John Locke; still, there was among them an emerging and widespread recognition of children's difference from adults and an acceptance of their need for play, at least if that play suited adult interests in suppressing youthful disorder. Even so austere a Puritan clergyman as John Cotton could concede that young children ought to "spend much time in pastime and play, for their bodyes are too weak to labour, and their minds to study are too shallow. . . . The first seven years are spent in pastime, and God looks not much at it."[19] Some Puritans even believed that a modicum of rebellious play might be necessary before a child could experience the desired conversion that led to personal salvation and the control of one's passions. And what historian Philip Greven has labeled as a "genteel style" of child raising, prevalent in New York, Pennsylvania, and the South, encouraged a style of play that inculcated leadership and organization rather than moral restraint.[20]

Indians, in their child raising, were perhaps more "Lockean" than whites, and they surpassed colonists' intentions in their encouragement of children's play. If whites idealized the kinds of play that taught reverence, obedience, and cooperation, natives infused the play of their young people with objectives of manual skill, mental tough-ness, and emotional independence. Preadolescent Indian boys, espe-cially, were turned loose into the woods to play their own games us-ing bows and arrows, throwing spears, and competing at running. In these ways, boys would learn from each other those skills they would need as men. They also participated in their own brand of sportive events during tribal festivals. Indian girls, less on their own than boys, mingled singing and playful banter into their household tasks. Slave children had somewhat similar gender divisions to those of Indians, with girls more confined to the master's household than boys, who ventured into the fields. (Girls also worked in the fields, but they were more likely than boys to have household tasks.) In the case of black youngsters, however, play and recreation usually had to be done surreptitiously. More than for other groups, play for slave kids was a luxury.[21]

Though threatened by hardship, disease, and the emotional trauma of separation from parents by death or sale, and beset by de-mands of labor, obedience, and religion, children of all colonial so-cieties nevertheless were allowed to play. All peoples of the New World valued children and perceived some larger rewards in granting youngsters opportunities for at least some kind of childish behavior, particularly if it would include educational qualities. And by recogniz-ing children as separate and distinct from their elders, these societies also provided children with spaces, materials, playmates, and freedom to nurture their own culture.

Children at Play

Silas Felton's complaint, noted at the beginning of this chapter, recog-nized a common pattern. In the British colonies, tensions between white children and their elders occurred over how the young occupied their time. As noted previously, parents were not necessarily unsym-pathetic to their children's needs for amusement, but with the older generation just how those needs should be satisfied, in God's eye and on behalf of the community, dictated that children follow particular paths of obedience, even when they were allowed to play.

In a society in which only a small minority of the white popula-tion and an even tinier proportion of blacks and Indians inhabited cities, and in which different generations shared indoor spaces where privacy was impossible, the sites for children's independent play consisted mainly of the outdoors. These spaces served as special locales for private reveries. Silas Felton admitted that he spent much of his time as a child reading and that he had little opportunity for play. Yet he also emphasized his love for "roving about" in the fields and forests that surrounded his father's Massachusetts farm, a pastime that he claimed was "generally the case with boys from ten to twenty-one years old." Felton's contemporaries, girls also, experienced similar pleasures. Future novelist Catharine Maria Sedgwick used nature as her "play-fellow" as she rambled through the woods near her native Stockbridge, Massachusetts. Daniel Drake, physician and booster of Cincinnati, noted that as a child in Kentucky he and his siblings enjoyed

> plays and rambles in the little fields and adjoining woods, which were close at hand. . . . The very loneliness of our situation [as pioneer children] led me to seek for new society and amusement in the woods, as often as opportunity offered. . . . To my young mind there was in them a kind of mystery. They excited my imagination. They awakened curiosity. They were exhaustless in variety.

And Levi Beardsley, who lived a pioneer childhood on the frontier of western New York State, found his most satisfying experiences in the forest. He wrote in his memoir:

> I can conceive of no place or circumstance so well calculated to impress the sensitive mind with awe and veneration, as the deep seclusion of the forest. Often, very often, when a mere boy, have I repaired to a secluded spot, where there was a clump of pine trees, and sat under them for hours together, listening to the sighing of the winds in the topmost branches.[22]

Such accounts no doubt reflected nostalgic reminiscences for an idealized youth; nevertheless, they suggest that nature figured powerfully in the childhoods of early Americans.

The countryside also provided a locale for more active children's play pastimes. Hillsides and ponds served as common venues for sledding and skating in winter and as locales for swimming, fishing,

SLAVE CHILDREN AT PLAY. A rare photograph of "Negro quarters" on a South Carolina plantation shows slave children playing in a circle separated from adults. *The New-York Historical Society*

and boating during warm weather. Both girls and boys engaged in these activities, but girls' domestic obligations, especially caring for younger siblings, usually kept them close to home. Boys more frequently and more freely appropriated the outdoors—building forts, trapping animals, wrestling, and racing. For both boys and girls, the outdoors also provided spaces for their various folk games of chase, ball throwing, and hoop rolling, and wealthier juveniles used open spaces for formal competitions such as "battledore and shuttlecock," an ancient game that evolved into modern badminton. Youngsters of all types, including slave children, also could merge amusement into outdoor labor, mingling singing games and informal competitions into or after such tasks as gathering berries, harvesting, raking, and barn raising. Levi Beardsley, for example, recollected that after a logging bee or barn raising in his Otsego River (New York) community,

> then the sports commenced. Almost invariably a ring was formed for wrestling, and frequently commenced with boys, the men looking on. The boy thrown would bring in one to wrestle with the victor, who could keep the ring against all comers; . . . I became skilful in all these sports, understood them well, and in a rough and tumble scuffle . . . there were but few of my age I could not throw.[23]

Indian boys carried spears and bows and arrows into the woods to practice their hunting skills on small animals and inanimate targets, and they organized lacrosse-like contests, which functioned not only as recreation but also as training for military combat. In the South, sons of white gentleman farmers also engaged in marksmanship and racing games, while black children raced and hunted in the fields.[24]

The home offered some opportunities for diversion, especially solitary ones. Probably the most common indoor amusement, at least for many white children, was reading. Silas Felton wrote that "at the age of nine or ten I was very fond of reading entertaining stories, and borrowed all the boy books within my reach. . . . I used at every convenient opportunity to take my book and step out of sight." John Bailhache, recalling his eighteenth-century Massachusetts boyhood, reminisced,

> Being naturally of a tractable disposition, I was generally considered a good boy, and seldom stood in need of correction. My habits were retiring and studious; and provided I could get a book to read, no matter on what subject—for I read everything that fell into my hands —I cared little or nothing for play, at which I was awkward and unhandy, and which seldom afforded me any gratification.

The diary of Ann Green Winslow, raised in Boston and the daughter of a British general, reveals that she spent most of her leisure time knitting and reading the Bible or other religious works such as *Pilgrim's Progress*. Daniel Drake's literary tastes leaned more toward secular edification, such as books on geometry, geography, and spelling, but also included lighter works such as *The Life of Robinson Crusoe*.[25]

Other indoor activities consisted of intergenerational amusements.

Card games, puzzles, and, among families of means, board games occupied parents and children jointly in the evening. Also, parents frequently read aloud, especially from the Bible, to children. Occasionally, at community social events or on visits to other households, children separated from adults to engage in their own special activities. Winslow's diary, written when she was twelve, noted an all-female gathering in which

> we had a very agreeable evening from five to ten o'clock. For variety we [played games of] woo'd a widow, hunted the whistle, threaded the needle [indoor games] and while the company was collecting, we diverted ourselves with playing of pawns [a kissing game], no rudeness Mamma I assure you. . . . [In all these games] the elderly part of the company were spectators only, they mix'd not in either of the above describ'd scenes.[26]

Games, whether outdoor or indoor, seem to have occupied less of colonial children's playtime than did unstructured amusements involving handcrafted toys and improvised playthings. Before the mid-eighteenth century, few items of what in the modern era could be called commercial toys could be found in American households, and, as noted above, the term "toy" denoted nearly any object used for amusement by anyone, adult or child. Dolls, rocking horses, miniature houses with tiny furniture, and a small number of other objects, mostly imported from England or Germany and intended as much for grownups as for children, comprised the most elaborate play paraphernalia. Also common—but rarely all in one family's possession— were domestically produced or homemade tops, hoops, kites, marbles, stilts, sleds, bows and arrows, puzzles, cards, blocks, and dolls, usually fashioned from wood, bone, ivory, or, in the case of some dolls, corn husks. A fifteen-item list of gifts that George Washington drew up for his stepchildren at Christmas time 1759 included bells, spinning musical toys, and dolls. Slave and indentured children owned few if any formal toys. For them, several objects such as tools and cooking implements served a combined purpose of amusement and instruction. The bows and arrows of Indian children and miniature farm and carpentry tools and cooking utensils used as play implements by white youngsters were also considered important training devices that aided the home economy and reinforced gender roles.[27]

↳ toys subconsciously did this

More frequently, youngsters of all races and regions entertained themselves with improvised playthings. Sometimes parents created these objects for their offspring, but more frequently children themselves made them. They carved and whittled sticks into fishing poles and into various objects for games of make-believe; fashioned and donned pieces of cloth to ornament their fantasies; and made use of corncobs, pieces of wood, and other discarded materials to construct mock-up forts and cabins. Samuel Goodrich, publisher and author of nineteenth-century children's books who wrote under the pen name of Peter Parley, grew up in Ridgefield, Connecticut, during the previous century and remembered how one simple object absorbed his time:

> During my youthful days I found the penknife a source of great amusement and even of recreation. Many a long winter evening, many a dull drizzly day . . . I spent in great ecstasy, making candlerods, or some other simple article of household goods for my mother, or in perfecting toys for myself and my young friends.[28]

Like memories of nature play, the recollections of playthings by Goodrich and others appear sentimentalized, yet they also strongly suggest that the homemade materials of folk culture held special meaning for children.

Even when they produced and used their own toys, however, kids did so in ways that represented distinct gender roles. Boys carved play weapons, tools, and horses in imitation of the material culture of adult male society. Girls employed their playthings and engaged in games that mimicked the activities of their mothers and other adult women. New Jersey Presbyterian minister Philip Vickers Fithian, for example, observed the young daughter of a friend "tying strings to a chair" and walking back and forth with them in order to simulate the spinning of yarn, "getting rags and washing them without water" to imitate the washing of clothes, and "knitting with straws" to replicate garment making.[29]

By the middle of the eighteenth century, formal toys began to be perceived as the materials of a separate children's culture. Portraits of children more frequently than in the past now included dolls, doll furniture, and doll dishes alongside girls, and hoops, wagons, balls, and miniature soldiers in scenes of boys. Contemporary writers on

FAMILY ENTERTAINMENT. In the early nineteenth century, reading occupied the leisure time of middle-class families and often brought generations together, both as listeners and as readers. *Picture Research Consultants and Archives*

childhood accepted the educational utility of what formerly might have been considered frivolous baubles. Locke, for example, argued that certain formal items of play could be given to children to aid their intellectual development, and he helped popularize sets of lettered blocks, sometimes referred to as "Locke's blocks," that were intended to aid the learning of the alphabet. By the 1770s, household inventories included numerous varieties of playing cards, jigsaw puzzles, and board games designed to teach geography, history, spelling, patriotism, and morality. In the cities, shops began selling educational toys and dolls. At the same time, adults claimed fewer of these items for themselves and associated them more explicitly with childishness. Didactic books exclusively for children also became more widespread. All of these developments reinforced a new attitude that toys and play belonged, according to historian Karin Calvert, to the "province of childhood," and they signaled a new dimension to the separation of generations.[30]

Because of the dispersed nature of most colonial settlements, children's playmates consisted largely of their own family members. Until the late seventeenth century, adults were much less self-conscious about what types of play were appropriate for different age groups than would be the case by the time of the American Revolution. Consequently, parents and children often amused themselves with the same games, such as blindman's bluff and find-the-bean, and with the same toys, such as cards, puzzles, and miniature figures. At other times, children and parents whiled away the time in each other's company, talking, singing, reading, and simply being together. For example, the diary of Esther Edwards, daughter of the celebrated Puritan evangelist, Reverend Jonathan Edwards of Northampton, Massachusetts, which she kept in 1742–43 when she was nine and ten years old, revealed that she spent most of her time in the presence of one or both of her parents, whom she called "Mr. Edwards" and "Mrs. Edwards." Esther described how she followed her mother around the house on most days, but on May 1, 1742, her diary entry related with pleasure that her father took her for a "wonderful ride . . . through the spring woods."[31]

There existed a separate children's culture, but both in the presence of and away from parents, that culture involved siblings more than peers. Often given responsibilities for childcare when mothers were tending to household chores or nursing infants, older daughters within all colonial societies—Indian, slave, and free—more frequently played with younger siblings than did older sons. But throughout the colonies, the dramatis personae of children's informal play commonly were sex-segregated, both by choice and by social prescription. Girls played with girls; boys played with boys. The Lowell mill girl Lucy Larcom grew up in the early nineteenth century, but her recollection about her childhood mirrored the experiences of earlier generations of girls when she remarked, "we were seldom permitted to play with any boys except our brothers." Catharine Maria Sedgwick also remembered the close bonds she formed with sisters, female cousins, and other girls. Like many girls, Sedgwick and her female kin played with dolls and other toys in ways that supposedly prepared them for the social refinements and nurturing skills they would need as women. Preteen boys, on their part, teamed with brothers and whatever other young male relatives were nearby to hunt, race, and roam together in their own male-only world.[32]

How much freedom children had when they engaged in playful activities rarely concerned adults because the inferior status of children was an assumed fact. No seventeenth- or eighteenth-century writer on childhood advocated that parents and other grownups should give children free rein to just be kids. Parents, clergymen, and educators all insisted that adults had a basic responsibility to guide a child's natural progress and to thwart bad habits such as disobedience, lack of self-control, and blasphemy. For example, Massachusetts minister Samuel West, reflecting on his childhood in the early eighteenth century and his adult role as parent and pastor, wrote in 1807 that the model of correct childhood development involved "a control over our feelings or passions, so as to prevent their ever betraying us into an impropriety either in words or actions." Another clergyman, Samuel Moody, advised that children should be "often thinking of Christ, while they are at play." Thus, adults held high expectations for their offspring and imposed various levels of control over them to ensure that they would develop without moral or intellectual corruption.[33]

When they roamed through the woods or invented games at home, children, however, did not always abide by these strictures and instead transgressed them, sometimes with guilt and sometimes guilelessly, prompting adult complaint. Thus one Puritan minister grumbled that juvenile rebelliousness was frequently expressed in an "inordinate love of play."[34] In his autobiography, Peter Cartwright, an Illinois Methodist minister raised in Virginia, precedes his religious conversion by confessing,

> I was naturally a wild, wicked boy, and delighted in horse-racing, card-playing, and dancing. My father restrained me but little, though my mother often talked to me, wept over me, and prayed for me, and often drew tears from my eyes; and though I often wept under preaching, and resolved to do better and seek religion, yet I broke my vows, went into young company, rode races, played cards, and danced.[35]

Conflict, both internally and with adults, has always characterized the process of growing up, as children have strived to find their place in a world full of limits and obligations. Though autobiographers commonly have created distorted histories of themselves, it seems clear that childhoods like that of Cartwright included willful acts that represented quests for independence from adult authority.[36]

Over the course of the colonial period, several factors opened paths for somewhat freer license for children to play that at least partially released them from prevailing behavioral codes. As the separate existence of childhood came more to be appreciated by the Revolutionary era, the play needs of children attracted more acceptance. Technological constraints still influenced how much children actually could play when a day's work and schooling were done. For example, the diary of Nahum Jones, a child living in colonial New Hampshire, remarked that darkness (lamp oil was scarce and, of course, electricity was nonexistent) severely limited what he and his family could do for amusement or edification at night.[37] Nevertheless, by the late 1700s, child's play increasingly included degrees of freedom and self-direction that previously had not existed.

An overlooked but critical component of the freedom to play that now became more common among children consisted of what they wore. Portraits of children in the seventeenth and eighteenth centuries reveal that changes in styles of clothing for both girls and boys began to enhance freedom of movement and, consequently, styles of play. Though the subjects of this artwork belonged to the wealthier white social classes, the designs and materials of their garments offer implications for children of other classes as well. The long, cumbersome skirts and bulky sleeves that girls wore in the seventeenth and early eighteenth centuries, for example, would have hampered play that involved running, bending, climbing, and reaching. Boys of that era, among the middle and upper classes, were permitted to wear breeches (pants that extended below the knee) rather than petticoats and other baby clothing at around age six or seven and thus were able to dress more like men, in part so that they could join fathers in the fields or shop. Certainly, these breeches, along with the trousers (somewhat longer than breeches) that laboring-class boys wore, served to emphasize a boy's gender distinction from girls as they provided freer movement that promoted more active play.[38]

After about 1770, important changes in clothing styles liberated girls for somewhat freer movement and further reinforced growing distinctions between childhood and adulthood. The simple frocks that preteen girls came to wear represented a somewhat modified adult costume that signified their role as mothers' helpers but still differed from the more complex gowns they would wear as mature women. Boys continued to exchange a baby frock for long trousers but in their formal attire began wearing suits, collars, and jackets that resembled the costume of their fathers. In each case, the simpler, looser clothing promoted freer physical movement for both work and play.[39]

Whatever they wore, children sometimes engaged in a kind of play that adults considered insupportable. New Englander John Barnard recalled that as a boy "I was beaten for my play, and my little roguish tricks."[40] Kids continued to fear retribution from parents and from God, but, like Peter Cartwright and Devereux Jarratt, exhibited a mischievous nature and broke their vows. Did the mischievous acts such as those by Barnard and Cartwright evidence a form of rebellion, an early breakdown of discipline that previewed the oppositional culture that, as some historians have hypothesized, fomented the American Revolution? Probably not. It is true that children born after the middle of the eighteenth century encountered a society that viewed children and their play more indulgently than had previous generations.[41] But for the most part, colonial kids were just being kids, seeking freedom and autonomy by testing adults and by exercising their own forms of amusement.

Thus while preadolescent children in colonial America—Indians, African Americans, and whites—made important contributions to the family economy, they were at times able to build their own play culture, more alternative than oppositional, around a mostly unstructured kind of play. Whether roaming through woods and interacting with nature along the way, or creating fantasies and games with self-fashioned playthings, or simply socializing with siblings and, when available, other children, young people in their preteen years manifested a definite play instinct. This is not to deny that challenges and hardship filled their lives; they toiled in fields and households, they fought illness and sorrow, they endured dry summers and harsh winters, and they struggled with warnings of dire consequences for defying parents and God. Still, they tried, and sometimes succeeded, to follow their own "inclinations."

2

The Attempt to Domesticate
Childhood and Play, 1800–1850

AS THE NEWLY independent American people launched their republic, and as important demographic, economic, and social changes accelerated, children encountered somewhat different circumstances than in the previous era. The transition in the way adults perceived children that had begun shortly before the Revolution now resulted in a society characterized by diverging generations and by a campaign to "domesticate" children: to nurture and educate them, in other words, so that they would become virtuous citizens. As in the past, the majority of youngsters, black and white, lived on farms, where chores and family obligations limited opportunities for free play. In addition, the rise of child labor in incipient industrial workshops and the expansion of plantation slavery filled the waking hours of preadolescent working-class and enslaved youngsters with toil that limited the amount of time they had for amusement. Yet, there is broad evidence that children did play, in the rural countryside and in cities, and that some of their play activities pleased adults while others distressed the older generation.

As in the colonial period, free white children grew up attentive to parental authority and to the devil's temptations, a consciousness that shaped and even curtailed their play. Maine native Fanny Newell, for example, recalled that in her late-eighteenth-century childhood she was haunted by fears for her soul and disdained playing with other children lest she fall "deeper into sin." Her parents encouraged her instead to prefer "joys on high." Her contemporary, New Jersey Quaker Joshua Evans, was made to believe that play was folly and equivalent to revolt against the social order. Children's amusement, especially in rural communities, still often took place with grownups watching and participating. Branson Harris, raised on the Indiana frontier in the early nineteenth century, spent most of his boyhood helping out on his family's subsistence farm. But he also recalled joining with married people at farm-related entertainments such as wood choppings, flax pullings, apple cuttings, and quiltings.[1]

More than previously, however, adults, particularly of the white middle class, looked at children as keys to, even guarantors of, not just the family's survival but also the nation's future. Influenced by ideas inherited from John Locke and by new attitudes derived from romantic thought, some parents now accepted a view that children had an innocent wholesomeness and should therefore delay their assimilation into adulthood so that they could complete a sheltered training, mostly under a mother's guidance, to become moral and productive adults. In this regard, the writings of Jean Jacques Rousseau were particularly influential. In his famous novel, *Emile, or On Education* (1762), Rousseau argued that children were not innately corrupted by original sin but, rather, were receptacles of the human virtue found in the state of nature. As such, they needed to be appreciated and cared for so that they might develop reason in their own way. This attitude generated a new tolerance for play and toys as inherent to the special qualities of childhood.

Though the family economy model of child rearing that had characterized the previous era still prevailed, more of the older generation now acknowledged the separate existence of youngsters and their independent play. Such recognition, however, rarely was free of consternation and disapproval. Caroline Clapp Briggs, born in Northampton, Massachusetts, the daughter of a local tailor and public official, wrote that her father never attempted to govern her when she was a child and that her parents rewarded her with toys for good behavior. At the same time, however, she grew up "wild as a deer" with such "a strange mixture of bravery and timidity" that she gave her mother "much trouble." Slave children had similar experiences, even when managed in harsher ways. Thus, Ebenezer Brown, who spent his childhood on a plantation in Amite County, Mississippi, told a WPA interviewer, "As a child, I played in de yard wid another black boy named Tom Hardin; but dey [his white masters] didn't 'low us to play much. We shot china berries frum er pop-gun, an' we made de shots hit de udder chaps an' wud git whup'ed fur it. We done dat all de time."[2]

Though they gave their elders "much trouble," children of the early nineteenth century nevertheless played, perhaps not "all de time," but in ways that symbolized the evolution of their own culture. As play became more acceptable, it also became more closely related to a distinct childhood, one with its own playthings and games. And, as children located play in their own "provinces," whether at home, in rural woods, or on city streets; as they joined playmates in common playful activities; and as they endeavored to construct a world that represented their autonomous culture, the generations increasingly inhabited different worlds.[3]

Children and Adults in the New Nation

The United States in the early 1800s was young not only in existence but also demographically. The median age of the population, which had been slightly under sixteen during most of the colonial period, remained at nearly the same level well into the nineteenth century. In 1810, half of all Americans were still younger than sixteen, and the median age rose only slowly for the next two decades. By 1830, it was just above seventeen for both whites and blacks, and though fertility decreased and life expectancy increased by mid-century, in 1850 almost half of the white population was under nineteen and the black population was even younger. (As mentioned in the previous chapter, the median age is thirty-six today.) Before 1830, it is not possible to determine the exact proportion of the total population that was in the posttoddler/preteen age group, the cohort that is the focus of this book, because federal census tabulators did not set apart that category, choosing instead to tabulate only inhabitants in the zero-to-ten and ten-to-fifteen age groups. But between 1830 and 1850, when the sums of those in the five-to-fourteen-year-old group were calculated, the category consistently contained slightly more than one-fourth of all Americans, and it is reasonable to assume that this proportion was much the same in the years between 1790 and 1820.[4]

In the early 1800s, American children lived in what still was a preindustrial society, but one with an ever more complex social structure. Expansion of a market economy altered economic functions, elevating larger-scale activities above subsistence economies of previous eras. Westward migration, accompanied and assisted by new transportation technologies (steamboats and railroads) and by internal improvements (roads and canals), urban growth, foreign immigration, new modes of finance, and, by 1840, early industrialization, helped create a social order that was more diversified and hierarchical than that of the colonial era. Work patterns shifted as production began to move out of the household and into larger sites, and investment opportunities opened paths to a new middle class consisting of entrepreneurs, traders, and professionals, who, though relatively small in number, exerted disproportionate influence on culture and institutions. At the same time, the plantation economy of the American South extended into new areas of what was then considered the Southwest (Alabama, Mississippi, Louisiana), and slavery touched the lives of an increasing number of both white and black families. For the working class in cities and mill towns, the rise of a capitalist economy created impersonality and a struggle to retain skills and independence in the face of mechanization, while the concentration of great wealth in the hands of a relatively small number of people called into question the belief in America as an egalitarian society. Culture clashes erupted with disturbing frequency, whether involving white efforts to remove Indians from desirable territory, attempts by the native-born to deny Irish and other immigrants access to jobs and housing, the severe discipline and fear of revolt that was inherent to the bondage system, conflict between militant laborers and obstinate employers, and more.

Perhaps most relevant of all for the lives of children was the separation of society into public and private spheres, with its accompanying reconstruction of gender roles. As fathers, young adults, and (in mill towns and cities) some children began working for wages outside the home, the public workplace and the private household became two distinct entities. Tradition and the law gave husbands legal authority over their wives, children, and property, but a broadening middle-class ideology assigned women explicit responsibility for maintaining the ideals of virtue and gentility in the sanctuary of the home. Mothers' duties included protecting children's innocence, not only by educating their offspring in the "moral arts" but also by sheltering them from death, crudeness, and sexuality. As household production began to decline, childhood dependency in families of means was prolonged, and school attendance, though not yet compulsory, increasingly occupied children's daily lives. As mid-century approached, birthrates began to fall, first among the middle class but eventually among the rural and working classes as well, resulting in fewer families with six or more children and more with three or four. The decline enabled parents to focus their material and emotional resources more intensively on fewer children and reinforced the new ideology that kids were special. Child and infant death rates remained high, but as households came to contain fewer children whose age ranges were more compressed, the household separated into two more clearly defined generations.[5]

Among whites, assumptions about proper gender roles applied to children as strongly as it did to the older generation, defining boyhood and girlhood in very different ways. Expectations about how boys and girls should be prepared for the future and how their behavior should be tolerated diverged, and the activities prescribed for each varied accordingly. Boys' inclination for physical activity and aggressiveness was tolerated, at least to some extent, and they were encouraged to form and function in groups. The concept of girlhood carried more complex qualities. On the one hand, they were deemed to harbor more delicate temperaments and more limited talents than boys; on the other, they continued to be given important domestic responsibilities for childcare and housework that kept them tied to the home more than boys were.

Indian and slave children of this period did not encounter the same separation of public and private social spheres as white kids did; their lives were filled with the same patterns and challenges that had characterized their forbears' existence. As in the colonial period, among most of the Indian groups and nations, gender strongly influenced children's roles. Girls generally participated in, and were obligated to learn, household crafts. As Thomas Wildcat Alford, a Shawnee-Creek native who grew up with the name Ganwahpeasaka, recalled, "Little girls played . . . mimicking their mothers' household tasks, making cakes, molding vessels of mud or clay. No doubt they 'kept house' and mothered small children." Native boys, as described by Alford, prepared for adulthood in the company of other boys, usually in activities involving hunting and mock-battle actions.[6]

Slave children lived under dreadful conditions in which hunger, disease, and early death, not to mention family separation and capital punishment, constantly threatened. Forced into fieldwork as soon as they were physically able, they had little time for themselves. Jim Allen, a former slave who grew up on a Mississippi plantation, told a WPA interviewer:

Did I work? Yes mam, me and a girl worked in de field . . . it took two chillerns to make one hand. Ole Marster . . . took me for a whiskey debt [from "Mars Bussey"]. Mars Bussey couldn't pay, and so Mars Allen took me a little boy out of the yard where I was playin' marbles. De law 'lowed the first thing the man saw, he could take.[7]

Nevertheless, slave families exhibited unusual strength in the face of disruption and hardship, and more than free children, slave youngsters could have multiple caregivers who included other adult kin and non-kin, as well as their parents. But bonded children often were trapped between the embrace of family and the authority of their owners. Denied education, beset by the fatigue of their toil, and recipients of, as well as witnesses to, humiliation and whippings, they struggled to adapt. Black youngsters in bondage experienced fewer gender distinctions than did others of their age, though girls more often than boys were assigned household tasks and as they grew older were more vulnerable to sexual exploitation from their white superiors.[8]

In white society, two new factors influenced attitudes about growing up: education and advice. After about 1800, churches began establishing Sunday schools as supplements to parental guidance, first for children of the poor but more commonly for middle-class kids, to fortify values of character and promote religious conversion. After 1830, however, public secular education rather than religious instruction altered the daily lives of many young people. Though attendance was inconsistent, school buildings scarce, and teachers poorly trained, an increasing number of children between the ages of six and fourteen found their way into schools for at least several months out of the year. What and how they were taught has been recounted elsewhere and need not be reviewed here, except to point out that the more frequently and longer children stayed in school, the longer their period of dependency at home would have lasted. But relevant to the discussion in these pages was the developing concept of play and toys as "educational." Child-rearing experts, for example, now advocated use of blocks, in school and at home, to teach values of order as well as building skills, and board games to enhance powers of planning and order.[9]

Advice manuals accompanied and reinforced prescriptions for fashioning the virtuous middle-class child. Authors of these books intended them to inculcate piety, respect, and, most importantly, proper (meaning acceptable to adults) behavior. One widely read writer, Harvey Newcomb, penned "how-to" books for boys and girls that lasted through numerous editions. Newcomb, adopting prevailing notions about the distinctiveness of childhood, would not have a boy or girl act like a full-grown gentleman or lady; rather, he advised that young persons should "take greater delight" in the "little fairy world in their minds" as long as such delight does not become a "passion." "There is no more harm," Newcomb admitted, "in the play of children than in the skipping of lambs." Still, he prescribed no fewer than sixteen rules for play behavior to prevent injury and, most importantly, to promote learning and "Christian duty."[10]

Early books produced explicitly for children included similar admonitions. An 1803 publication, for example, offered a poem on "Good Advice for Children":

Be just and true, and kind to all,
Play with a top, a bat, and ball,
He who does what good he can,
May gain the love of God and man.
And he who does no hurt all day,
May go some other time to play.[11]

A small cloth book titled *Boys and Girls Illustrated Primer* represented each letter of the alphabet with a brief didactic verse. The letter "B," for example advised

Bo Peep is a sluggard:
Her sheep go astray,
For she spends her moments
In sleeping and play.[12]

The social context of childhood in the early nineteenth century, then, evidenced an ironic, sometimes contradictory tension between appreciation and regulation. Those writers who were most smitten by the purity and playfulness of children, such as school reformer Horace Mann and children's author and editor Lydia Maria Child, were also the ones who recommended strict child-rearing methods and rigorous, age-graded schooling.[13] The romantic ideal of childhood also inspired proponents of a sheltered childhood to wish to "save" destitute, working children, whom they believed were not only exploited and mistreated but also denied their, the reformers', version of a republican childhood. This childhood now included an expanded acceptance of play, but one that adults wanted to define with their own terms even more precisely than previously.

The Transformation of Formal Play

If throughout most of the colonial era writers, educators, and parents had considered childhood a time when youngsters, though loved, needed to surrender their innately willful qualities and begin to "earn" adulthood, the enhanced appreciation for the special innocence and vulnerability of children that emerged in the nineteenth century included the notion of childhood as a time of play. As Samuel G. Goodrich, one of the era's most successful children's authors, who wrote under the pen name of Peter Parley, urged,

> If God places our offspring in Eden, let us not cause less or carelessly take them out of it. It is certainly a mistake to consider childhood and youth—the first twenty years of life—as only a period of constraint and discipline. This is one-third part of existence—to a majority, it is more than the half of life. It is the only portion which seems made for unalloyed enjoyment.[14]

As in the previous two centuries, no adult endorsed frivolous play; rather, in the nineteenth century, utilitarian play, exclusive to childhood, acquired new value. Middle-class parents came to accept, even encourage, children's special games, hobbies, and toys as a means to develop what a contemporary author described as "a habit of reflection and observation." Even among poorer white children, especially boys, whose penchant for physicality and prankishness was considered normal (girls, either by necessity or ideology, remained more "domestic" in their daily activities), play was assumed to require a practical quality. Writers advised that as long as toys and games were "judiciously chosen," children could learn as well as enjoy. English author Maria Edgeworth, whose works were widely read in the United States, exemplified the consequences ensuing from such choices:

A little boy of nine years old, who had a hoop to play with, asked "why a hoop, or a plate, if rolled upon its edge, keeps up as long as it is rolled, but falls as soon as it stops, and will not stand if you try to make it stand still upon its edge?" Was not the boy's understanding as well employed whilst he was thinking of this phenomenon, which he observed whilst he was beating his hoop, as it could possibly have been by the most learned preceptor?[15]

Some of the most detailed insights into the kinds of play that adults preferred can be found in children's chapbooks, a form of literature that arose in the eighteenth century and flourished in the early nineteenth. "Chap" was a corruption of "cheap," a quality identified with the small size—usually around three inches by four inches—and cloth binding of these works. Often containing ballads and popular tales, a number of the books detailed games and playthings, accompanied by illustrations, that their compilers deemed suitable for young readers. Significantly, the books blended encouragement and caution, reflecting the new acceptance of "childish" games yet expressing an obsessive desire for sheltering youngsters from harm. Thus an 1802 catalog of games, titled *Youthful Sports,* advised against an extreme version of leapfrog called "flydown":

Jumping over backs is a harmless amusement, but children should not often play at Flydown, which is a violent pitching upon another's back from some stated distance. A little boy was one day playing at Flydown, when, pitching too far, he missed the back, and falling on one side, broke his arm!

Even the common game blindman's bluff evoked anxiety, with the warning: "Blindman's Bluff is rather dangerous play, unless it be in some open place, or very large room. It seems to be very amusing . . . but if the blinded boy should fall down and break his nose, what then!" Kite flying, though it "employs the ingenuity of children," had limits; it could frighten horses and cause accidents. Trundling a hoop was "innocent amusement," but "Little Tommy" neglected to watch where he was going and "got hurt by stepping in a hole in the street." Playing "the tow" (marbles) was a "pretty diversion," as long as it was not played "for money or one another's marbles." The only games that *Youthful Sports* listed as completely safe were dressing a doll, riding wooden horses, spinning a top, battledore and shuttlecock (badminton because there was "not much danger except for breaking windows") and tossing a ball.[16]

The urge for control and protection pervaded other publications. A chapbook titled *A Present for a Good Boy* presented an illustration of a boy and girl crying and observed how ugly they looked. "It may be," the author indicated, that "they want to be running about in the street to play, when they should be in the house. Well, what can be done to quiet them? I suppose they must have a little Picture Book or something else to play with." On the next page, a new drawing shows the children playing with a mask, and their faces are beaming with joy.[17]

Other publications used play as a prompt for instilling morality and good behavior. Author Sarah Josepha Hale, best known for her long tenure as editor of *Godey's Ladies Book,* a magazine for women, also edited a chapbook of advice stories for children titled *A Gift to Young Friends.* Among its contents is "Two Good Boys," a story about a pair of youngsters who played ball indoors while their mother was away. In their recklessness, the youngsters broke a glass inkstand and spilled ink on a new rug. They confessed right away and were forgiven, showing that their play was of less consequence—and thereby somewhat indulged—than admitting up to their negligence.[18] Given confidence and encouragement, authors maintained, children would become the vanguard of a new age in spite of their play.

The swelling body of children's literature, as well as a modicum of new toys and games, denote the optimistic celebration of childhood and acceptance of the need for kids to be entertained. But adults remained the gatekeepers, evincing a strong sense of what was suitable. The prose in many of the chapbooks suggests that they were written to be read to, as much as by, children. In somewhat the same way that Bible reading had formerly served as a means to impart moral messages, the play-oriented chapbooks and other advice publications became secular means for parents to sympathize with children's efforts to pursue their playful impulses and, at the same time, to guide children's behavior within the framework of a new juvenile world. Thus as Nathanial Willis, editor of *The Youth's Companion,* which one historian has called "one of the most influential periodicals of the entire nineteenth century," proclaimed, "Our children are born to higher destinies than their fathers; they will be actors in a far advanced period."[19] Yet, as the mischief of the boys and girls depicted in the chap-book literature signified, that world was full of tension between what kids did and what adults prescribed.

Antebellum Kids at Play: Places and Playthings

Among his several reminiscences, author and critic William Dean Howells wrote *A Boy's Town*, a third-person account of growing up in small-town Ohio in the 1840s. His childhood, common for the era, re-vealed a divided quality. In one half, seemed earnestly willing to share with his parents "the world of foolish dreams half of him lived in," while his "other half" indulged in an independent existence in which he "swam, and fished, and hunted, and ran races, and played tops and marbles, and squabbled and scuffed in the Boy's Town."[20] Split be-tween the traditional milieu of family and the expanded opportunities for informal, sometimes secret, play, early-nineteenth-century young-sters such as Howells attempted to negotiate a balance between obedi-ence and self-gratification. As they came to cherish newfound auton-omy, they began to realize that theirs was a different world that only they appreciated. As Catherine Elizabeth Havens, daughter of a New York merchant, wrote in her diary when she was nine, "I don't think grownup people understand what children like."[21] What children now liked was expressed in the places where they played, the things and the other kids they played with, and the ways that they played.

As had previous generations of youngsters, children in early-nine-teenth-century America used both the home and the outdoors as ven-ues for their play. Contemporary attitudes about the distinctiveness of childhood, however, seemed to prompt a more liberal use of those environments and opened up new places for self-structured amuse-ment. For kids of means, the family abode offered an expanded play arena. As new architectural components, such as attics, cellars, and children's own bedrooms, became more common, young people could claim spaces that adults did not always monitor. Author and Unitar-ian minister Edward Everett Hale recalled in his autobiography how he and his brother exploited the attic of their Boston home for all kinds of imaginative play in the 1830s where "we had perpetual mo-tion to discover." The Hale brothers converted their attic into a make-believe schoolroom, communicated across it by connecting jars with a string, rehearsed theatrical performances and composed a newspaper there, mapped out and fought naval battles on the floor, and painted portraits of their "belles" and friends on the walls.[22] Other household rooms provided opportunities for creative enjoyment as well. New Englander Emily Wilson remembered a childhood delight from the 1840s:

> Our kitchen boasted a cook stove, the like of which I have never seen elsewhere. It had a rotary top turned by a crank at the side, thus obviating the necessity of changing the pots and kettle from the front to the back. [My sister and I] very soon recognized the possibility of using it for our own amusement and one, seated on the top, rode round and round while the other operated the crank.[23]

Most youngsters of course lacked the privacy and freedom that middle-class offspring such as Hale and Wilson enjoyed. Brown Thurston, who grew up in rural Maine during the 1820s and later became an abolitionist editor, recounted in his journal that he and his sister slept in a trundle bed that rolled out from under his parents' bed and rarely had the opportunity for unsupervised play. But like other children, he could always find "great pleasure" outside the house.[24]

Indeed, more than in the home, it was in the woods, pastures, streets, yards, and empty lots that antebellum children of all races and classes fostered their own play culture. For some kids, the outdoors served as a place of escape, somewhere to seek and to welcome the joys of solitude. Henry Clark Wright, later an educator and abolitionist, spent a demanding childhood in the 1810s on a farm seventy miles west of Albany, New York, where he often had to look after his stepsisters and stepbrothers, as well as tend to household chores. But, just as Silas Felton relished "roving about" in the eighteenth century, Wright found solace by wandering in the woods alone. He reflected that "to see and feel the gathering gloom of night settling around me, to feel myself shrouded in forest darkness, far from the footsteps of man, with a dog, seemed to me the consummation of earthly felicity."[25] For children such as Wright, isolated on the frontier, nature was not necessarily a playground, but it did serve as a private retreat where a child could indulge in personal reverie.

More commonly, however, nature inspired some of the most rhapsodic memories and experiences of childhood fun. Emily Inez Denny, whose family settled on the Puget Sound of Washington in the 1840s after journeying across the West from Illinois, epitomized the effect:

> Ah, we lived so close to dear nature then! Our playgrounds were the brown beaches or the hillsides covered with plumy fir trees, the alder groves or the slashing where we hacked and chopped with our little hatchets in imitation of our elders. . . . Running on long logs . . . and jumping from one to another was found to be an exhilarating pastime. When the frolicsome Chinook wind came singing across the Sound, . . . girls ran down the hills, performing a peculiar skirt dance by taking the gown by the hem on either side and turning the skirt over the head. Facing the wind it assumed a balloonlike inflation very pleasing to the small performer.[26]

Another frontier child, Rachel Butz, who grew up in Indiana, loved to take playmates into the woods, "where the interlacing boughs of the majestic trees formed an almost perfect shelter for the cool, moist, earth."[27] Obviously, wistful remembrances such as these reflect selective, exaggerated memory, but the frequency of references to nature as a playground in memoirs and diaries signifies a very strong relationship between children's play and the outdoors in the early nineteenth century.

Limited in the flexibility of their time and in the accessibility to play spaces, slave children nevertheless made good use of yards, trees, fields, barns, and wharves. Some, such as Laura Ford of Hinds Country, Mississippi, could only remember a childhood of "wuk, wuk all through de week from daylight 'til dark." Others, such as William Flannagan of Attala Country, Mississippi, stole time for singing and amusing themselves while doing fieldwork. Still, the WPA narratives contain numerous allusions to informal games in outdoor places. Recalling plantation life in Simpson County, Mississippi, Tony Cox recounted, "All us had to amuse us wuz what us found in de woods, wid de trees, streams, an' de hillsides." Cox especially remembered swinging from the supple branches of pine trees until they bent almost to the ground and then flying back up. "Dat was fun," he mused, "swingin' through de air lak dat an see de trees whiz back up." Another Simpson County slave child, Hannah Chapman, used discarded

rope to build a swing in the plantation barn, and Emily Dixon revealed how much a simple natural object such as a tree could mean to
a youngster:

> Did yo' eber take time ter think jist what a hickory-nut tree is to
> chillum? Deir's de shade ter play under, de tree ter climb, de big
> limbs ter hang swings from, de leaves ter pine tergether wid pine
> straw ter make dresses an' hats, de nuts ter eat an' throw at each
> uder, if yo' all wants ter fight. . . . Den yo' can hide 'hind der trunks
> in playin' hide an' seek, or hab hit fer de base.

Occasionally slave kids appropriated indoor spaces for play, as when
Isaac Potter and his brother, who had "run out ob nothin' to amuse
us," donned gunnysacks for aprons and tried to cook in their cabin's
fireplace that had been temporarily abandoned by "Milly, de cook."
But the most common pattern was exemplified by Minerva Grubbs:
"Befo' I wuz big 'nough ter wuk, I played 'round de cabins in de
shade ob de trees."[28]

As might be expected, Indian children, especially boys, found
their greatest pleasures outdoors. Because native boys spent their
youth learning the hunting and martial skills they would practice as
adults, mostly through play and imitation of adult males, their activities took place beyond their encampment or village. Ohiyesa, a member of the Wahpetonwan band of the Santee Sioux in Minnesota, asserted in his memoir, which he wrote under his Christian name of
Charles A. Eastman, that "the Indian boy was a prince of the wilderness. He had but very little work to do during the period of his boyhood." Mostly, he retold, he and his friends played in and appropriated nature:

> Our games were feats with the bow and arrow, foot and pony races,
> wrestling, swimming and imitation of the customs and habits of our
> fathers. We had sham fights with mud balls and willow wands; we
> played lacrosse, made war upon bees, shot winter arrows . . . and
> coasted upon the ribs of animals and buffalo robes.[29]

Much of the play of Indian kids was recorded by white settlers
who as youths had played with them. James Langdon Hill, the son
of a missionary on the Iowa frontier, recalled how in wintertime he

shared his sled with Indian boys, who joined him in the joy of careen-ing down nearby hills. The Indians, Hill wrote, "soon appeared with [their own] sleds, made of a hickory sapling, which had been split in two for runners." But, reflecting prevailing racial bias, Hill reported that the Indians seemed to perform unusual cruelty on animals, tor-menting turtles and frogs, showing their descent from a "remote sav-age ancestry." Hill observed also that "there used to be a touch of hardship in their [outdoor] play, and penalties and pain were intro-duced into their games."[30] In all probability, Hill and other white boys may have been as savage and sadistic as their Indian playmates, but Hill's descriptions may also hint at a different style of outdoor play culture that Indian children practiced.

In addition to the home and the outdoors, children appropriated sites whose existence reflected broader developments in the new at-tention paid to children. The school, especially its surrounding yard, offered opportunities not only for learning but also for play. Wide-spread public schools and compulsory attendance loomed in the fu-ture, but enough kids, especially those of means, now attended so that school life became a source for a multitude of memories. Edward Ev-erett Hale liked to arrive at his school early, where he could engage in games of tag and "all of the fun of the school [that could be] enjoyed before the bell rang." New Englander Henrietta Dana, daughter of au-thor Richard Henry Dana, found that at her Cambridge, Massachu-setts, school, "the large grounds gave us ample opportunity to play a variety of games." And Caroline Cowles Richards, raised by her grandparents in upstate New York, learned the "fun, but rather dan-gerous" games of snap-the-whip and mumble-peg during school re-cess. Schools also prompted new temptations for escape, as several memoirists noted that they had skipped their classes to pursue goals of amusement over those of enlightenment. Brown Thurston, for ex-ample remembered how he often "played truant" in order to go fish-ing in a pond near his home.[31]

In addition, city youths discovered ways of invading public spaces that were never intended for their use. Stables, warehouses, shops, and docks lured youngsters who exploited such locations for recreation and exploration. Girls used man-made structures as props, such as stoops and sheds that they found in these places, for make-believe dramas and for games such as hide-and-seek. Boys played war games around and in the built environment and simply roamed

@ school, children played before classes or played hooky to play without regard for trespass. Hale, recalling that he and his friends wandered across Boston's wharves, admitted, "I do not remember that . . . it once occurred to me to ask whose property we used on these occasions."[32]

Antebellum children, both black and white, used their own and others' objects to play with, and they applied considerable inventiveness to the existing material culture. As in the past, formal toys were scarce; the American toy industry barely existed before the Civil War, and imported toys were few and costly. Families with means could buy their children game paraphernalia, such as dominoes, checkers, backgammon and chess pieces, and rackets for "battledore and shuttlecock." In addition, sleds, hoops, hobbyhorses, dolls, tin soldiers, marbles, playing cards, puzzles, and board games all found their way to store shelves. But resourceful kids and the adults in their lives could make facsimiles of these things themselves. Thus, manufactured toys remained secondary to improvised playthings.

The least fortunate children had to be inventive by necessity. The most common play articles that former slaves recounted to WPA interviewers were balls and marbles, but Salem Powell, once a Mississippi plantation slave child, summed up the normal state of affairs: "We made up de things us played an' what us played wid." He and his friends crafted primitive slingshots to shoot sparrows, used planks to slide down hills on which they had spread pine straw to grease the way, and converted the same planks into miniature sailboats. Other former slaves recalled winding balls out of discarded yarn, constructing dolls out of sticks and rags, and fashioning fantasy clothing out of leaves and flowers. Slave kids also appropriated farm animals as playthings. Georgia slave Melvina Roberts would cover her master's two hogs with wood shavings and play "ketchum" with them, while Barney Alford chased chickens. One time he "tied a bundle uf fodder on de tail uf er horse an wus 'bout ter sot it on fire when de oversee kotch me."[33]

Underprivileged white children also used what little material they could find as play materials. Brown Thurston could not afford to buy a sled, so he contrived one out of "rough pine or hemlock boards [fastened] together in the shape of a sled." Jeannette Leonard Gilder, born on Long Island but forced by unfortunate family circumstances to live with a maiden aunt in Birdlington, New Jersey, amused herself "with a few odds and ends of toys," such as a broken cookstove, an unused bureau, a washboard, and a one-legged doll that someone had discarded. "These were my greatest treasures," she reminisced, "because I could really use them."[34]

How children used the myriad objects they found and created confirms that a lack of store-bought toys was no disadvantage. John Albee asserted that in his Massachusetts boyhood all movable objects were playthings to him; he straddled a stick to pretend he was riding a horse, converted his mother's knitting needles into swords, and used clothespins as toy soldiers. Even in wealthy families, informal playthings seemed more important than formal toys. Cornelia Gray, daughter of a well-off Chicago family, entertained herself with ribbons in innumerable ways, while Connecticut-born Caroline Stickney, daughter of a paper mill owner, cut up discarded bedsheets for doll clothes, supplying her "ever-increasing family" of dolls with "many and variously colored dresses, coats, hats and aprons." Edward Everett Hale improvised playthings from "whalebone, spiral springs, pulleys, and catgut, for perpetual motion or locomotive carriages; rollers and planks for floats." And countless boys whittled toy boats and weapons from sticks and discarded pieces of wood, and they fashioned kites from paper, cloth, and string that they had collected.[35]

Adult clothing, cast off or purloined, offered special opportunities for fantasy play. Mary Crosby, born in New York City in 1822, recalled "dressing up in various characters and making use of old-time costumes, brocade coats of our grandfathers. . . . My mother had preserved various bonnets of different fashions from the extremely large to the extremely small, the high top and the poke, these always created great amusement." Garments belonging to grownups also were among the items most commonly appropriated by slave children. Ann Drake, of Pike County, Mississippi, testified that "sumtimes we wud dress up in mammies dresses, an' play lak we wus fine ladies. Sum time we wud break down er bush an hol' it ober our heds an lak dat wus er par'sol."[36]

Reading materials cannot be deemed toys in the same way as other playthings are, but they often have served the purpose of inspiring the impromptu games and play items that occupied children's time. In the early nineteenth century, the Bible provided young readers with stories and characters that they adapted into their fantasy play, but books such as *Robinson Crusoe*, read by or to children, served the same purpose. The journal of David Clapp, son of a Boston printer,

Books, such as Bible, inspired playing

and the diary of author Louisa May Alcott, written when she was eleven, exemplify the way literature occupied their childhoods, inspiring them to create impromptu dramas in which they assumed the role of various literary characters.[37]

In addition, children created their own publications, sometimes in imitation of adults. Numerous examples exist of amateur newspapers, typeset (though sometimes written in longhand) by neighborhood kids or siblings. These publications, such as they were, had very short runs and presented mostly family and local news plus fiction stories and poems. For example, the "Juvenile Key," printed by "Z. J. & J. W. Griffin" of Brunswick, Maine, in 1830 (probably with the help of a parent), identified the publishers as ages seven and nine and included listings of lost items as well as brief parables. The "Minute Gun," published by Samuel Foster Haven Jr. of Worcester, Massachusetts, in 1845–46, came out on four-inch-by-five-inch sheets with a subscription price of three cents per month. It, too, included listings of lost items along with jokes, short stories, and poetry. And "The Casket," a longhand journal of three editions, compiled by Sarah J. Davidson and Eunice W. Brewer of unknown location, presented jokes and riddles, plus stories and articles submitted by girls who apparently were friends of the editors.[38]

In the twenty-first-century, when formal play sites have replaced woods, streets, and attics and when manufactured toys and games glut most children's everyday life, it is hard to imagine that the surfeit of designated play spaces and the dearth of commercial playthings did not prevent antebellum kids from amusing themselves. Indeed, the creativity that early-nineteenth-century youngsters revealed has bequeathed an impressive legacy to American play culture.

Antebellum Kids at Play: Playmates and Rebellion

Left to their own devices, in what William Dean Howells called "a world of foolish dreams," antebellum children appropriated and transformed their environments and the materials that filled those surroundings in ways that enabled them to impart to their play a special quality. Sometimes they pursued those foolish dreams alone; at other times, they did so with others. Sometimes their pastimes won approval from adults; at other times, they defied the ideals that the older

INDIANS IN "CIVILIZED" PLAY. These Crow Indian girls, ages ten, twelve, and thirteen, had been sent East from their reservation in the 1880s. They are shown here dressed in "American" clothes and playing with common toys, including a checkers game, a rag doll, and a doll chair. *President and Fellows of Harvard College, Peabody Museum, Harvard University*

generation prescribed. Sometimes, play was innocent and instructive; at other times, it was cruel and dangerous.

In a society that valued children yet also strongly desired to control their actions, adults tried to integrate children into "constructive" activities that often included intergenerational grouping. As much as

he reminisced about his independent boyhood, Edward Everett Hale
also spent much of his youth in adult-directed activities linked to his
church and his school. His autobiography mentions, for example, being sent to dancing school and attending lectures sponsored by organizations such as the Society for the Promotion of Useful Knowledge,
the Mercantile Literary Association, and the Natural History Society.
After a lecture, he would accompany his parents to some family's
home for an evening dinner, "and thus," he wrote, "the lyceum lecture
of that time played a quite important part in the social arrangements
of growing boys and girls." Other kinds of formal entertainment also
brought generations together. A diary of an unidentified young girl,
written between 1828 and 1831, frequently mentions "having tea"
with various adults, not just those from her own family.[39]

Many children, by circumstance or by choice, played alone. William Johnston, son of a Pittsburgh printer, suffered a temporary physical disability that prevented him from actively playing with other children. A hip abscess and subsequent infection confined Johnston to his
house where he amused himself in "quiet ways," building model fire
engines and ships. As his condition improved, however, William was
able to join in "more active sports." Other autobiographers recalled a
preference for private reverie. Elizabeth Buffum Chase, daughter of a
leading Rhode Island manufacturer and abolitionist, claimed, "When I
was a very little girl I used to be very fond of going off by myself."
Looking back from old age, Chase might have been appreciating her
solitude with exaggerated sentimentality, but there seems to be a gen-
uineness to claims such as those by her and by Henry Clark Wright
who, upon reflection, believed that he disliked playing with other
boys because he had an aversion to competition and the "damage" to
his spirit—probably meaning self-esteem—that boys' aggressive play
caused.[40]

The most accessible partners for group play in the early nineteenth century were siblings and other kin, a pattern that reflected
both the enduring importance of family ties and a not-yet-fully-devel-
oped peer-oriented youth culture. Children on the frontier, distant
from neighbors, relied largely on brothers, sisters, and cousins for
playmates. Sabrina Loomis Hills, whose family moved frequently
through Vermont and upstate New York, played almost exclusively
with her two siblings. Rachel Butz, who grew up in rural Indiana,
recalled, "As the rest of the family were much older than I, Sammy

[her brother, four years older than she] and Mary [a cousin] were my only playmates, except when we had company or visited away from home." Margaret DeLand, raised on an estate on the Ohio River, occupied her free time mostly with her many cousins who lived nearby, though she also enjoyed staying at her grandmother's house where she played with the "colored children" who worked there.[41]

Once they became involved in playgroups of peers, antebellum children more regularly separated by sex than when they played within their family. John Burroughs, raised in the Catskill Mountains of New York and who became a farmer and writer, was born into a family of five children that eventually increased to ten, giving him ample play partners within the household. Yet, he spent most of his childhood outside the family circle in the company of male peers, with whom he engaged in shooting competitions and expeditions into the woods. "A boy friend could throw the witchery of romance over everything," he rhapsodized. Caroline Stickney, the Connecticut girl mentioned previously who cut up bedsheets for doll clothes, also liked to summon neighbor girls and create a "sewing society" that met in an outdoor field. And, as was their tradition, Indian children continued to grow up in strictly sex-segregated circumstances. The previously mentioned Thomas Wildcat Alford, born into the "Absentee Shawnee" tribe that had been removed to Oklahoma, described competitive games played exclusively by boys and emphasized that "Indian girls never were allowed to play with boys."[42]

Gender-integrated play did sometimes occur, especially when choices for playmates were limited. Jeannette Leonard Gilder recalled that in her New Jersey neighborhood, "Our playmates were of necessity boys, which suited me very well, for we had tastes in common." Mary Esther Mulford, a Long Island sea captain's daughter, played dolls with her cousin Amanda but averred that she liked playing with boys more than with girls. Sarah Brewer-Bonebright moved from Indiana to a log cabin in Iowa when she was eleven. Constrained by her isolation to socializing with the four households who had migrated with her family, Sarah and other girls played various games with the boys of her tiny rural community.[43] Memories of these integrated associations seem to have been recalled mostly by female autobiographers and diarists, possibly reflecting both the selective memories of women and the selective forgetfulness of men. If so, the gender separation would have been even more common than the evidence suggests.

In the plantation South, slave children played with each other in both same-sex and mixed-gender situations, often in ways that mimicked the conditions of their parents. Some of their games, such as reenactments of whippings and auctions, may have prepared them psychologically for their futures, though some historians have challenged this theory as overly speculative.[44] While slave kids mostly played with others of their station, it is clear that interracial play was common. WPA narratives contain myriad references such as that by Harriet Miller of Pile County, Mississippi, who stated that "I played wid de white chilluns all de time, " and by Dempsey Pitts of Coahama County, Mississippi, that "all the white and colored children would go to the grove and ride saplings for horses all day." Charity Jones of Amite County, Mississippi, testified, "We played in de yard wid de white an' nigger chilluns," and Randall Flagg of Columbus, Georgia, recalled, "The white and colored children up to eight or ten years of age, played and frolicked together."[45] Often these integrated amusements reproduced prevailing racial hierarchy, such as when black youngsters played the part of a mule in a game of wagon or assumed servile qualities in games of house. But also, in ball playing, hunting and fishing, and other games, preteen black and white children appear, at least on the surface, to have disregarded their differences in status.

How emotionally close these interracial relationships were may have been distorted by memory, but former slaves retold of them as if they were natural to both black and white childhoods. Abe McKlennan of Lincoln County, Mississippi, told his WPA interviewer, "Marster Burkett had three sons [and] four gals. . . . Me an' his son Jim growed up together. We loves each other mighty, an' we plays togethah all the time." Westley Little of Smith County, Mississippi, recalled, "I played wid Marse [Master's] chillum lak I did my own brothers an' sisters. A heap o' nights after we had played hard all day an' until late I has crawled in de bed wid Marse's boys an' slept all night." And Joe Coney of Pike County, Mississippi, remembered that one day while rabbit hunting with some white boys, one of them saved him when he fell into a creek.[46]

Though the play sites and play materials of antebellum children —white, black, and Indian—shifted daily, perhaps hourly, from home to yard to street to the countryside and back, there seems to have been a consistency in playmates, at least more so than would become apparent by the end of the twentieth century, when instructional activities, organized playgroups, and television and video games created varied types of contact. Geography and demography certainly influenced how playgroups were constituted, within the family and within a community. But because children lacked the kinds of formal, nonschool activities that began to emerge later in the nineteenth century, and because work consumed most waking hours of children's lives, the day-to-day dramatis personae of their play worlds consisted mainly of the same people: siblings, cousins, and small groups of neighbors. In addition, however, whether playing by themselves or with others, children conspired to challenge adult authority.

The first half of the nineteenth century remained, as in the past, a time when religious concerns normally prevailed over the mundane, and fear of God as well as obedience to parents governed the lives of most children. Though perhaps an extreme case, William McKnight, who was raised on a farm in Portage County, Ohio, and who later became a circuit-riding preacher, set his childhood religious conversion at the center of his autobiography:

> I was a wicked boy until I was about thirteen years old, . . . [but then]
> I attended a prayer meeting one evening. . . . A strange feeling came
> over me, . . . and I called on the name of the Lord for mercy and the
> brethren prayed for me and before the meeting closed that evening,
> the Lord spoke peace to my soul.[47]

Given his adult calling, McKnight understandably wanted to emphasize how he found God; yet, his recollection of being a wild youth represents a quality of play that often characterized various childhoods, a quality that included risk, cruelty, and, especially among boys, aggressiveness and simple disobedience of society's rules and prescriptions.

The notion that children came into the world with innate wickedness was fading, but in the adult mind, kids still needed to be firmly steered away from idleness and toward reason. Parents increasingly shared chief responsibility for this task with schools, but also a heightened tolerance for play included prescriptions for the kind of domesticated childhood that was most desirable. Especially among middle-class families, the judicious selection of toys, games, and books was intended to set children's play on a proper course. Advice literature regularly distinguished the home, where youngsters could be supervised and trained, as a necessary alternative to street play, and writers proposed diversions such as games, hobbies, and collecting various items as means to instill what one advocate identified as "habits of order and arrangement."[48]

Children themselves absorbed these values and usually complied with the directives of their elders. William Hoppin, son of a Providence, Rhode Island, auctioneer, filled his diary with references to play activities that supposedly cultivated efficiency, self-improvement, industry, and achievement. Daniel Drake, physician and booster of early Cincinnati, recalled that "I was preserved from many temptations and practically taught self-denial. . . . I was taught to practice economy." Future Massachusetts senator George F. Hoar and his brothers were strictly forbidden to play on the Sabbath. They "could not play at any games or talk about matters not pertaining to religion . . . [and] not permitted to read any books except such as were 'good for Sunday.'" Joseph Hodges Choate, son of a Salem, Massachusetts, physician, spent much of his spare time attending lyceum lectures and observing proceedings at the local courthouse. He stated that he and his siblings "were not much given to sport," but there was one exception: "We played cards a great deal. Father had a theory that if he taught us all the games of cards that he knew or could learn himself, there was no danger of any of the children taking to gambling when they grew up, and so it proved." And, some youngsters rarely if ever had opportunities for leisure activity because their poverty and the needs of their family prevented it. For example, Sallie Hester began keeping a diary in 1839 when her family picked up stakes in Indiana and traveled by wagon to California in hopes of finding a healthier home for her ailing mother. Sallie's diary contains almost no reference to play, only to pioneer hardship.[49]

When youngsters' play mimicked adult activities and, especially, prepared children for the demands of adulthood, the older generation usually did not object. As already mentioned, slave and Indian children often practiced for the rigors and hardships they would encounter once they were old enough to shoulder tasks in the cotton fields, households, and hunting grounds. Among whites, girls, more than boys, tended to engage in daily activities such as childcare, sewing, and housework that were intended to foster feminine skills and to encourage reserved, nurturing behavior. Boys were allowed to exhibit more self-assertion and aggressiveness, within certain boundaries, because such qualities were deemed essential to adult masculinity. Still, boys tended to resist formal, adult-sanctioned games that too rigidly channeled their energies. Edward Everett Hale, for example, noted, "We play all the tame games, such as checkers, chess, lotto, battledore and shuttlecocks, graces, vingt-et-un (a card game), cup and ball, coronella, and the like, but I think under a certain protest."[50]

The mode of preparation for adulthood, however, was gradually drifting in new directions, and children themselves, girls as well as boys, were finding ways to use their play in defiance of what adults expected of them. Such activity evoked varying reactions. Sometimes a child's assertion of freedom and playful spontaneity gained endorsement from adults who had discarded the traditional model of restrictive parenting. Richard Henry Dana, who grew up in Boston in the early nineteenth century, believed that his father overcame a fear of dangerous play and gave Richard and his brothers leeway in their pastimes. "He felt," Dana later wrote, "the habits of self-reliance and self-help, and familiarity with exposure and risks, to a boy not foolhardy, are a greater protection than all the guarding and watching of the most careful parents."[51]

Other caretakers were not as lenient, so kids rebelled. They found secret places where they devised their own innocent amusements but also where they got into mischief (sometimes getting caught and punished; other times eluding authority), courted danger, and exhibited both creativity and callousness. Brown Thurston's journal contains numerous references to disobedience and misbehavior. He defied his father's opposition to circuses and ran off to see one without consent, he escaped his aunt's watchful eye and tried to learn how to chew tobacco, he nearly drowned while playing with a friend on a homemade raft, and he snuck a quaff of rum punch that caused him to pass out. Edward Everett Hale singed his eyebrows after igniting some gunpowder while secretly playing with a magnifying glass. Girls, too, demonstrated wayward qualities. Orleana Ellery Pell, daughter of a judge in New Orleans where she was raised, often was punished at school for being naughty, but, she asserted with self-congratulation, "I enjoyed it immensely." Harriet Doutney's self-promotional autobiographical account claimed that she had two distinct lives as a child. "The one, bright and joyous; mischief and prank filling the house with sunshine. The other, dreary and sad; included by emotions and difficult to explain, but with which my playmates had no sympathy."[52]

A thirst for violence and cruelty also accompanied independent play. The recollections of future naturalist John Muir, who emigrated from Scotland to Wisconsin when he was ten, represent a common pattern of many boyhoods:

> One of our amusements was hunting cats without seriously hurting them. These sagacious animals knew, however, that, though not very dangerous, boys were not to be trusted. . . . After we learned that [cats] had nine lives, we tried to verify the common saying that no matter how far cats fell they always landed on their feet unhurt. We caught one in our back yard, . . . and somehow got him smuggled up to the top story of the house. [They dropped the cat and it landed on its feet uninjured.] . . . Again—showing the natural savagery of boys —we delighted in dog-fights, and even in the horrid red work of slaughter-houses, often running long distances and climbing over walls and roofs to see a pig killed.[53]

For enslaved children, play could combine freedom and resistance in ways that free children would never experience. As historian Steven Mintz has observed, "Children were not simply slavery's victims; they were also active agents, who managed to resist slavery's dehumanizing pressures. . . . Play taught enslaved children that they were equal or even superior to their white counterparts." Mintz quotes former slave Felix Heywood of Texas: "We was stronger and knowed how to play, and the white children's didn't."[54] More than among white children, the play of slave youngsters involved risk, some of it unavoidable but at other times courted. Many former slaves interviewed by WPA workers, for example, recalled play that involved petty pilfering: stealing eggs from the master's henhouse, climbing trees in the orchard to grab apples, taking a horse for an unauthorized ride, and the like. White kids who were apprehended in such transgressions faced physical punishment, but seldom as severe or capricious as what befell slave children. Playing away from the master's premises always meant eluding the "patrollers," and if captured without a proper pass, the young offender soon felt the lash. One day when Emmaline Sturgis and her friends stole away from their Georgia plantation to play in the woods, "dey wuz waitin' for us and massa had whipped me an' de oberseer whipped my little sistah." Mischievous play with white children could bring unwanted repercussions to all concerned. Prince

Johnson, from Coachana County, Mississippi, recalled, "One day master's children and all the colored children slipped off to the orchard. They were eating green apples fast as they could swallow, when who should come riding up but Master himself. He lined them all up, black and white alike, and cut a keen switch and there was not a one in that line that didn't get a few licks."[55]

Just as in previous generations, American youngsters in the first half of the nineteenth century took the opportunity, when it presented itself, to pursue their own forms of amusement. Whatever their race, class, or gender, children strayed from adult supervision alone or with others to invent games and playthings, engage in solitary reverie and prankish behavior, and simply be childish. But evidence suggests that in this pursuit of independence, whether innocent or purposefully rebellious, the feelings of guilt that pervaded transgressions of earlier eras were more absent. John Muir's recollections were typical; though his stern father constantly warned him of the reprisal that awaited disobedience, John perceived his independent play as almost sacred:

> Like devout martyrs of wildness, we stole away to the seashore or the green, sunny fields with almost religious regularity, taking advantage of opportunities when father was very busy. . . . No punishment, however sure and severe, was of any avail against the attractions of the fields and woods.[56]

Even Henry Clark Wright, who confessed that he had "a sabbatarian feeling," secretly engaged in pastimes that his parents would not condone. "I could not help it," he confessed. "I used to try very hard to be good, and to keep my restless, merry thoughts from wandering on Sunday; but it was of no use; they would rove about the pastures and meadows, and in the woods; and I never thought of condemning myself for it."[57]

By 1850, children's play was in full transformation. Society's attitudes about the young now recognized the playful rather than the corrupt quality of their natures, and writers accepted the notion that childhood was, and should be, a time of play. As long as they respected authority, kids' play could receive a stamp of approval. Even their "cunning" behavior—the nineteenth-century term for "cute"—could be seen as tolerable and sometimes even delightful. But this appreciative view also was giving youngsters opportunities to broaden their own culture and to explore new environments and new ways to claim independence. More than in previous generations, preadolescent children were developing a dual existence, as expressed by both Harriet Doutney and William Dean Howells: an acceptable one that occurred in the presence of adults and a separate one that was flourishing beyond what adults observed or accepted. The tensions of this duality, one part structured, the other part uncontrolled, would widen in the latter half of the century.

3

The Stuff of Childhood, 1850–1900

JACOB ABBOTT WAS one of the most popular and prolific children's authors in nineteenth-century America. A Congregationalist minister dedicated to teaching Christian duty, Abbott was best known for penning a series of twenty-eight adventure books published between 1836 and 1863 and featuring Rollo Holiday, a plucky boy who imparted practical skills combined with moral lessons to other children. In his later years, Abbott wrote a widely read child-raising manual titled *Gentle Measures in the Training of the Young* (1871). Influenced by both John Locke and contemporary energy theory, Abbott believed that character formation in childhood was critical to human progress and that children needed to be able to release their innate stored-up energy lest dangerous consequences ensue. The means for unleashing that energy, he advised, was through unrestrained play.

Abbott was no libertarian. "The only government of the parent over the child," he wrote, "is one of authority—complete, absolute, unquestioned *authority*." But he believed also that the establishment of parental authority involved "gentle measures," meaning "those which tend to exert a calming, quieting, and soothing influence on the mind, or to produce only such excitements as are pleasurable in [a child's] character." Gentle measures also implied encouragement of children's natural playful impulses rather than expecting young people always to act rationally and purposefully. Abbott advised:

> In a word, we must favor and promote, by every means in our power, the activity of children, not censure and repress it. . . . In encouraging the activity of children, and in guiding the direction of it in their hours of play, we must not expect to make it available for useful results, other than that of promoting their own physical development and health.[1]

In identifying play as a special attribute of childhood, Abbott was articulating an outlook that built on the appreciation of children's innocence and freedom, an attitude that had arisen early in the nineteenth century. But by the time Abbott and others like him were writing their guides, an important evolution had occurred. In the minds of many, by the late nineteenth century, play had become what one writer has called the "stuff of childhood."[2] Play served to channel excess energy and provide intervals of relief between more sober tasks of work and learning, and it was considered an enjoyable, rather than a serious, way to rehearse for adulthood and master the emotional challenges of growing up. Harmless fantasy rather than moral strictures, happiness more than subservience and prayer, became the norm for a child's existence. To promote that happiness, many parents rewarded their young with an expanding array of toys. Educators and psychologists now deemed too much serious activity and denial of fun as detrimental; instead, they argued, youngsters needed a balance between labor and amusement. According to George Ellsworth Johnson, an early playground administrator, a child "should be taught that a life of play-work is the ideal, and that it is his privilege to seek it."[3]

When it came to defining how, where, and with what children played, however, a new generation of experts distrusted both children and parents. They opposed child-generated spontaneous play, stressing instead that guidance and control were paramount. Maria Kraus-Boelte, who helped introduce the German concept of kindergarten into the United States, typified this view when she wrote in 1875, "American children must be taught *how to play*."[4] As part of their child-guidance movement, reformers promoted educational games, playgrounds, and athletics as means to achieve "healthy" play. Moreover, these reformers believed, because of their emotional and physical immaturity, children needed to be protected from the dangers of a society that was growing increasingly complex from industrialization, urbanization, and immigration. City streets, especially, harbored vice, "bad" kids who could taint childhood innocence, and physical hazards that could do even worse harm. Thus, professional child workers, fearing that the social fabric was unraveling, tried to employ organized play as a means for "saving" kids from the street, the marketplace, and even other kids.[5]

But as has always been their wont, children had their own ideas about play, and perhaps more than ever before, they took advantage of their status to craft their own amusements, sometimes compliant with adult wishes, sometimes alternative, and sometimes outright oppositional. Indeed, as the separation between adult and children's worlds widened, the tensions over young people's autonomy became more apparent. Even as the availability and sale of manufactured toys and games expanded, youngsters often favored their own brands of free and unstructured play and their informal, improvised playthings. Children in preteen years did not usually revolt from adult supervision, but—given more things to play with, more time for recreational activity, and more opportunities to socialize with peers—they elaborated an alternative culture that by 1900 placed them on the threshold of a golden age of independent play.

The Celebration of Childhood

As urbanization, industrialization, and immigration overspread the nation in the second half of the nineteenth century, a number of factors set apart and complicated the status of children. These included a general decline in birthrates, the separation of place of work from place of residence, a budding consumer economy, the emergence of a middle-class ideal of longer residence within the family and greater socialization role for mothers, widespread imposition of compulsory school attendance, and heightened age-consciousness and age-grading with resulting formation of peer cultures. Largely prevalent among economically advantaged families, some of these factors nevertheless had effect on other children as well.

Between 1850 and 1900, the drop in birthrates in the United States was substantial. The estimated number of live births for every one thousand women in the most fertile age range (fifteen to forty-four years of age) fell from 194 at mid-century to 87 by 1900. This plunge ultimately influenced the proportion of youngsters in the preadolescent age cohort, the group under consideration in this book. While young people aged five to fourteen comprised around 25 percent of the total population just before the Civil War, their share declined each decade thereafter, to slightly over 22 percent at century's end. Concomitantly, the median age of the population rose: for whites from nineteen in 1850 to slightly more than twenty-three in 1900, and for nonwhites from seventeen to almost twenty. (It is thirty-six at present.)

Higher life expectancies and increased adult immigration accounted for part of these changes, but family limitation was involved as well. Average number of births per mother, around five in 1850, fell to just above three by 1900. As demographers and historians have pointed out, fewer children per family enabled parents to devote more attention and resources to their offspring, and because the ages of children in any given family did not stretch across a broad span of years, a more definite gap developed between generations.[6]

With the rise of large factories, offices, and retail establishments in cities and with the spread of mechanized agriculture in rural areas, income-producing work was removed from the household, and children were less likely to be involved in the family home economy than in previous eras. On farms and in tenement sweatshops, young people still engaged in demanding labor, but many kids had more time and energy for non-work activity.[7] School, especially, occupied more of a child's daily life than it had in previous eras. The campaign for widespread public education that had begun in the 1830s intensified after the Civil War with the passage of compulsory attendance laws in numerous states and localities. As a result, by the late nineteenth century, city children attended school for nine months a year into their teen years, though in rural areas, where children's labor was still necessary, especially during spring planting and fall harvesting, the school year was often much briefer—around six months—and kids stayed in school only until they were ten or eleven.[8]

The organization of schoolchildren in age-graded classrooms reflected a major cultural development in American society of the late nineteenth century: the application of age norms to social organization and resulting strengthening of peer-group influence. By the 1880s, a consciousness of normal—meaning desired—human development, coupled with a reliance on numbers and predictability stemming from the standardization and regulation of industrial production, had created a series of expectations about experiences and achievements related to age. These expectations were applied most rigorously to children, and they included not only what young people should be taught at specific ages but also age-related norms of physical and psychological development. The establishment of the American Pediatric Association in 1886 exemplifies the belief that there were age-related standards of physiology and morbidity unique to childhood. These standards soon were applied to intelligence and emotional growth as well.

Childhood increasingly came to be seen as a distinct stage of life with distinctive properties and needs. Numerous laws set children apart from adults, and children began to have their own unique clothing, furniture, literature, games, and social worlds. Though they slept and ate meals at home, youngsters in school and out now were grouped with, and socialized by, peers more than ever before.[9]

Also, from the 1860s into the 1880s, families felt aftershocks of the Civil War. In both North and South, thousands of children experienced the absence of fathers, who were casualties of war, and grew up in economically strained circumstances that necessitated their participation in farmwork and in the industrial workforce. In the Far West and on the Plains, rural children were perhaps even more important to the family economy than in the East; geographically isolated, they shouldered many tasks and exercised considerable independence. Children of emancipated slaves had new opportunities to attend school, and though their labor on family sharecropping and tenant farms remained vital, they were freer to engage in new kinds of independent activity than had been the case when they were in bondage. Their continued poverty, however, left them with fewer places in which to play and deprived them of most newly available consumer goods.[10]

Indian children, especially in the West, encountered some of the most difficult challenges. Disruptions from endemic white invasion and warfare, exacerbated by poverty, disease, and destruction of natural resources such as crops, bison, and salmon, made life insecure. Of perhaps even greater impact on children themselves, beginning in the 1870s the federal government and several religious organizations removed thousands of Indian children from their families and placed them in boarding schools created to teach them values and skills for assimilating into white society. At these institutions, Indian youngsters were deprived of native clothing and hairstyles, given Anglo names, forced to replace native religious customs with Christianity, prohibited from speaking their native languages, and regimented into a daily routine of basic education, vocational training, and domestic chores. Nevertheless, even as they labored and learned, disadvantaged children still managed to steal time for leisure and amusement.[11]

In the culture at large, childhood was celebrated and sentimentalized as never before. Prevailing ideology among the middle class —and, to some extent, the working class as well—cherished the

Indian Children forced to become "Americanized"

innocence and exuberance of children as special and charming qualities, not only in a romantic way, as influenced by Rousseau, but also
in a rationalized way. Indeed, in keeping with the scientific spirit of
the times, children in late-nineteenth-century America became objects
of serious study as educators, psychologists, and physicians moved
learning and play, both deemed critical to children's singular existence
and development, under the magnifying glass.

The goal of shaping character, inherited from teachers and clergymen of previous generations, now became the purview of social scientists who emphasized secular more than spiritual guidance. Beginning
in the late 1880s, the leading spokesmen in this endeavor were G.
Stanley Hall and Luther Halsey Gulick. Hall was a psychologist at
Johns Hopkins University and later president of Clark University.
Gulick, a physical education professional at the Young Men's Christian Education (YMCA)Training School in Springfield, Massachusetts,
founded the Boy Scouts of America, the Campfire Girls, and New York
City's Public School Athletic League for boys. Hall and Gulick subscribed to a Darwinian-influenced "recapitulation" theory, believing
that an individual's personal and intellectual development recapitulated human evolution from savagery to civilization. From their studies of children's behavior, Hall and Gulick concluded that each phase
of childhood required particular forms of education and other activity
appropriate to a child's biological and cultural development.[12]

Drawing from recapitulation theory, Hall and Gulick asserted that
play, the natural inclination of all animals, was a part of a child's des-
tiny, just as there had once been an "animalistic" era of unrestrained
behavior that had preceded the more civilized stages in human history. They appreciated the spontaneity of children and did not consider play to be a tool by which adults could dominate children's
lives. Rather, they asserted, adults needed to intervene in children's
activities only to ensure that play, like learning, was appropriate to a
child's growth. Parents and teachers, they said, should tolerate cas-
ual, unstructured play, especially among younger children, but when
youngsters became old enough to play in groups, experts might be
needed to provide guidance. To Hall and Gulick, play reflected a
child's instinct for freedom and enjoyment, but whether or not play
was "fun" was secondary to whether or not it conformed to what they
called the "cultural phase" of recapitulated evolution.[13]

For social scientists seeking to understand human development,

[handwritten margin note: Psychologists began to study play as essential to biological/cultural development]

such as Hall and Gulick, childhood was serious business. While psychologists were observing various facets of children's behavior, anthropologists and folklorists were investigating the games, rhymes, and songs of children and comparing them to preliterate, "childlike" Indian societies. For example, William Wells Newell, a founder of the American Folklore Society, pioneered the collection of children's activities, publishing *Games and Songs of American Children* in 1883.[14] This compilation of some 160 forms of play represented one of the first attempts to identify the folk culture of children.

But even as many of these investigators placed great value upon —and even romanticized as pure—the activities that kids engaged in by themselves, social reformers worried about the harmful influences that the perceived decline of home life and the objectionable qualities of the urban terrain might have on children. Anxious about dangers lurking in anarchic streets and tenements inhabited by foreigners and loath to trust the influence of the peer group, a number of reformers endeavored to guide the process of growing up by creating separate public environments where young people could overcome what one contemporary writer called their "lawless tendencies." In consequence, these reformers established orphanages, settlement houses, playgrounds, and organizations such as the YMCA and YWCA as safe alternatives to the unsupervised, after-school activities that they believed were endangering youth.[15]

Thus, the American playground movement, which flourished after the turn of the century, began in the 1880s. The earliest playgrounds, influenced by German precedents, were sand gardens, constructed in Boston and other cities to provide educational play spaces for very young children of the slums. Soon, government agencies, aided on occasion by private contributions, established summer school playgrounds, followed by year-round play areas, in cities of the industrial Northeast and Midwest. Viewed as one of several methods by which to instill immigrant children with "American" middle-class ideals, playgrounds served as a preferred alternative to unsupervised play in the home. As one New York City reformer declared, "That which parents do not or cannot control in the private sphere of the home, the city must control in the public spheres of park, playground, schools, and recreation centers."[16]

For many youngsters of the late nineteenth century, then, childhood was not idyllic; as in the past, it could be filled with pain and confusion. Yet by 1900, childhood—meaning a period of freedom, joy, and learning—came to be regarded as every person's birthright. But believing that children could succumb to "bad" influences and that kids posed potential disruptions to the status quo if left to their own devices, professional child savers left what historian Gary Cross has called a "contradictory legacy." Leaders of the movement, such as Hall and Gulick, extolled the uninhibited joys of youth, yet they also endeavored to tame kids and to foster purposeful play.[17]

Toys, Games, and Books

As labor in industrial America became more systematized, distinctions between work and play became more definite: one activity produced goods and income; the other produced happiness. Because happiness was considered the normal state of childhood and because happiness and play were equated, it followed that writers who concerned themselves with childhood urged that parents should not only provide for moral, educational, and material well-being but also encourage their children's play instincts. The image of play as the devil's workshop had faded, and a set of new, more secular experts had new ideas. Thus, T. Benjamin Atkins, who laid the foundation for the future psychoanalytic approach to children's play, asserted in his aptly titled book, *Out of the Cradle into the World of Self Education through Play*, that play was not only healthful but also desirable.[18]

Some psychologists now argued that rewards for good behavior should replace punishment for misconduct, and in many families rewards now took the form of toys. The availability of mass-produced toys increased dramatically after the Civil War as technology combined with higher expendable incomes to create a profusion of, and demand for, games, dolls, play paraphernalia, and books. In 1850, the federal census listed only forty-seven American toy manufacturers; by 1880, there were 173, not including carriage and sled makers. Sometimes overlooked, but centrally important to the rising American toy industry, were technological developments such as sheet-metal stamping for making tin toys, molding machines for the manufacture of more lifelike dolls, improved printing techniques for the creation of more attractive board games and books, along with countless new techniques for using textiles, woods, metals, ceramics, and glass. All these and more made toys cheaper, more plentiful, and more appealing than ever before. Advertisers hawked these products in colorful new displays, targeting adult consumers by accentuating a product's durability and educational value and touting brand names of toys in the same ways that they proclaimed the virtues of Uneeda biscuits and Pears soap.[19] Also, just as housing design, with its expanded spaces that promoted both privacy and recreation, represented a rising, child-centered middle class, so did the advent of mass-produced toys enter a new middle-class culture of childhood. Once considered either as unnecessary trifles or as educational aids, toys now assumed functions of fostering pure joy and fantasy.[20]

At the same time, a new form of instructional literature began to appear, one in which self-styled experts produced elaborate compendiums that both encouraged play and prescribed how to play. One such author was Daniel Carter Beard, an illustrator and naturalist who founded a version of boys' clubs known as the Society of the Sons of Daniel Boone and later helped Luther Gulick establish the Boy Scouts of America. Beard penned a tome titled *The American Boys Handy Book* (1882) that prescribed "what to do and how to do it." The book's chapters included instructions for making kites, fishing poles, blowguns, boats, and theatrical costumes and for raising dogs, stuffing animals, stocking an aquarium, and camping. Beard's sisters, Lina and Adelia Beard, wrote the companion *American Girls Handy Book* (1888), which outlined appropriate activities for young females. Other manuals, such as John Dennison Champlin and Arthur Elmore Bostwick's *The Young Folks' Cyclopaedia of Games and Sports* (1890), included a treatise on tiddlywinks as well as instructions—as if youngsters needed them —on how to organize snowball fights.[21]

Fictional literature created by adults specifically for young people also reflected the new distinctiveness of childhood. Before the nineteenth century, publishers of books for children aimed their products at parents, who would be reading to, or buying for, their kids. Mostly biblical tales that taught obedience and self-control and religious-based child-rearing manuals, these publications rarely catered to children's fantasies. But as attitudes about childhood began to shift, a market designed for youngsters' tastes arose, and books containing fantasy tales and adventure stories competed with didactic works. By the 1840s, the stories of Hans Christian Anderson reached American bookshops, and native writers of children's literature began producing works to entertain youngsters directly. Tales of heroic characters, far-away places (in time as well as distance), the "Wild West," animals (dog and horse stories), and adventure on the high seas reinforced the new outlook that childhood was a special period that should be enjoyed.[22]

To some extent, authors of this fiction masked their fantasies behind avowals of moral instruction. For example, William Taylor Adams, a Massachusetts schoolteacher who between 1850 and 1900 wrote hundreds of books and stories under the pen name of Oliver Optic, promised that he intended his writing to inspire "moral and social duties" in his readers. But in fact, as he also claimed, he made his tales almost exclusively "full of dash and vigor." With works such as his Riverdale series (six volumes for boys), his Great Western series, and his *Oliver Optics Magazine* (appropriately subtitled *Our Boys and Girls*), Adams helped introduce the genre of children's adventure fiction that offered examples of virtue and Christian forbearance only in passing, not as the major theme. He also penned such books as *Poor and Proud* and *Onward and Upward*, tales of children making their way in the world that influenced the career and writing of his contemporary, Horatio Alger.[23]

In the mid-1860s, the number of magazines published explicitly for children also mushroomed. A few of these publications predated the era, led by the long-lived *Youth's Companion*. Founded in 1827 with the object of providing both edification and entertainment, by the 1850s this magazine included more straightforward fiction than religious lessons, along with biographical sketches and poetry. By 1885, *Youth's Companion* boasted 385,000 subscribers. The other highly successful children's magazine, *St. Nicholas*, began publication in 1873 and ultimately absorbed several similar periodicals. These well-known periodicals for children attracted contributions from notable writers such as Harriet Beecher Stowe. Youngsters might have read these journals selectively, however. According to journalism historian Frank Luther Mott, when *Youth's Companion* began prefacing its popular "anecdote" feature in 1869 with a moral lesson printed in leaded type, juvenile readers learned to skip over the serious introductions and read only the smaller-type but more entertaining anecdotes.[24]

By the 1880s, the respectable journals for children were being forced to share the market with weeklies created especially for young readers to buy and devour independent of parental guidance. What Mott has labeled "blood-and-thunder" serials for boys, such as *Boys of New York,* derived from the genre of action-oriented dime novels for adults and found their way to haylofts and attics where youngsters secretly poured over them, much as boys of a few generations later read comic books. Girls, too, had their own inexpensive publications such as *Girls of Today,* though these journals found less success—generally fewer subscribers—than those produced for boys.

A shift in children's reading habits was not abrupt. In many households, the genre of moralistic literature continued to prevail. This type of publication, inherited from previous eras, reflected the ongoing and contradictory attempt to inhibit children's playful activity amid growing appreciation of play. The "Sunnybrook Stories," a didactic series compiled by Asa Bullard, for example, explicitly exhorted—even frightened—young readers to serve God and keep the Sabbath holy. In one such tale, two boys ignored their Sunday religious duties and stole cherries from a farmer's orchard. While they were in the act, a large dog attacked them and the farmer imprisoned them until the next morning. The more benign *Girl's Story Book* by Francis Woodworth featured counsel such as "Stay where you are, and make the most and the best of what you have and are likely to have, and you will be happy enough."[25]

Still, by the 1880s, literature that stirred the imagination as much as, if not more than, one's piety was capturing young readers. For example, Theodore Dreiser, growing up in Evansville, Indiana, devoured the Alger books and others of their ilk. He recalled:

> It was a colorful world which they presented, impossible from a practical point of view and yet suggesting that freedom of action which we so often experience in dreams. How often at that time I trotted over the plains of Africa or Australia or Asia with these famous boy heroes whose names I have long since forgotten, but who possessed some practical device or other—iron horse or buggy or man, and bullet or arrow-proof jacket and suits even—in which one could travel in safety, if not peace, and at the same time defy and destroy all manner of savage and wild animals, and so with impunity invade the wildest, the most dangerous and therefore the most fascinating regions![26]

To be sure, children's reading habits in the late nineteenth century varied widely and are difficult to interpret. Class and gender exerted considerable influence, and the subject matter ranged along a spectrum from pious to taboo. Nevertheless, new forms of literature were emerging as a component of children's entertainment culture. The homilies of church and school had to compete with—and often give way to—books, stories, and magazines chosen by peers rather than by teachers and parents. And, as Dreiser's recollection illustrates, styles and content of the literature imprinted themselves in the memory in indelible ways, and the words acted as intermediaries between the storyteller's intentions and the child's imagination.[27]

Thus, in a society of complicating demographic, economic, and social change, the world of preadolescents also became more complicated. Yet, as playrooms began to fill up with games, toys, and books, children did what they had always done: they adopted play styles that incorporated spaces, things, and playmates in their own ways.

Incorporating Play Places and Playthings

Urban planners and architects seldom have intended their structures as children's play spaces, but in the late nineteenth century, youngsters in America's burgeoning cities and towns incorporated and transformed streets and buildings in impressively inventive ways. In the countryside, kids had always romped in fields and forests, and they had appropriated barns and sheds as play spaces. But after 1850, a massive expansion of the urban-built environment provided countless new sites and objects to be used. The advent of asphalt pavement and better street lighting; the planting of telephone poles, hydrants, and fences; the erection of walls and stoops; and the construction of other new edifices—all fueled youthful imaginations. Balls bounced higher on pavement than on dirt, nighttime no longer halted outdoor activity, new hiding places and bases could be found for old games, and inanimate objects could be appropriated as play partners. The roadways and buildings increased hazards as well as adventure, but in an era before automobiles and a public policy that catered to them pushed youngsters out of the way, opportunities for creative outdoor play multiplied considerably.[28]

As it always had, nature still gave both city kids and country kids myriad locations for solitude and adventure. To describe their most common activity in woods and fields, diarists and autobiographers applied the term "roaming," much like their predecessors earlier in the century had used the term "roving." Roaming meant walking aimlessly, observing, imagining, and, mostly, exhilarating in the freedom of the outdoors. The writer Robert Luther Duffus, growing up in Vermont, recalled, "We weren't roaming for any definite purpose, although I believe the theory among us was that we were Indians, or pioneers looking for Indians. The theory didn't matter too much. It was wonderful just to be alive and out of doors." Novelist Isabel Bolton expressed her memories with even more rapture: "Release! Completely cut off from the human tether we ran straight into the bright acres of earth and sky and sea. We appeared to have no objective; our need was to run to release our happiness." And Della Lutes, raised on a farm in central Michigan, relished "hours of childish leisure passed . . . lying full length upon the grass where wind falls spent their wasted opulence."[29] Literate and poetic, these passages represent a sentimental quality of childhood that memory might have embellished; nevertheless, their details invoke a quality of experience that other children may have felt but could not articulate so lyrically.

In rural areas, hunting, fishing, swimming, sledding, and bicycling characterized active outdoor play. Indian boys, as they had done for generations, combined nature play with practical training, catching and learning about birds, deer, and fish. Luther Standing Bear, born Ota Kte on the Pine Ridge Reservation in Dakota Territory, recalled using miniature bows and arrows to shoot at bushes and throwing sticks as if they were spears in order to prepare for his principal adult vocation of hunting. White boys also trapped or shot small prey. Southern lawyer Aubrey Lee Brooks, raised in North Carolina, liked to take his dog with him to hunt for rabbits and opossums, and journalist Ralph Blumenthal often swam in the river near his Wisconsin boyhood home—he was once arrested for bathing nude—and caught frogs along the shore. Future heavyweight boxing champion Jack Dempsey spent much of his Colorado boyhood hunting deer and setting traps. Girls, too, converted the woods into a playground. Novelist Edna Ferber made frequent excursions into the forest outside her Wisconsin home to collect flowers and nuts, and poet and historian Sarah Bixby Smith, growing up on a California sheep farm, built sand houses and impromptu gardens alongside a nearby river.[30]

STREET PLAY. Immigrant children used city streets, including in front of a saloon, for a common play site. *Chicago Historical Society*

Sarah Bixby Smith, however, soon moved to Los Angeles where, like countless preadolescent youngsters, she incorporated the streets and sidewalks into an informal but treasured playscape. "The level street at Court and Hill," she wrote, "protected on three sides by grades too steep for horses, was our neighborhood playground. . . . [There] we played school, jacks, marbles, tag, and an adaptation of *Peck's Bad Boy*, and, between whiles, dolls." Future editor and critic Henry Seidel Canby and his friends incorporated the yards and fences of Wilmington, Delaware, into a "series of city states to play in," and they transformed vacant lots into a "true frontier, where fires could be built to roast chestnuts and potatoes." Working-class children, short on private play sites, were especially inventive in taking over public spaces and creating a rich play life in the urban outdoors. Catharine Brody, reflecting on her childhood on New York City's "unfashionable" West Side, wrote that "we could not go into the woods hunting for the first violets, but on the day that the sidewalks bloomed with the boxes and numbers of 'potsies' [hopscotch], on that day we knew that spring had come."[31]

In his 1891 pioneer survey of street play in Brooklyn, anthropologist Stewart Culin noted how children adapted and invented games to conform to the urban environment. Autobiographers such as Sarah Bixby Smith, Henry Seidel Canby, and many more exemplified such an observation, presenting countless ways that urban youngsters incorporated and transformed objects and structures to meet their play needs. Canby and friends used fences as both boundaries for informal ball games and runways across which they walked in a precarious balancing act. Bixby Smith and comrades employed assorted objects as goals for games of "prisoner's base," while other youngsters appropriated streets and common objects for diverse kicking and throwing contests. Culin described one elaborate game called "kick-the-wicket" that illustrates how creatively urban youngsters could use their surroundings:

> A lamp-post or a tree is chosen as "home" and several bases are agreed upon, usually four, around which the players run. The boy who is "it" places the wicket, which is sometimes made of wood, and sometimes of a piece of old rubber hose, against the tree or post chosen as home, and then stations himself at some distance from it, ready to catch it when it is kicked by the other players. They take turns kicking the wicket. If it is caught by the boy who is "it," the kicker becomes "it." If the boy who is "it" does not catch the wicket, he runs after it and puts it in place, and any boy whom he catches running between the bases, where the wicket is up, becomes "it." The players run around the bases as they kick the wicket, and when they make the circuit and touch home, they form in a line, ready to kick the wicket again.[32]

When weather and parents prohibited outdoor play, children, especially those who occupied spacious middle-class dwellings, could convert the home into a fertile place of amusement. Equipped with roomy attics and basements, the detached, one-and-a-half-story bungalow and larger two-story Victorian house also usually included separate bedrooms for children and in some homes even special playrooms. Situated in the center of a relatively large lot, these structures had front, side, and rear yards, often fenced in, that offered additional private play sites. By the 1880s and 1890s, simple balloon-frame construction and standardized features such as mass-produced window frames coupled with huge demand and the suburban ideal to make these homes desirable and affordable even to some working-class families.[33]

Children were just as creative in their appropriation of domestic space as they were of the outdoors. Writer Eleanor Hallowell Abbot, growing up in Cambridge, Massachusetts, in the 1870s, observed how her brother and cousin "roamed the house as free agents, from attic to cellar with great clatter of boots and unmitigated hoots of joy." Henry Seidel Canby recalled that the houses of his childhood "were big enough for the child's affairs to bubble out from repression, finding their own space." Girls invaded their mothers' closets and attic trunks to play dress up in adult clothing, while boys found hiding places in nooks and crannies of all floors for games of hide-and-seek.[34]

As mentioned above, parents and other concerned adults who attempted to isolate children from the perils of modern society often used toys as a means of occupying kids' time. Manufacturers fashioned many of the era's mass-produced toys to appeal to parents rather than directly to children themselves. Toy banks were among the most popular—meaning that they were bought by parents—commercial items for youngsters; they were intended to promote both entertainment and thrift. Conveying another adult ideal, several board and card games had patriotic themes; a number of tops, bell-ringing toys, and miniature vehicles carried patriotic motifs. Miniature horses and wagons often included racing insignias intended to channel boys' competitive instincts.

As girls' toys, dolls served particular functions for the adults who produced them and for those who purchased them. During the late nineteenth century, the American doll-making industry rapidly expanded but did so in two directions. Drawing on the age's fascination with technology, the dolls produced by male inventors in some ways resembled machines. Manufactured from sturdy materials such as metal and wood, these dolls came with appendages that duplicated mechanical movements. According to doll historian Miriam Formanek-Brunell, the designers of these dolls applied a male point of view. The patents for their dolls and doll parts rarely mentioned children or play, instead describing the technical details of their inventions. By contrast, Formanek-Brunell points out, female doll makers seemed to display more sensitivity to the needs of children, particularly girls. Martha Jenks Chase, for example, founder of the highly successful M. J. Chase Doll Company, created dolls that instead of resembling mechanical devices gave girls more realistic ways to play. Chase and other female doll designers used materials such as cloth and fiber stuffing that were soft to touch and safe to handle. Their dolls looked like real babies, and their goal was to enable girls to actively learn and practice mothering tasks such as fondling, dressing, and carrying their dolls around. Mary Scarborough Paxson, age nine, revealed the popularity of such dolls when she confessed to her diary her disappointment that the doll her father gave her only had "wax hair and painted shoes." "I do want a baby with real hair and real shoes," she pined.[35]

For preadolescent boys, a few almost universal toys seemed to dominate play: sleds, bicycles, marbles, balls, and, to a lesser extent, guns and knives. In snowy Vermont, recalled R. L. Duffus, "Not to have a sled was to be, or seem, undressed and impoverished." Even more than a sled, a bicycle defined Duffus's boyhood. "I don't suppose I can make anybody understand," he wrote, "what it meant to a boy then to ride a bicycle from the town where he lived to another and larger town. . . . The bicycle opened up a whole new world, and I suppose it meant more to us boys than the automobile meant some years later."[36]

Marbles freighted their own meaning. Iowan James Langdon Hill pronounced, "When the boys appear, playing at marbles, on their way to school, it is like saying in unmistakable language, that spring is here." Western novelist and critic Harvey Fergusson saw himself as both typical and unique when he wrote about his youth: "Nearly all boys then played with weapons more or less and most of the older boys owned guns, but to me weapons were an almost exclusive interest." And to many a lad, a pocketknife served not only as a plaything itself—for popular games such as mumble-peg—but also as a tool for fashioning new toys.[37]

Yet in spite of the growing profusion of dolls and other manufactured playthings, a lingering ambivalence also suffused toy consumption. While middle-class parents subscribed to the view that toys should impart useful skills and encourage wholesome exercise, they still distrusted objects that stirred utter fantasy, and they fretted about overindulging their children. Children's author and educator Kate Douglas Wiggins voiced a common concern when she warned that "the more you give to the child the less chance he has to develop his own resources."[38]

Wiggins did not need to worry about youngsters losing the use of their own resources. Though they showed special loyalty to certain manufactured toys such as dolls and bicycles, children, as they always had, created playthings out of objects they found in nature and invented their own functions for manufactured goods not intended for use by children. Those improvised playthings that never could be found on the store shelves represented the real resourcefulness of childhood. Recollections of the appropriation and transformation of everyday objects are so recurrent, so diverse, that their role in children's culture had to have been vital.

A host of family possessions, for example, enhanced indoor amusement. Eleanor Hallowell Abbot and her siblings conscripted an ancestor's antique sword for playing "many a gallant battle in the living-room or behind the impregnable bulwark of the kitchen washtubs." She also wielded her great-great grandfather's four-foot cane, "with which we thumped out innumerable parades up the front stairs and down the back." James Langdon Hill enjoyed playing stagecoach by "harnessing up chairs, one before the other, and then I would mount, behind them, in a high chair, having long reins in my hands." Pierrepont Noyes created play money by punching out the tops of cans for preserving fruits and vegetables used by the Oneida community where he was raised—until his father, the community's founder John Humphrey Noyes, confiscated his handiwork because it violated the community's anticommercial proscription.[39]

Nature especially sparked youthful inventiveness. Poet Lizette Woodworth Reese, who spent her childhood in the small town of Waverly, Maryland, recollected an experience common to many girls of making mud pies to supplement their games of house and bakery.[40] John Albee, raised in Bellingham, Massachusetts, alongside the Charles River, penned a vivid expression of childhood improvisation. "All movable objects are playthings to him," he recalled, referring to himself in the third person:

> He makes them also, like the Creator, out of nothing; if he wants a horse he has one in an instant by straddling a stick or tying a string to a companion. He has epic uses for his father's tools, his mother's knitting needles; they can slay a thousand foes at one stroke and the

button bag contains them alive and dead. Six marching clothespins are his army and conquer the world in an afternoon.[41]

Kids also applied their own skills to make replicas of formal toys. Kansas journalist William Allen White remembered the homemade sleds, wagons, and bows and arrows, as well as the whistles, stick horses, and "little railroads with whittled ties" that he crafted himself. Taylor Gordon, an African American born in White Springs, Montana, improvised accessories for the toy train that his brother built for the two of them. And Bellamy Partridge, forbidden by his strict father from card playing but encouraged to make his own toys, secretly transformed dominoes—which his father did approve—into playing cards for extemporaneous games.[42]

As children, particularly those in cities, began to become involved in the emerging consumer economy, they entered a transitional stage in their relationship to playthings. The informal, self-made toys that young people always had used now had to share the toy box with an increasing array of formal, mass-produced games and objects. Thus, middle-class children such as Bellamy Partridge, who had made his own toys, also owned "every game obtainable at the period: Backgammon, checkers, squails [a game resembling tiddlywinks], parchisi [sic], lotto, crokinole [a game in which disks are propelled on a board by sticks], tiddlywinks, authors, go-bang [known today as Go], a wide choice of travel games and inescapably a game of Bible characters."[43]

Bostonian Walter Brooks improvised a valued plaything by building a fort out of newspapers and, like James Langdon Hill, turned over chairs to create a make-believe horse coach; but he also owned an elaborately dressed boy doll, a toy house made out of "sanded cardboard," and a brightly-painted Noah's ark. The extent to which children actually played with each toy, whether homemade or not, is impossible to discern. What is evident, however, is that kids continued to enjoy the freedom of their self-defined and unstructured play, alone and with each other.[44]

Controlling Play, Alone and Together

In the latter half of the nineteenth century, two factors affected the composition of preadolescent play groupings. For one thing, the decline in average family size meant that children had fewer siblings to play with than their forebears enjoyed. To be sure, contemporary diaries and retrospective autobiographies from that era make references to sibling play partners, but the kinds of family play partners romanticized by writers such as Louisa May Alcott were becoming increasingly rare. Perhaps more importantly, the increasing pervasiveness of graded public schools, with their enrollments swelled by compulsory attendance laws, herded kids together and fomented peer-group associations that kept same-age—and usually, but not always, same-sex—youngsters together for the better part of their waking hours. These groupings, initially imposed by educational policy, extended into before-school, after-school, and general out-of-school activities. As early as 1863, a popular children's story could exult, "What happy times are spent in the district school in study, and what happy ones, too, in play, during the long noon-time and 'recess.'" Moreover, the rise of children's peer groupings, when combined with the now-dominant attitude about the separate, special quality of childhood, widened the generation gap, especially in children's minds. For example, even though Ethel Spencer, daughter of a Pittsburgh steel company agent, grew up in an unusually large family of seven children, she could write, "Though relatives were an integral part of life during our childhood, they were not, since they were mostly grown-ups, on quite the same level of importance as the friends of our own age with whom we played every day."[45]

Peers did not always occupy children's time. The proliferation of toys, games, and books enhanced the instances and even the desire of some youngsters to play alone. Mary Church Terrell, born in 1863 to slave parents, grew up after emancipation in Yellow Springs, Ohio, where her favorite play activities were solitary ones that included reading the Rollo books and *St. Nicholas* magazine, and, especially, solving the puzzles that were published in the back of the magazine.[46] Dolls, toy soldiers, miniature vehicles, and more occupied the time of youngsters who played by themselves. As James Langdon Hill's recollection exemplified, amusement involving the imaginative conversion of home furnishings often occurred when a child was left alone.

Other examples of solitary play abound. During his San Francisco childhood, future writer and reformer Lincoln Steffens could envision himself as a teamster, a gun-playing, bronco-busting vaquero, or a hearty steamboat man. . . . I remember having a leaf from our dining-room table on the floor, kneeling on it, and taking hold of one end, jerking it backward over the carpet, tooting like a steam boat whistle. Three or four big chairs and all the small chairs in the house made me a mountain train of wagons and mules; a clothes line tied to the leader and strung through the other chairs was a rein which I could jerk as the black-bearded teamster did.[47]

Theodore Dreiser claimed that he "preferred to play by myself" and recalled creations similar to those of Steffens. Dreiser wrote in his autobiography:

One of these games I can best describe was "train." It consisted of placing half-size cigar boxes in a row, end to end, on the floor of our parlor . . . , and there "switching" or making up a train, with which I traveled from station to station, whistling as I went. . . . In summer . . . I transferred this process to the yard. Here I laid out a series of stations built of twigs along the fence nearest the house, and between these I traveled . . . , hour after hour.[48]

More literate, perhaps more ingenious than other kids, Terrell, Steffens, and Dreiser nevertheless represent common experiences. Moreover, the trials and errors of solitary activity not only exercised the imagination but also provided vital educational experiences. As James Langdon Hill asserted, "No amount of learning can teach a boy to swim, or to catch, or strike a ball, drive a horse, or sail a boat. He must educate himself. The real art is acquired almost unconsciously." Still, most diarists and autobiographers of the era highlighted the importance of peers as playmates and the increasing sex segregation that peer associations entailed. As Hill declared, "I craved the companionship of boys of my own age. It was the stirring in me, of the gang forming spirit. If I had a top, after trying it a few times, I was inclined to go over to the next house to show it and to spin it."[49]

As mentioned previously, Indian boys traditionally were grouped together, often imitating adult activities. The memoir of Charles Alexander Eastman, a Wahpeton Dakota (Sioux) whose native name was Ohiyesa, vividly described how groups of boys competed in various physical games and mimicked their elders by making war on bees' nests. "We imagined ourselves about to make an attack upon the Ojibways or some [other] tribal foe," he wrote. "We all painted and stole cautiously upon the nest; then, with a rush and war-whoops, sprang upon the object of our attack and endeavored to destroy it." Offspring of emancipated slaves also engaged in sex-segregated play. Taylor Gordon, for example, took pride when a group of older African American boys accepted him into their gang and allowed him to join in their version of "Stray Goose," a game in which the group chased their fastest member. "If they caught him," Gordon related wryly, "they could do anything they wanted, except perform an operation or kill him."[50]

Of course, white boys, too, had keen inclinations for same-sex pastimes. Growing up in Texas, Charles Nagel observed, "In the school room we were one group of pupils. Outside, the girls and boys each followed their own kind of play." The diary of Francis Bennett Jr., who lived in Gloucester, Massachusetts, includes "good sleighing" with male friends in January and firing off fireworks with them in May. Boys, as Massachusetts senator George F. Hoar recalled, did things together in ways that they only could carry out away from the company of girls. Reflecting on how the boys of his neighborhood would gather at a nearby river to swim, Hoar wrote that they would all "sit down on the bank and have a sort of boys' exchange, in which all matters of interest were talked over, and a great deal of good-natured chaff was exchanged."[51]

Girls also understood gender differences and engaged with their peers in activities that often contrasted to those of boys. Isabel Bolton and her neighbor, a girl named Julie, liked to watch boys at play, "but were never allowed to join them. They were rough and terrible," she wrote. Wisconsin playwright Zona Gale had a similar experience with boys. "Their whole world was filled with doing, doing, doing," she reflected, "whereas ours was made wholly of watching things get done." And Frances Parkinson Keyes, born in Virginia but raised in Boston, played quietly with dolls and books in a garden "to my heart's content with Ruth French, the little girl who lived next door." The diary of Mary Scarborough Paxson made mention of fishing with her sister but most frequently described her sedentary doll playing with a friend named "Maggie."[52]

Some girls resented their status. Californian Loretta Berner complained, "At the age of nine, I was sorry I was a girl because I too wanted to roam the world free as a bird." But others deeply immersed themselves in their own female world and ignored how boys were playing. Much of girls' peer play involved imitating their elders by engaging in dress up and homemaking fantasies. Eleanor Hallowell Abbot and her girlfriends organized make-believe craft fairs, and Edna Ferber reveled in playing "grownup" with her friends:

> We would don our mothers' long skirts pinned tight around our hips, top this by a discarded waist, all revers [turned inside out to show the lining] and braid and high collar, skewer with long hatpins a two-story hat of the day; ferret out a sunshade and gloves if possible, and in this regalia go flouncing down the street, walking with a mincing gait, speaking in an affected tone, discussing our children, our hired girls, our cookery, our clothes, our husbands in unconscious and deadly imitation of our elders.[53]

Other girls rebelled by acting "unfeminine" and mistreating their toys. Some evidence suggests that girls abused their dolls, even "killing" a doll by breaking it in order to hold a funeral for it. Girls also used dolls aggressively as weapons to hit animals and boys.[54]

It would be a mistake to assume, however, that preadolescent children of the late nineteenth century inhabited completely sex-segregated worlds. The composition of playgroups depended on availability—sometimes only opposite-sex relatives were at hand—as well as age and culturally determined choices. North Carolinian William Cox, sent to live on his grandparents' plantation when his mother became ill, had a "wonderful playmate" in his grandparents' youngest child, an aunt just two and half years older than he. Sarah Bixby Smith played hopscotch, jacks, and tag with girls but also enlisted her slightly younger cousin Harry into collecting bottles and leaves with her. Frances Cooper Kroll, raised on an isolated farm outside of Santa Barbara, California, before her family moved to Los Angeles, recalled that between ages six and ten she skated and biked with her brother and his male friends because no girls lived nearby.[55]

Other autobiographers claimed that they actually preferred to play with the opposite sex. Though memory might have embellished the experiences, recollections of mixed-gender activities were frequent, though not predominant. Some girls eagerly sought "rough" play with boys. Lizette Woodworth Reese claimed that she liked to join boys after school for "some instant deviltry" and lurched with them across fields and hollows on sleds. Eleanor Hallowell Abbot played war games with a neighbor boy in a toy fort, climbed trees with boys, and sometimes clashed with them. "I know we fought a good deal among ourselves," she wrote. "Not just word battles, I mean, but real fisticuffs." And Harvey Fergusson recollected that in his native Albuquerque boys and girls played together and that there were "a certain number of 'tom-boy' girls who pushed their way into almost every masculine activity except football."[56]

It is difficult to determine from recollections long after the fact how much consciousness of sexuality existed in the gender-integrated play of this era's preadolescents. Memories of these matters, more so than of others, were probably selective. More reflective about cultural prescriptions than many writers, Frances Parkinson Keyes had ambivalent experiences with boys. She recalled that she played with boys in a "sexless" way (remarking that on these occasions "the word sex was never actually used") but also observing that "girls knew—I think almost instinctively—that they were not welcome at the swimming hole and why; and boys recognized that they were similarly debarred from certain feminine pastimes and prerogatives." When Henry Seidel Canby spoke about exhibiting affection toward a girl he was "stuck on" by throwing mud balls at her from behind a fence, he most likely was referring to something that actually happened and had special meaning to him, but such an incident was unlikely to have been as recurrent as his play activities with boys. Certainly, there were both innocent play experiences and stirrings of sexual awareness between boys and girls, much of which depended on age. Novelist Irving Bacheller, raised in upstate New York, recalled playing with a local girl when he was about eight or ten years old and that "her red cheeks and bright eyes and dark wavy hair and smiling face started in me a vibration which I had not felt before." Perhaps more self-conscious than many youngsters, Bacheller told of engaging in kissing games— probably "post office"—a year or two later and being nervous "until a pretty young miss pulled me in. When I got kissed everyone laughed at me and I covered my face for shame, but, after all, this first disgrace was delightful."[57] Reminiscences such as these, however, represent perceptions about romance and sex shaped by adult culture, not necessarily a full reflection of children's attitudes.

Whether they played alone or in groups, same-sex or mixed, children found ways to elude adult supervision. Frances Parkinson Keyes spoke for many a venturesome young person when she retold how she and her friends determined to explore a "subterranean chamber" under a sandbank near her Boston home. "We did not seek . . . advice from any of our elders" in making their decision, she wrote; "in fact, none of us felt it necessary to inform them of our decision." Even a youngster such as Pierrepont Noyes, sheltered in the utopian Oneida commune of Upstate New York, took pleasure in sneaking away to play in a field on the settlement's outskirts. The locale gave Noyes and his friends "a pleasant sense of freedom" because of its distance from adult oversight. He and his "gang" also constructed a secret club-house in the attic of a storage building, where "we found joy in the knowledge that we were beyond the reach of authority." Alas, however, their habit of climbing down from their clubhouse to help themselves to the brown sugar that was stored beneath them was discovered, and a whipping painfully ended their conspiracy.[58]

As Noyes found out, the adult world did not always appreciate children's unrestrained playful activity. Imposition of restrictions could stem from official public authority, such as when New York City made kite flying illegal below 14th Street. Or, it could take the form of countless family restrictions, such as when Eleanor Hallowell Abbot's grandfather pasted specific regulations on a toy boat, dictating that

> this rocking boat was made for girls; girls accordingly have preference over boys in the use of it. Whenever, therefore, any girls come into the [play] room, any boys that are in the boat must leave it at once to give the girls the opportunity to occupy it. If they do not occupy it the boys may return; if on the other hand they do occupy it, no boy must get into it or touch it except by invitation from the oldest girl in the boat.[59]

Or, restraints could come from institutions, such as when Stephen Littlefield imparted to his diary that he received harsh punishment for misbehaving at school.[60]

Control over youthful behavior had always been a chief concern of the older generation, but by the closing decades of the nineteenth century, new ambivalence and more permissive viewpoints began to be voiced. Although some adults considered both play and reading material too important to be left to the judgment of children, a few involved in the emerging fields of child psychology and child study cautioned that children needed leeway to use their "play instinct" for their own purposes. Social scientists began undertaking surveys of how youngsters actually played as a means to understanding their culture. Anthropologist William Wells Newell's survey of *Games and Songs of American Children,* mentioned previously, prompted him to value the "inventiveness of children" and for the continuity of favorite games and songs across generations. Likewise, in 1891, ethnographer and museum curator Stewart Culin interviewed a ten-year-old Brooklyn boy and compiled from him a list of street games that provided a further foundation for the appreciation of children's self-made amusements. And in 1896, psychologist T. R. Crosswell asked almost two thousand schoolchildren in Worcester, Massachusetts, to specify their play preferences and concluded that free, unstructured play—as distinct from work or school and taking place without strict adult interference—had beneficial effects. He advised that "it is vastly more important that teachers and parents see that conditions are favorable for profitable employment of children's leisure than that they graft 'the play instinct' upon methods used in school."[61]

Crosswell's data revealed what was probably the most remarkable yet unanticipated pattern in the play of preadolescents. In spite of the formalization of children's amusements in settlement houses and clubs, in spite of the widespread availability and sales of manufactured toys and their acquisition by young people at birthday and Christmas time, and in spite of the incipient establishment of playgrounds, what children liked to do best deviated from what the older generation created for them. Even though about one-fourth of the nearly one thousand boys and one thousand girls whom Crosswell surveyed occasionally played checkers and other formal board games, only 87 boys and 34 girls named these commercialized games as their favorite kinds of play. Though 621 girls owned dolls, only 233 considered doll play as their favorite pastime. Among the boys, only 27 mentioned toy trains as their favorite play activity, only 37 identified blocks, and just two mentioned toy soldiers. A similar study of eight thousand South Carolina children, undertaken by Zachariah McGhee, revealed a slightly higher penchant for organized play. Among boys, 66 percent named baseball as their favorite and 55 percent listed football, but these were most often informal games and in all probability were performed independent of adult management. Girls' preferences as expressed to McGhee spanned a long spectrum of formal and informal games and lacked any consistent pattern that would have suggested a positive effect of new manufactured toys.[62]

Most children would not have known about these surveys, but many no doubt would have offered that their own amusements gave them the most fun. Henry Seidel Canby remembered that in his childhood, "There was no 'organized play,' wither athletic or otherwise. Any yard did for ball throwing and one or two for crude tennis. . . . Such a let-alone life may seem not to have made for introspection, but that is not true, there was always space for solitude—trees, and hidden corners." John Albee found his greatest play pleasures in accompanying friends to engage in berry picking and creating informal games of hide and chase away from adult supervision. Pierrepont Noyes testified that when he became "a boy" at age seven, "I looked on time and space as mine. They seemed mediums in which to enjoy and multiply the things I myself could do." And Ervin King, who spent his boyhood in Los Angeles, remembered his penchant to roam at will, interacting contacts with plants and wildlife, and "getting into trouble."[63]

Ah, that tendency to get into trouble. This is what defined many a child's autonomous activity. As in the case of sexuality, accounts of misbehavior were selective and probably exaggerated, but beyond the self-congratulatory tales that people of all ages relate about their youth, the breach of adult constraints signifies a vital dimension of children's play. Preadolescence was, and is, a time of exploration and challenge, qualities that involve risk as well as growth, and the expanded peer culture of childhood in the late nineteenth century furnished numerous opportunities for mutually inspired mischief—what observers at the time called the "gang instinct." Kids both bragged about and confessed their transgressions. In her diary entry of August 28, 1881, nine-year-old Maggie Scarborough Paxson revealed the unexpected consequences of trying out an improvised plaything: "We made bows and arrows and the first thing I did when I shot my arrows was to brake [sic] a window pane, because my arrow went the wrong way."[64]

More commonly, youngsters seem to have unconsciously endangered themselves by ignoring hazards or simply tempting fate. Rufus

Jones, growing up in rural Minnesota in the 1870s, labeled himself and his peers as

> the usual run of boys [who] walked high beams . . . , climbed per-
> ilous roofs, . . . dived off bridges into brooks with our clothes and
> boots on . . . and ventured out on thin ice in the early freeze-up of the
> lake, daring one another to see who could carry a stone the farthest
> out on the ticklish, bending ice.[65]

Edna Ferber recalled a pastime of "bobsled-catching" which consisted of grabbing onto the sides of a horse-drawn sleigh moving down the street and then leaping onto another sleigh as it passed in the opposite direction. John Albee verified the way peer association encouraged a competitive quality to misbehavior, boasting that he outdid his male peers in mischief when he "looted the best apple trees, beat them at ball and managed to escape my tasks oftener."[66]

A prank recalled by Aline Bernstein perhaps best exemplifies both the way an autobiographer creates a persona for herself and how children could guide their improvised play toward wayward, rebellious ends. Born to theater performers and raised mostly in New England boardinghouses, Bernstein spent many hours with a male friend named Jesse, who lured her into impish pursuits. Together they concocted ways to harass their elders:

> The rubber balls we used to play stoop ball and jackstones were hol-
> low, with a tiny pin-hole in them. Jesse filled them with water and
> said it would be a fine idea if we went up to his mother's room and
> squirted water on the people in the street as they passed under the
> window. We gave them a sporting chance for we only squirted men
> who wore gray derby hats.[67]

Pranks and creations that adults would never sanction sometimes included cruelty and destruction. One illustrative act comes from the remembrances of John Albee:

> I manufactured quite an assemblage [of play figures] out of one thing
> and another and gave them names, mostly of older boys whom I dis-
> liked. . . . I added a few pretended animals of corn cobs, a dead
> snake, a live frog. . . . I surrounded the whole with sticks, paper and

pine cones and then came the exciting moment when I "touched her off," as boys say. What fun, what glee I experienced at that moment; no one can know, who does not keep in his bosom a fragment of his boyish heart. Creation may please the gods, but it cannot equal the boy's pleasure in destruction, especially by fire.[68]

The diary of Granville Howland Norcross, son of a Boston lawyer, also reveals a boy's interest in starting fires.[69]

The risks that kids such as John Albee and Edna Ferber took could be truly hazardous, and undoubtedly some of them backfired, with sorry, if not tragic consequences. The physical perils of child labor have been well publicized, but few statistics were collected that might reveal the extent of injury and worse that occurred from playful acts gone bad. Street play and the rising dangers from wheeled vehicles prompted child-saving reformers to embark on a crusade to create spaces and activities ostensibly to protect children's physical safety, but youngsters often avoided these places in favor of play sites that they controlled themselves. Also, as Aline Bernstein's reminiscence suggests, preadolescents could be truly obnoxious in their quest for autonomy and their disobedience of social conventions. As Adeline Atwater, born to wealthy Chicago parents, admitted, "I had a dare-devil spirit—or was I just a brat?"[70] The defiance of adults thus involved drawbacks as well as freedom.

The components of children's play in the late nineteenth century differed from those of the previous half century in that in the later period social and economic change intensified important qualities of both private and public life. The growth of cities, the expansion of peer socialization in schools and neighborhoods, the rise of consumer society, and the broadened appearance of mass-produced toys mingled with heightened attitudes about the worth of childhood to create new opportunities for young people to pursue playful amusements, both in view of and beyond adult vigilance. In this pursuit, youngsters had both allies and adversaries, basically because now more than previously the adult world was ambivalent about how much leeway to give kids in their unstructured time. Adults never abandoned their ambition to direct and protect the young; the health of family, society, and republic depended on such guidance. But a few educators and psychologists were beginning to advocate a more noninterventionist view of child development, one that was not completely indulgent but that did recognize children's abilities to play on their own.

Continuities from previous eras still pervaded children's play culture, and to some extent these intensified as well. Class distinctions, never absent from American society, had an enhanced impact by affecting how many and what kinds of toys a child could have and by defining how much play time was available. Gender, too, made a difference in whom children played with and how they played. And location—region and whether urban, small town, or rural—continued to distinguish playgroups and play activities. Growing up remained perilous; though infant mortality was declining, disease, poverty, accidents, and abuse were always present to endanger the vulnerable child. Nevertheless, the notion of fun as a desired quality of childhood, had new credence, and at least a few observers of children's behavior were willing to tolerate their independent play and understand that children often resisted attempts to dictate their play. Thus, contemplating the ways that young people perpetuated their own amusements, William Newell wrote in 1883,

> There is something so agreeable in the idea of an inheritance of thought kept up by childhood itself, created for and adapted to its own needs, that it is hard to consent to part with it. The loss cannot be made good by the deliberate invention of older minds. Children's amusement, directed and controlled by grown people, would be neither childish nor amusing. . . . Children will never adopt as their own tradition the games which may be composed or remodeled, professedly for their amusement, but with the secret purpose of moral direction.[71]

Both the new patterns and the dilemmas of the era are embodied in an innocent short narrative in Asa Bullard's compilation of *Aunt Lizzie's Stories,* a volume published in 1863. One scene of the tale describes a "gentleman of wealth and character" taking a walk one day and chancing on a group of boys playing on the sidewalk. When the boys fail to yield a path to him, the man chastises them for ignoring his need for passage, and one of the boys mutters as the man passed by, "I wonder if that thing was ever a little boy." Significantly, the unnamed author of this story was expressing the child's view rather than what in an earlier era might have represented the principle of respecting one's elders. Thus, the author remarked, "If the boys were in [the stroller's] way, while engaging in their amusements, would it have been a very great inconvenience for him, remembering his own boyhood and its sports, just to have stepped quietly around them?"[72] This depiction of some children engaging in self-structured play activity and the contest with an adult over the use of space marked the most important development in children's play of the late nineteenth century, one that would become full-blown in the new century.

4

The Invasion of Children's Play Culture, 1900–1950

IN 1930, AMID rising concern over the Great Depression's effect on children's welfare and happiness, President Herbert Hoover convened a White House Conference on Child Health and Protection. The meeting brought together professionals from fields of education, psychology, medicine, and social services to discuss and present reports concerning child care and protection on all governmental levels. In addition to preparing a Children's Charter—a set of nineteen principles that addressed issues of health, education, child labor, family welfare, and growth and development—conference delegates declared that play was "every child's right." But that right bore a serious attribute, for as the conference concluded, "With the young child, his work is his play and his play is his work."[1]

Such sentiments were clearly reminiscent of an attitude that was more than a century old: in the minds of experts, play was not the opposite of work; rather, it should be a productive activity through which a child rehearsed for modern adulthood by following the guidance of wise, rational adults. In the twentieth century, however, as a new brand of specialists endeavored to define the concept of play more scientifically, the prevailing attitude included an appreciation of both the serious and the fun components of play. Some believed that children's culture could enrich older generations. Thus, physical educator B. F. Boller could proclaim early in the century that the "overflowing, joyous, radiant life of the child" would serve as the legacy to the adult, who would add to work "the zeal and energy of earnest, joyous play."[2] But "joyous play" could take place only under proper adult tutelage. As child psychologists Harvey Lehman and Paul Witty announced in their 1927 volume, *The Psychology of Play Activities*, "educators should assume the responsibility of training children for profitable use of leisure."[3]

Many children of the time, however, had different ideas. They followed their own age-old principle: to them, childhood represented a realm that they wanted to define and control by and for themselves. They often resisted the imposition of adult-defined activities and restrictions. Their position was articulated by author Robert Paul Smith, recalling his own insubordinate youth: "I think we were right about grownups being the natural enemies of kids, because we knew that what they wanted us to do was to be like them. And that was for the birds."[4]

Even more than in previous eras, the divergence between what adults wanted for kids ("his play is his work" and "profitable use of time") and what kids believed ("that was for the birds") became a major theme of play history in the first half of the twentieth century. These years, bounded roughly by the onset of a full-fledged child-saving movement during the Progressive era at the dawn of the century and the appropriation of kids' culture by television in the early 1950s, mark what I believe to have been a much more highly organized adult incursion into childhood than in the past and, somewhat paradoxically, children's most successful, though transitory, assertion of play independence. In large part, this incursion derived from shifting attitudes about the social role of children. Before 1900, a family-economy model of childhood, in which parents endeavored to integrate children into domestic activities as quickly as possible, prevailed among farm and urban working-class families—into which the bulk of children were born. As one historian has aptly observed, "Working-class girls . . . were less likely to 'play' house than to run it."[5] By the turn of the century, however, growth of the urban middle-class broadened the acceptance of a sheltered-child model. Under this version, which had arisen in the mid- and late nineteenth century, the state and its institutions set apart children by age and status, and family ideology as well as public concern channeled young people toward a protected physical and emotional development.[6]

The sheltered-child model shaped play in several and sometimes contradictory, ways. Before 1900, adults had dominated children's play, and when possible had determined the kinds of toys young people received and the games they played. After 1900, however, adults—mainly middle and upper class, but increasingly working class as well —allowed play and toys to become more child centered and more often defined by children's desires. As a result of reduced responsibilities to the family economy and of influence from peer-based associations formed in schools and neighborhoods, preadolescent boys and girls now had more time and opportunities for unstructured play. And in contrast to the late twentieth century, not many kids were locked into regimented after-school, weekend, and summer regimens of lessons, leagues, clubs, and camps where they were unable to control use of their leisure time.

Child centeredness, however, was not child indulgence. Progressive reform united a phalanx of parents, teachers, psychologists, and social welfare professionals who mounted an earnest effort to ensure that children's play interests would be functional, healthy, and safe. Their efforts expanded as the century proceeded, resulting in the creation of playgrounds, schoolyards, organized sports, and "educational" games and toys, all with the goal of preparing children for the demands of living in a consumer-oriented, technological society. However, countervailing, even ironical, viewpoints circulated, as experts in the field of child study who advocated "directed play" for youngsters at the same time stressed a child's need to develop a sense of independence, individuality, and self-discovery. More importantly, personal accounts, though they must be treated with care, indicate that within the tightened bonds of a sheltered childhood, kids found ways to conspire alternatives, giving the era a quality of freedom that had not existed previously and that would fade afterward. The culture of childhood during this period was rich with imagination, mutuality, and self-centeredness. Robert Paul Smith summed up a child's outlook:

> What we knew as kids, what we learned from other kids, was not tentatively true, or extremely probable, or proven by science or polls or surveys. It was so. I wrote on the flyleaf of my schoolbooks . . . in descending order my name, my street, my town, my county, my state, my country, my continent, my hemisphere, my planet, my solar system . . . it started with me . . . the center point was me, me me. . . . [Grownups are] always around pumping kids full of what we laughingly call facts. [Kids] don't want science. They want magic. . . . If you cut yourself in the web of skin between your thumb and forefinger, you die. That's it. . . . Grasshoppers spit tobacco. Step on a crack, break your mother's back. . . . We really knew that what came out of

grasshoppers was not tobacco juice. But facts were one thing, and beliefs were another.[7]

In this chapter I summarize the goals and paradoxes of the adult
"invasion" of children's culture in the first half of the early twentieth
century and examine how adults tried to define how, where, with
what, and with whom youngsters should play. In the next chapter I
follow up on Smith's evocative portrayal as I explore how children actually played and examine the ways they ignored and manipulated
adult prescriptions in their quest for control of their own culture.

The Social Context Surrounding Childhood in the Early Twentieth Century

By the turn of the nineteenth century in America, childhood had fully
acquired the reverence and empathy that had been gravitating toward
it for several decades. Like all stages of life, it was not idyllic; pain and
stress beset children of all social ranks, especially those of the native
and foreign-born working class. But now, as the White House Conference confirmed, a healthy, happy childhood was deemed to be a fundamental right, promoted and protected by society's institutions, as
well as by parents. Infants and young children became objects of considerable attention, as concerned workers in public and private welfare institutions strived to reduce infant mortality and ensure healthy
growth. But also, preadolescent children received keener consideration than in the past, as educators and psychologists endeavored to
understand their needs and improve their lives.

Children were revered more intensely in part because there were
relatively fewer of them. As immigration, disproportionately containing young adults, increased and as birthrates continued to fall, children of preadolescent age constituted a smaller segment of the American population than in previous eras. During the mid-nineteenth
century, this cohort had averaged around 25 percent of the total population. Then, their percentages began to fall so that in 1900, those aged
five to fourteen comprised just over 22 percent of the total. By 1920,
their share had declined to under 21 percent, and by 1940 it stood at
just 17 percent. The 1940 figure to some extent reflects postponed

births during the Depression, but not completely because the proportion fell even further by 1950, when it stood at 16 percent. African American children in this age group constituted a somewhat larger component of the total black population, chiefly because life expectancy for this group was lower than that for whites; but the proportions of black preadolescents declined also, from 24 percent in 1910 to 19 percent in 1950. The whole population's median age reflected the declines, rising continuously from 22.3 in 1900 to 30.2 in 1950. As the baby boom gathered steam thereafter, the number of preadolescents ballooned, but in the first half of the twentieth century youngsters of elementary school age were proportionately much less numerous than they had been in earlier eras.[8]

These demographic patterns occurred within years of shifting and complex political, social, and economic patterns: the eras of Progressive reform, World War I, the "Roaring Twenties," the Depression, World War II, and the onset of the Cold War. Technological evolution seemed to accelerate, with new wonders such as automobiles and electric appliances increasingly dominating everyday life. As well, changes related to immigration, migration, consumerism, urbanization, and suburbanization spanned these periods, giving gender, ethnic, racial, and class identities special salience. As the workweek shrank and electricity broadened the possibilities for nighttime activity, mass popular culture expanded, with movies, radio, and recorded music joining print media and live entertainment as leisure-time amusements for all ages. At the same time, educators, physicians, and psychologists tightened age-linked expectations for all segments of society but especially for children's growth and behavior, applying age grading and age norms to institutions such as juvenile courts, elementary and junior high school curricula, medical diagnoses and treatments, and boys' and girls' organizations.[9]

All childhoods, of course, were not the same. Socioeconomic and gender distinctions especially determined paths by which kids would grow up. These factors also shaped patterns of play, influencing the environments, play groupings, and, especially, the playthings that constituted the major qualities of children's culture. I have no intention of minimizing these elements. Yet it seems important to point out certain cultural uniformities and continuities, as I do here and in the next chapter. Play remained a vital component of all children's lives, and though contextual conditions changed and though youngsters generally accepted the guidance of their elders, they at times still sought to assert control over where, with what, and with whom they played. Styles, opportunities, and resources differed to be sure, but as the consumer society matured, youngsters of all types increasingly became active members of it. Compulsory schooling and the changing nature of work drew children out of the labor force—though in most rural areas young people remained involved in the productive economy—and they now encountered a new assortment of formal and informal establishments, ranging from parks to movie houses to penny arcades to candy stores to gymnasiums, where they could indulge in recreational pastimes and spend whatever nickels and dimes they could accumulate. At the same time, however, they found themselves objects of intensified study and institutional concern.[10]

Studying and Saving the Child

Taking their cue from Locke and Rousseau, intellectuals had drawn a boundary around childhood during the course of the nineteenth century, providing a backdrop for defining the sheltered model of the twentieth century. Viewed as a precious resource in need of attentive welfare, children had become both a means to an end (Locke's aim of creating a civilized populace) and repositories of humankind's natural joy (Rousseau's vision of children as pure and uninhibited). These two views assumed a scientific tinge at the turn of the century in the writings of Sigmund Freud and John Dewey, both of whom expanded on the idea of children's uniqueness. Freud insisted that children possessed a special sexual and psychic nature that developed through uniform stages. He said that during ages six through twelve, children's sexual desires were in a "latent" stage and they became preoccupied with other pursuits, such as same-sex friendships, hobbies, and athletics. During this stage, Freud noted, children acquire skills that will enable them to integrate into society. He thus implied that parents needed to take particular care at this time to ensure that a child would develop into a healthy social being. Dewey believed that a young person's needs must be met in terms of what the child is, not necessarily what the child will become. Thus he advocated that the child's own instincts, activities, and interests should be appreciated and used in their education. The paradigms created by Freud and Dewey thus extended the somewhat ambiguous view that pervaded earlier eras: that adults must acknowledge the natural charm and exuberance of a child while at the same time parents and teachers must contain those qualities so that important values such as self-control and logical thought may be cultivated.[11]

These ideas fed the child-study movement that flowered in the early 1900s and then branched in several directions as the century advanced. As discussed in the previous chapter, the influential figures G. Stanley Hall and Luther Gulick had helped launch the movement in the late nineteenth century. Hall, who as president of Clark University invited Sigmund Freud for his first visit to America, became especially influential with his blending of Darwinian and Freudian theories. Using an evolutionary model that perceived human development as recapitulating the stages of the progress of civilization, Hall believed that adults needed to make certain that each phase of childhood matched the natural impulses, rather than some imposed spiritual scheme, appropriate to that stage. This premise meant that children should not be prematurely forced to adopt adult standards of comportment and that their instinctual drives should not be shackled. A well-rounded, "adjusted" child could not be left scot free, however. While Hall, Dewey, and others argued that education and nurture should be child centered, they also asserted that adults must control the processes. Thus children needed to be protected—sheltered—from the demands and perils of modern society.[12]

Those who observed and advocated on behalf of children in the early twentieth century viewed them, in historian Harvey Graff's words, "as the hope of tomorrow and the fear of today." With both optimism and anxiety, those in the child-saving movement reasoned that children resembled mechanical devices that could be fine tuned. Thus pediatrician L. Emmett Holt Jr. in his influential child-rearing manual, *The Diseases of Infancy and Children,* referred to a child as a "delicately constructed piece of machinery" whose nutrition needed to be matched to their age-related needs lest they perform poorly in school.[13]

Yet also, reformers in the Progressive era viewed children as more than machines. They were apprehensive about the exploitation of child laborers, still in the early twentieth century involved in heavy sweatshop and farm labor, and about the temptations confronting city kids on streets and in tenements. Settlement-house workers, charity workers, educators, physicians, and others feared that unwholesome environments had especially injurious influences on children, who were too naïve and dependent to protect themselves. Some child savers also believed that immigrant youngsters needed to be rescued from their incapable (meaning impoverished and un-Americanized) parents, but generally the urban environment outweighed the family as the source of endangerment. All these hazards, reformers reasoned, called for intervention to protect children, now deemed to have sentimental rather than economic value. Middle-class optimism of the age, however, also assumed that, properly guided, working-class youngsters could be rescued from their plight and more advantaged youngsters could be encouraged to use their time in ways worthy of their families' aspirations. The result of such management would be a "normal" childhood.[14]

The components of child saving—labor laws, juvenile courts, health care, educational programs, and others—have been analyzed elsewhere. Here, the relationship between reform and play is what matters. Hall and Gulick had argued that because play characterized a vital evolutionary stage that all children must experience before maturing into productive adulthood, youngsters should not lose their "play instinct." John Dewey agreed, writing in 1916 that "the idea that the need [for play] can be suppressed is absolutely fallacious, and the Puritanic tradition which disallows the need has entailed an enormous crop of evils." Though their ideas meshed with the scientific management of industrial production current at the time, Hall, Gulick, and Dewey focused more on what they believed was "natural" about play. Unlike some of their nineteenth-century predecessors, analysts of the early twentieth century did not necessarily deem the spontaneity and precociousness of childhood to be unacceptable; rather, children's innate energies needed to be carefully channeled. Such guidance was especially important for reining in the tendency for boys to become disorderly, but it also intended to divert girls from unhealthy associations that could lead to sexual dissipation. By engaging in healthy games and playing with proper toys in protected places, young people of both sexes would be deterred from joining gangs and engaging in other objectionable activities that would prevent them from becoming responsible fathers and nurturing mothers. In contrast to earlier theorists, however, Hall, Gulick, and Dewey warned that too much intervention might stifle a child's creativity. Thus Gulick advised in his

1920 book *The Philosophy of Play*, "The role of the teacher appears to come in when the child has exhausted his own ability to invent."[15]

By the 1920s and 1930s, the child-study movement had incorporated most of the precepts of Gulick, Hall, Dewey, and Freud. For example, in their book *The Psychology of Play Activities*, published in 1927, Harvey C. Lehman and Paul A. Witty, psychologists at the University of Kansas School of Education, concluded, like Dewey, that teachers must notice, evaluate, and then guide children's play. "Most persons would agree," they wrote, "that it is sometimes best for the play supervisor to adopt a doctrine of 'hands off.' However, it is none the less desirable for [the supervisor] to make careful studies of the child's play behavior." Lehman and Witty listed four tasks for those involved with child study and welfare: to discover the games and play activities that children most commonly played; to identify the games and play that children liked best; to measure the time that children spent playing their favorite games; and to analyze the effects on play of variables such as age, sex, race, season, intelligence, and locale. Their ultimate goal was to ensure that play promoted healthy personality development and enable educators to "take remedial steps if they find a child who engages too much in solitary play or too much in social play."[16]

Commercial interests reconfigured the impulse for healthy play to meet their own needs. In 1926, retailers and manufacturers in New York City formed the Better Play for Childhood League with the stated purpose "to stimulate normal play" and the "right kind of play" for children. To promote their goals, the league tried to establish a national Children's Day, to be celebrated on the third Saturday of June, a time in which parents could display their love and reward youngsters for school achievements by buying gifts for them. Though the organization included child-saving reformers on its board of directors, the league clearly wished to create a Christmas-type shopping season during the slow summer months and a complement to the recently established Mother's Day.[17] Nevertheless, promoters of Children's Day adopted child-saving rhetoric, warning of the dangers of unsupervised street play and advising mothers that it was their duty to provide for their children's safety when out of school by encouraging their sons and daughters to become involved in youth groups and supervised playground activities. Given that these exhortations came mostly from commercial enterprises, however, it is not surprising that mothers also were exhorted to purchase "proper" toys. Doll makers, for example, were especially prominent among such advocates, informing mothers that a doll would help girls learn etiquette and domestic skills.[18]

Reining in City Play

As the rhetoric behind Children's Day suggests, cities, with their bustle, diversity, and allurements, more than any other institution stirred child savers to intrude on children's play. In 1910, sixteen American cities contained at least 300,000 inhabitants, eight claimed over 500,000, and three topped a million. By 1920, over half of the American population lived in urban places. Central-city, as opposed to metropolitan-area, growth slowed during the Depression and World War II, but as late as 1950 there were eighteen places with over 500,000 inhabitants and five with a million or more. Perhaps more important than the big cities, countless middle-sized and small cities expanded. In 1950, at least 65 places claimed between 100,000 and 250,000 people and 128 contained between 50,000 and 100,000, about the same number as in 1940 but up from 23 and 40, respectively, in 1900.[19]

The bulk of population expansion derived from migration: from rural areas and from abroad. Foreign immigration peaked between 1900 and 1910, and although legislation in the 1920s restricted entry, Europeans and Latin Americans continued to arrive thereafter, adding new cultures to urban life. White migrants from the native countryside to the city joined the procession, and two "Great Migrations" of African Americans moving off southern tenant farms, chiefly before World War I and after World War II, altered the racial composition of many cities, especially in the North and West.

Because large proportions of migrants and immigrants were working class, reformers, showing both compassion and cultural biases, were concerned that urban newcomers, especially their children, learn values that would enable them to become moral, pliant American citizens. As believers in the environmental effect on behavior, reformers feared that the crowding and poverty of bursting neighborhoods forced working-class children out into the streets, where their recreational needs would be endangered and their moral character corrupted. Street life, to child savers, was too anonymous, too unsupervised, so that boundaries between safe harbor and vicious, promiscuous influences were too fragile. Nostalgic for an idealized community of the close-knit family and the rural village, reformers romanticized about private homes, quiet neighborhoods, and untainted nature where children could play safely and soundly. As one reformer wrote in 1911, it was one thing for five hundred boys to "vent their energies upon five square miles of hill, wood, and greensward around their town," where their parents could supervise them. It was quite another matter "when these five hundred must play upon a street a quarter mile long, crowded with traffic, shops, and saloons."[20]

Behind such rhetoric lurked the view that children playing on city streets and sidewalks were nuisances to adult endeavors. Youngsters might be susceptible to immoral influences, but they also created noise, blocked traffic, pilfered goods, and destroyed property. Urban space was, after all, a valuable resource, important to numerous public and private functions. By the late nineteenth century, city streets had become contested territory as merchants, deliverymen, carriage drivers and others demanded more and more room for their needs. These economic interests mounted campaigns to control access and rights of way, and they pushed kids off the streets in formal and informal ways.

The automobile's speed and appetite for space created a watershed. By the 1900s, burgeoning motorized traffic was curtailing street play and imperiling young lives. In 1922, automobiles caused 477 children's deaths in New York City; in 1925, children numbered almost half of all people killed by cars in Hartford, Connecticut. In fact, the model for Children's Day was a "No Accident Day," declared in 1925 to alert New York City residents to the need to protect kids on the streets from cars and trolleys. Increasingly, local governments, under pressure to reserve urban thoroughfares for motorized vehicles, passed ordinances to prevent street play and, more frequently, private interests pressured police officers to sweep children out of the way. In several cities, juvenile courts, newly established by child-saving efforts, processed thousands of cases of youngsters arrested for obstructing street activity with their play.[21]

The street culture of boys particularly unnerved adults. Some boyish pastimes were harmless annoyances: boys often engaged in games such as tag, hide-and-seek, marbles, and baseball that appropriated sidewalks and kept pedestrians and merchants alert to scampering youngsters. According to one report, a "winning tactic in the chase game of hare-and-hounds was running through a store and out the back—the hares usually made it through quickly enough to avoid interference, but the shopkeeper was roused to anger in time to stop the pursuing hounds." Boys' ball games incorporated stationary objects— walls, posts, hydrants, telephone booths, parked vehicles—as bases and boundaries to the irritation of their owners; meanwhile, the ballplayers aggravated drivers by blocking traffic. Other young male amusements provoked more distress. Youths stole rides on streetcars and delivery wagons, badgered both fixed and moving targets with snowballs, upset sidewalk displays, pulled pranks on draft horses, and filched food and merchandise from shops. Most menacing were the brawls some youths waged and the fires they capriciously started. Gang rivalry, usually among older boys but sometimes including younger ones as well, created an unofficial social map, making some streets safe and others dangerous.[22]

Responding to pressures to remove kids from public places and assimilate immigrant children, settlement houses and other social agencies undertook efforts to create alternatives to street play. Hull House in Chicago and settlements in other cities, as well as the YMCA, YWCA, and YMHA, established clubs where neighborhood youngsters could gather in protected spaces and engage in supervised play. Several sponsors provided gymnasiums and roof gardens to help working-class children learn values of cooperation while they partook of recreational activities. Reform associations also organized competitive sports, hoping that unruly boys might be drawn in by the lure of athletics and assuming that if boys would participate in a sport they might also be cajoled into being involved in educational activities. Recollecting his own experiences with the Good Will Club of Hartford during the 1910s, Morris Cohen testified, "All I know is that they [the club sponsors] did not want us on the street so we went to a club where we could not get into trouble."[23]

What concerned the experts most was that children of the city were not using their time out of school and away from parental supervision in approved ways—in a word, they were "idling." When recreation advocate George Ellsworth Johnson surveyed the play sites and activities of nearly fifteen thousand Cleveland, Ohio, schoolchildren on one day, June 23, 1913, he discovered that six thousand of them were, in his words, "doing nothing." Among the others, seventy-four hundred were "playing" and fourteen hundred were "working." That

ADULT-SPONSORED ACTIVITY. Eager to remove children from the streets and instill appropriate values of obedience and order, adult-run associations organized an increasing number of formal play activities during and after the Progressive era. *Chicago Historical Society*

same year, a study counted half of 120,000 New York City children as "inactive." An earlier count in Milwaukee tallied half of 1,419 children likewise unoccupied. The terms that the studies used—"idling," "hanging out," "loafing," "just fooling"—highlight the value judgments that the researchers applied to their categories. "Playing" to reformers entailed active but acceptable pastimes such as baseball, kite flying, jacks, and the like. Though some admitted that "doing nothing" could involve innocent social interaction and deciding what to do, they observed that it more commonly was the first step on the road to gambling, thievery, vandalism, and fighting. Johnson granted that children should have certain latitude in selecting their play and that they deserved to achieve happiness through those choices, but he also reinforced the idea that play should be functional. Thus, he classified over four hundred games according to their "educational value" and appropriateness for each stage of childhood.[24]

Concern over "just fooling" and what others called "marginal play" had always worried parents and clergymen. Now, however, there was a growing conviction that professional intervention could deter the ill effects of unsupervised activity. The inference was that some kind of boundary needed to be drawn around play lest young people, striving for self-definition but incapable of making good decisions, endanger themselves. As one play reformer put it, "Children not knowing the best that is in play, will be apt to find their fun in smoking, playing marbles for 'keeps,' pitching pennies, predatory raids, truancy, and sex delinquencies—all of which are violations of our best ideals of social conduct."[25] In order to promote acceptable conduct in one particular way, educators Evelyn Dewey (wife of John) and Katherine Glover recommended a regimen of organized activities for schoolchildren during summer vacations. Their argument reflected the outlook that carried over from the Progressive era when they wrote in 1934,

> In how we shall deal with this marginal play time of youth we have a most serious challenge. It is so rich in potentialities for good or for ill. The boy can spend it in scout activities or in gang warfare, he can go camping or hiking; or he can play craps and hang around in back alleys.[26]

Among reformers, however, the most desirable way to confine children's marginal play was to situate it in the parent-controlled home and at an adult-supervised playground.

Delimiting the Play Site

As the previous chapter notes, the playground movement in the United States arose in the 1880s when, influenced by the German model, reformers established sand gardens in parks and schoolyards to promote constructive play among very young children. Shortly thereafter, play equipment and apparatus for older children were added to these spaces, followed by ball fields, buildings for indoor recreation, and organized programs for competition and entertainment. In accord with Progressive-era goals of rational organization and expert management, in 1906 Henry S. Curtis, a psychologist who had studied under G. Stanley Hall, joined with Jane Addams, Luther

THE PLAYGROUND MOVEMENT. Child-saving reformers created controlled spaces, such as this Colorado playground, where children could play safely under adult supervision, but often children avoided such places in favor of their own play environments. *Library of Congress*

Gulick, and Joseph Lee to formed the Playground Association of America. Their new organization marked the professionalization of playground work. The association began publishing a journal the following year; by the 1910s, staffs of college-trained experts were overseeing playground activities. By 1917, there were 3,940 public and private playgrounds in 481 cities, and they employed 8,768 playground directors.[27]

Playground reformers desired to remove children, especially working-class, immigrant children, from the dangers and enticements of the street and put them in an environment where expert adults— usually trained, middle-class women—could keep an eye on them. Their goal was to make the playground more than just an alternative play space. According to literature of the movement, planned play could supplement the schools, and supervised playgrounds could serve as incubators of cognitive skills, social values, and citizenship.[28] Thus, Curtis advocated in 1907:

> Supervision not only trebles the attendance at the playground, but makes it a school of character and of all the social virtues, whilst the

unsupervised playground is apt to get into the hands of older boys, who should be working, and train the children in all of the things they ought not to be trained in.[29]

Steeped in the language of social control, playground advocates wanted to impose public authority in order to supplant the influences of unhealthy institutions such as pool halls and penny arcades. Creating formal playground space and training instructors, however, still were not enough. Children also needed appropriate equipment for safe, regulated activity; otherwise their tendency toward noise and misbehavior would prevail. Thus the movement generated a number of manufacturers of swings, slides, jungle gyms, and other apparatus all eager to help restrict activity to precise spaces—and profit from it, too—where adults could more easily, promote safe, orderly play.[30]

Themes of security, discipline, and development—physical and moral—characterized the playground movement. Significantly, a fence surrounded a typical playground to thwart children from straying from view, to prevent intrusion from unwanted influences, and to create an orderly exterior "room" that, like an interior room of a home, contrasted with the rowdy, dirty street. The protective management of female playground supervisors contrasted with the unsympathetic harassment from the street's mostly male shopkeepers and policemen. Not all playground activity was prearranged. Of eleven public playgrounds in Hartford, Connecticut, in 1912, for example, seven offered structured play and four left kids to play freely on the equipment and on the grounds. But even "free" playground activity was regulated, usually by employees of the school system.[31]

Inside the grounds, play was sex-segregated, sometimes even divided by interior fences. Here, too, unhealthy influences from mixed-sex activity were to be excluded. Henry Curtis defended such separation by stating, "The reason for [sex-segregation] are obvious and sufficient. . . . There are often loose girls and always loose boys coming to the playgrounds, and it is better not to have them together, or where they can corrupt other children." Though girls' activities tended to be less physical than boys,' the looser clothing and flexible footwear that girls now wore enabled them to partake in more active running games, and there was some cultural tolerance for "tomboyism," at least in girls who had not yet reached puberty. Most organized playground games were segregated by age as well as separated by sex.[32]

In 1911, the Playground Association of America changed its name to the Playground and Recreation Association, later becoming the National Recreation and Park Association. The evolution, by adding the term "recreation" and eventually dropping the term "playground," signified an important shift. In the minds of the professionals, recreation had become a means for adults to find relief from the pressures of modern society, while children's play remained serious business, vital to their growth. By the 1920s, the profession of playground management had transformed into recreation specialists whose goal was to provide service to entire communities. Meanwhile, playgrounds, though still present in many parks and school yards, assumed tighter connections with school curricula and the notion that physical fitness reinforced learning. During the Depression of the 1930s, the playground movement stalled as communities across the country cut budgets, closed playgrounds, and laid off employees. Even the return of better economic times after World War II left playgrounds in less favorable light than at the beginning of the century.

Perhaps most importantly, researchers discovered that even where playgrounds were relatively abundant and accessible, they did not attract as many children as reformers desired. According to surveys, only about 4 percent of school-age youngsters frequented playgrounds in Milwaukee and Cleveland, and only a slightly higher percentage did so in Chicago. Attendance records for young people ages five through eleven in Hartford in 1915 showed that boys especially avoided playgrounds as sites for play, and in several places gangs seized playgrounds as their own fiefdoms or turned them into battlegrounds. Hartford's Parks Superintendent George A. Parker undoubtedly was voicing wishful thinking when he wrote in 1912 that "the playground has solved the juvenile problem for us. We have none now, for the children are off the streets." But as one Worcester, Massachusetts, eleven-year-old remarked, "I can't go to the playgrounds now. They get on my nerves with so many men and women around telling you what to do." Most children, it appeared, preferred the unsupervised byways, yards, and vacant lots in which to play.[33]

To a certain extent as well, the playground movement declined because a growing number of middle-class families provided their children with their own play accoutrements at home. Authorities on child care in the first half of the twentieth century feared for the decline of the family as much as they feared the dangers of the street, and they urged parents to provide home-centered play spaces as a means of restoring family unity, as well as keeping children safe. Thus, at least in middle-class families who could afford them, playrooms became another panacea, along with playgrounds, for dangerous play. A well-designed playroom, said the experts in agreement with new psychological theories, could stimulate a child's need for self-expression. The experts were not of one mind, however. While some advised parents to yield control of playroom activities to their children, others advocated that parents participate at home in play with their children as a means of promoting family togetherness. Though no data exist that can be used to assess how many families actually set up playrooms in their homes, the ideal of designating a separate and special area for children's play was a new one.[34]

Backyard playgrounds became another home-oriented space that competed with public play areas. By the early 1930s, 46 percent of families of means had backyard swings and 58 percent had sandboxes. Working-class parents also acquired these items but in much lower proportions: 25 percent owned swings and 17 percent had sandboxes. Like playrooms, in the minds of child experts these places could draw children into the safety of the home. As one advocate wrote in *Parents Magazine* in 1934, "The child with a backyard playground develops the habit of contentment at home. Home becomes the center of his life, not merely a place to eat, and sleep, and have his ears washed."[35]

In addition, other venues arose to compete with playgrounds. In 1922, for example, Chicago boasted 76 public baseball diamonds, 15 skating rinks, and 250 tennis courts.[36] Child-welfare professionals in organizations such as the YMCA and settlement houses recruited working-class children into their gymnasiums and yards to participate in team sports, using baseball and basketball games to inculcate middle-class values of teamwork, fair play, and accomplishment in poor youths. Indeed, organized sports became a basic method by which adults colonized childhood. Little League Baseball, for example, founded in 1939 in Williamsport, Pennsylvania, stated as its purpose:

> Through proper guidance and exemplary leadership the Little League program assists youth in developing the qualities of citizenship, discipline, teamwork and physical well-being. By espousing the virtues of character, courage and loyalty, the Little League Baseball

and Softball program is designed to develop superior citizens rather than superior athletes.[37]

This attitude has continued to pervade organized sports for children to the present. But even more than formal play spaces and organized play activities, between the early and mid-twentieth century momentous developments in the lives of children—and in American consumer culture—involved the proliferating availability of mass-produced toys.

The Expanding Toy Box

Just think about the toys that stir the childhood memories of today's older generations who grew up before the age of television. Teddy bears, erector sets, Monopoly games, baby dolls, kewpie dolls, fantasy characters, Tinkertoys, yo-yos, Patsy dolls, Lincoln Logs, model trains —all these and more, many more, emerged in the first third or so of the twentieth century to offer youngsters play opportunities that their forebears never had. The American toy industry, like other manufacturing concerns, matured during this period as mass production, widespread distribution, mass marketing, and new technologies enabled toy makers to feed on—and bolster—the growing child-centered society. And just as soap, cigarettes, automobiles, and crackers became associated with a particular brand name, so did toys. Indeed, a budding synergism arose, linking toys to characters identified with other consumer products: dolls depicting the Campbell Soup Kids and the Cracker Jack Boy, to name just two examples. In a society where childhood had become protected and sentimentalized, toys, purchased and given by loving parents and other family members, became the customary way to express affection and reward good behavior. At the same time, toys represented both the older generation's nostalgia for a lost innocence and their hope for a rosy future. Though still small compared to what it would become after 1950 when dollar revenues soared from millions to billions, the American toy industry now increasingly joined the effort to redefine childhood.[38]

The new mass-market toys reflected two dichotomies affecting children's relationship to them: gender divisions and the tug between "free" play and educational play. To a large extent, trends in boys' and girls' toys moved in opposite directions. Building blocks and minia-ture tools early in the century, followed by electric trains, toy cars and airplanes, Tinkertoys, erector sets, and Lincoln Logs after World War I, anticipated a boy's future manhood that would be filled with machines, competition, and teamwork. These various types of boys' toys idealized mechanics and construction, and they encouraged their users to find pleasure in technology and how things worked. Girls' toys, on the other hand, avoided connections with an adulthood de-fined by science and business and instead reinforced time-honored female social roles as nurturing mothers and homemakers. Newly designed, more realistic baby dolls encouraged girls to learn tasks of feeding and caring, and paper dolls drew them into the world of fash-ion and friendship. Even though many girls played with their broth-ers' toys and some boys liked to play with dolls, toy makers and adult consumers overlooked exceptions to their shared definitions of sex roles.[39]

The intended educational function of toys derived from the pre-dominant middle-class aspiration for self-improvement. Once consid-ered foolish baubles, toys increasingly came to be seen as instrumental to a child's intellectual development. Realizing changing attitudes to-ward childhood, the American Toy Manufacturers' Association in 1903 began promoting the use of their products for educational and so-cialization purposes. An editorialist in *Playthings*, the industry's chief publication, pronounced in 1907, "There is no doubt that children are perfect imitators; they want to do things their elders do and any and all toys that will educate at the same time that they amuse are good." Noted companies such as Parker Brothers, Playskool, and Milton Bradley promoted their games and objects as "educational" in that they not only were designed to be entertaining but also were sup-posed to teach children to play together and follow rules.[40]

But as psychologists began to place more emphasis on a child's personality development and needs, the role of toys as instruments of joy and freedom shared prominence, and sometimes competed with, their role as educational tools. Parents, following advice for promot-ing their offspring's self-expression and imaginations, often were com-plicit with manufacturers in disregarding toys that supposedly helped in skill development, instead buying fantasy toys that represented heroines and heroes of radio, comics, and the movies. By the 1930s, nonutilitarian toys linked to celebrities such as Shirley Temple, Charlie

McCarthy, and Mickey Mouse and to heroes such as Superman, Buck Rogers, Little Orphan Annie, and Dick Tracy began filling children's toy boxes across the country.[41]

Many of the new toys and games, if they actually had occupied most of children's playtime—but they often did not—would have had the effect of increasing solitary and small-group play and keeping youngsters indoors. Doll play among girls did indeed become more elaborate and isolating. Many girls spent considerable time alone cutting out dresses and other apparel from newspapers and fitting them onto paper dolls or dressing and otherwise tending to baby dolls.[42] Also, "New Kid" dolls such as Raggedy Ann and Andy, which were flexible character dolls made of soft and washable materials, gave girls cuddly playthings for private amusement. During the 1910s and 1920s, companies such as E. I. Horsman and Effanbee expanded the child-doll (as opposed to baby-doll) population by producing companion dolls, whose rosy cheeks, sparkling eyes, and sometimes-mischievous expressions made them girls' fantasy friends, to serve as, and even replace, human playmates.

Among the most popular companion doll was Effanbee's "Patsy," born in 1924. Patsy was an early version of a wardrobe doll, who had her own line of clothing—outfits that replicated those worn by middle-class children but also those, such as a surgeon's gown, to enlarge the doll's roles. By the 1930s, Patsy had her own accompanying doll family that included siblings Patsy Ann, Patsy Joan, and Patsy Babykin. Effanbee also extended the trend of making baby dolls look, feel, and act more realistic, coming out with "Dy-Dee Baby" in 1934. Like Ideal Toy Company's "Betsy Wetsy" of the same time, Dy-Dee Baby drank and excreted real water. In the 1930s, character dolls from film and comics, such as Shirley Temple and Little Orphan Annie, occupied girls' attention when alone or in small groups. Girls also played singly with other gender-reinforcing items inherited from earlier generations: tea sets, doll houses, homemaking equipment.[43]

The popular participation of boys in sports, organized and informal, gave them greater opportunities for group play, but they, too, could use new toys in solitary ways. Construction sets such as Gilbert erector sets (created in 1913), Tinkertoys (1914), Lincoln Logs (1916), and Lego bricks (1932), along with chemistry sets (made by A. C. Gilbert) and model railroads (Lionel began manufacturing electric trains in 1901, though the 1920s was the company's "Golden Age"), gave boys opportunities to experiment on their own and be introduced to aspects of modern science and engineering. Following contemporary norms of age grading, manufacturers of these items produced series of sets that became more complicated, and therefore more age appropriate, for boys as they grew older. Multifeatured miniature vehicles—cars, trucks, fire engines—also encouraged single or small-group players. Fantasy toys, which expanded in connection with radio and movie adventures in the 1920s and 1930s, included items such as Superman paraphernalia, cowboy guns and outfits, and the Daisy Company's Buck Rogers air rifle, all of which could encourage private or group amusement. Also, new children's crafts (Crayola crayons first appeared in 1903), card games (Rook, for example, debuted in 1911), board games (Monopoly in 1935), and cardboard jigsaw puzzles (made more intricate after 1900 by invention of the die-cut process) all enhanced indoor play for both boys and girls.[44]

Though reading continued as a solitary childhood activity, new types of amusement and the expansion of commercially produced toys altered reading habits. Certainly by the beginning of the twentieth century, the ritual of reading aloud at home was fading. Parents still read to very young children—the bedtime story persisted—but the practice of school-age siblings or peers reading to each other was being supplanted by the emerging toys listed above. In schools and libraries, age-graded books and magazines filled shelves, and educators imposed restrictions on what they believed to be unsuitable literature. But it appears that many children now had what historian David Macleod has called an "uncertain appetite for reading." Macleod cites an 1896 survey of schoolchildren in Worcester, Massachusetts, that found only about 10 percent of both girls and boys expressing reading as an important amusement activity. How much or how often young people read is difficult to assess. Another study involving fewer children of immigrants than in the Worcester group indicated more widespread reading, and it seems plausible to assume that, at least until movies and television enveloped children's culture, books remained important stimulants and sustenance for children's imaginations.[45]

More important was the type of literature that kids were beginning to consume and that librarians could not restrict. After 1900, pulp series books for boys that presented crime mysteries and stories about sports and science heroes, as well as animal tales written mostly for girls, flooded the market. Already avid readers of comic strips, children by the 1930s were devouring comic books that featured cartoon characters such as Mickey Mouse for younger children and superheroes, horror stories, and romance tales for older kids. By 1944, a survey reported that 95 percent of boys and 91 percent of girls between ages six and eleven regularly read comic books. After World War II, comic books became a hotly contested issue, pitting adult regulators against children's consumer tastes, but long before then the genre, inexpensive and appealing, offered children a tempting opportunity to spend their own money and make their own consumer choices.

Parents, now supportive of children's self-expression and cautiously tolerant of children's precociousness, largely relinquished the role of feeding youngsters' fantasies to comic book publishers and producers of radio programs and movies. But the older generation remained uncomfortable with what their excitement-seeking youngsters were doing and reading when they were out of sight and how these semi-illicit media had dangerously enticed them. Thus Katherine Glover and Evelyn Dewey lamented that "ready-made amusements have impinged too much on the wits and creativeness of American youth. We have let slip into the hands of the commercial entrepreneur most of those amusements which used to be created in the home." As one remedy, Glover and Dewey suggested that boys no longer be allowed to build and listen to radios on their own; rather, they should be obliged to sit and listen passively under adult supervision. Such a goal was unrealistic, however. Mass media were now entering and widening the generation gap.[46]

As much as new mass-produced toys, games, and literature created a "solitariness" to play that had not been as much a part of previous childhoods, other toys, inherited from the past, still were popular and still involved children in group play. Diarists and autobiographers continued to mention balls, marbles, hoops, skates, bicycles, kites, sleds, and jackknives, usually more often and more devotedly than they talked about newer playthings that were more ephemeral. Of course, social class also determined the kinds and quantities of toys that kids had at hand. Consequently, testimonies by children from lower-income families referred frequently to improvised playthings that were imagined to represent some of the newer toys: for example, a companion doll made from straw and cloth rather than Patsy or

Betsy Wetsy; building materials consisting of scavenged bricks and wood rather than Lincoln Logs and erector sets; games improvised from buttons or stones rather than formal board games such as Monopoly or Rook.[47]

Still, two developments overrode, at least partially, the constraints of class. For one thing, mass production lowered costs, and toy manufacturers tried hard to offer products that could fit as many household budgets as possible. Train sets and dolls, for example, came in sizes and intricacy that spread across the cost spectrum. In addition, new toys helped underpin a bourgeois society in which more uniform consumer tastes were created by marketers and retailers. Though advertisers were coming to realize that children comprised a special consumer community that could express a powerful demand, toys continued to reflect adult attitudes, negative as well as positive. Factory-made playthings that expressed racist images, for example, occupied many a merchant's shelves. In the 1890s, just as Jim Crow legislation became increasingly formalized in the South, toys such as shooting games with African American characters as targets, a "Chopped Up Nigger" jigsaw puzzle, and "Pickaninny Tenpins" reflected prevailing racism. After the turn of the century, some doll manufacturers marketed characters with racial and racist features, such as Horsman's Cotton Joe (1911) and the Louis Marx Company's "Alabama Coon Jigger" (1921). These figures and other toys that represented blacks as plantation mammies, urban dandies, and erratic fools no doubt transferred demeaning stereotypes to children's attitudes.[48]

Through the 1920s, as in the past, most toys were selected and purchased for children by adults. Christmas and birthdays remained the major occasions when a youngster received toys as gifts. But among middle-class households that subscribed to the precept that children needed to be cherished and their self-expressiveness encouraged, two portentous trends were invading parental jurisdiction over the world of playthings. First, manufacturers and marketers began to realize that young people harbored their own tastes and aspirations that were nurtured in peer groups at school, on the streets, and in backyards. The older generation's willingness to grant youngsters some degrees of freedom gave toy producers and advertisers an opportunity to stimulate children's demand for toys, a demand that could exert pressure year round. With spendable cash of their own, resulting from gifts and rewards, many children also could satisfy some of their own wants. Late in the nineteenth century, several American school systems began setting up school banks in which students were encouraged to make weekly deposits as a means of teaching them thrift and responsibility. The movement flourished in the 1920s, but at the same time children ignored the intended lessons and spent their nickels and dimes for their own purposes.[49] Though they often spent their money on candy, novelties, clothing, and movies, children also bought commercial playthings such as games and dolls.

Second, the flowering of new mass media—radio, movies, books, and comics—sparked children's fantasies and consumerism in ways that had not existed previously. Children's programs on the airwaves, the Saturday afternoon movie matinees, and published tales about Tom Swift and Anne of Green Gables catered to an enriched children's culture and a broadened youth autonomy. With allowance money in their pockets and banks, youngsters increasingly could access goods and media on their own schedule, not on holidays and birthdays, and not with the rest of the family. And importantly, many of the media products and programs included role models of spunky children challenging and outwitting naïve or wicked adults. Parents' nostalgic vision of play was fading behind new, more exciting modes of kids' pleasure.[50]

Putting Children at the Center

Katherine Glover and Evelyn Dewey opened a chapter titled "On Their Own: Play and Adventure," in their 1934 book on child care with a seeming confession:

> Our adult world owes children many apologies, but one it owes more than any other. This special apology is for having intruded upon their play. That, at least, one feels, might have been left to them uninvaded, free, without scrutiny and imposition. . . . We have cut peepholes in fences and spied on children at play, have written theses and treatises about what we saw, have created organizations about their play life, have made artificial places for them to play in and set organizers and supervisors over them. We have seized on their love of play and capitalized and commercialized it.[51]

Their mea culpa stopped short, however. "The intrusion has become necessary," Glover and Dewey reasoned, because cities had usurped play space, families had shrunk and reduced play companions, and play had become more complex so that it called for expensive equipment and trained supervisors. Most of all, Glover and Dewey warned, "We need to remind ourselves over and over that we are living in a world undergoing transition." That world was creating challenges to teachers and children alike:

> Through play we have to create opportunities for children, physical and mental challenges, which once were offered by life conditions before we began to live altogether in a push-button civilization. We see children in large cities skating in the street, dodging in and out between cars for the sake of the thrill because so little chance is left them for adventure other than to court death under the wheels of the modern juggernaut. And the hold which the movies have, the vogue of the "Westerns" and the wild-life pictures, is that they satisfy vicariously a hunger which in children's own experience is unsatisfied.[52]

At the time that Glover and Dewey were reviewing the state of American childhoods, researchers such as themselves had been observing, counting, testing, and construing children for several decades. They also had convinced parents at least to pay attention to their counsel. A survey of parents in the early 1930s found that nine out of ten mothers and three-fourths of fathers of high socioeconomic status read works of child-rearing experts; more than a third of lower working-class mothers did so.[53]

More than ever before, the advice was grounded in emotional and ascriptive qualities of the child, qualities that related directly to play. The maturing field of child psychology devoted increasing attention to play as the twentieth century advanced, and researchers used newly defined fundamental concepts such as mental age and IQ, along with characteristics such as sex and race, in drawing conclusions about how young people were—and should be—acting. For example, psychologists Harvey Lehman and Paul Witty concluded that black children were more social in their play than were white youths, who preferred solitary play more than blacks; that the higher the mental age of a child, the more likely the child was to play with fewer toys and avoid physical play; that between ages five and a half and twelve and a half, boys engaged more frequently in active play, while girls were more sedentary in their pastimes; but also that both sexes participated about equally in some thirty-five different play activities. Such discrete qualities, the result of supposedly scientific observation, defined and reinforced norms that prevailed for the next half century.[54]

Moreover, by the 1930s, toy manufacturers were on their way to putting children's fantasies, rather than parents' objectives, at the center of their enterprise. Themes of boys' toys that previously had entailed the imitation of adult male pursuits increasingly moved in the direction of powerful, imaginary heroes who both fed a youngster's caprice and, at least during the Depression, provided emotional relief from pressures of economic insecurity. Futuristic toy guns, toy soldiers, and gadgetry that related to popular media characters such as Dick Tracy, Buck Rogers, and Superman gave boys opportunities for self-expression and romance through role-playing that insulated them from, rather than joined them to, their fathers' real world. The trend in girls' toys did not signify as dramatic a break from the past as boys' toys did, but toys associated with characters such as Shirley Temple and Little Orphan Annie were commercial playthings that represented for girls a world of romance and adventure that existed outside the domestic sphere. It was no accident that the Better Play for Childhood League designated Peter Pan, "the boy who would never grow up," as the "patron saint" of Children's Day, because Peter's fantasy life symbolized the spirit of play that toy makers now promoted.[55]

Probably no one of the immediate pre– and post–World War II era enriched children's commercial culture, as well as their fantasies, more than Walt Disney. The cartoon shorts of Mickey Mouse and Donald Duck blended slapstick humor with conflict and chaos in a way that enabled young people to accept the frustrations and fragility of everyday life. The Disney Studio's animated feature films, beginning with *Snow White* in 1939, created a new kind of children's folktale, one that included wholesome, lovable characters who sang and danced—all lavishly illustrated—and that always involved the triumph of good and tempered the foreboding that had darkened traditional folk stories. More importantly, the animated characters presented in Disney cartoons and feature films carried with them extraordinary merchandising potential.[56] Though the most explosive influence of Disney was to come after the success of television programming and the opening of Disneyland from the mid-1950s onward, toys and games linked to

Disney characters and stories already were becoming staples of toy boxes and desires in the 1930s and 1940s.

Thus, over the first half of the twentieth century, both sexes of children were becoming more deeply immersed in consumer culture. Though it always must be kept in mind that socioeconomic class and external events such as the Depression and World Wars I and II shaped the consumer experiences of children as it did those of their entire families, even relatively deprived youngsters entered the realm of commercial amusement in the 1930s and 1940s. Whether they were attending—or sneaking into—a movie, haunting the penny arcade, spending a nickel at the candy shop, going into a five and dime store to purchase a set of jacks or a spaldeen (a high-bouncing ball used in street games), or prevailing on a parent to buy them a Shirley Temple doll or a Buck Rogers spaceman outfit, preadolescent children were exercising a kind of autonomy that defined a culture, a time, and a social space that was their own. Radio, billboards, comic books, and, most of all, peer groups gave kids the "vicarious hunger" that Glover and Dewey lamented and enabled them to travel, figuratively and literally, away from the adult society that simultaneously wanted to nourish their "love of play" while at the same time constrain it. On their part, children wanted to claim the birthright that the 1930 White House Conference had ratified for them, but they often wanted to do so away from the regulated and, to them, uninspiring designs that their elders had for them. That quest is the theme of the next chapter.

5

The Golden Age of Unstructured Play, 1900–1950

SAMUEL NATHANIEL BEHRMAN was one of America's most important dramatists and scriptwriters of the 1930s and 1940s, but just twenty years before that time he was an ordinary kid growing up in Worcester, Massachusetts. He swam and canoed in nearby Lake Quinsigamond (often to the consternation of his protective parents), played baseball, and hung out at the neighborhood drugstore. Looking back on his youth, Behrman recalled that one of his most vivid memories was joining a group of friends "to walk boldly downtown on Main Street on Saturday morning and ride up and down in the elevators of the Slater Building just for a fling at the illicit."[1]

Ruby Berkley Goodwin, an African American writer, was a near-contemporary of Behrman but from a very different family and a very different part of the country. Born in 1903, Goodwin was raised in southern Illinois, daughter of a coal miner and granddaughter of an ex-slave. She had what she considered an ordinary childhood, a time when, she recalled, "everything was a game. . . . Every season had its own special type of game, and the long winters did not tax our ingenuity." Poor but creative, young Ruby had few toys, so she fabricated playthings out of household objects and played games using leftover corn kernels as prizes.[2]

Growing up in the 1930s, Jane Gray never became famous, as Behrman or Goodwin did, but her childhood in Rochester, New York, resembled that of her more literate contemporaries. Like Behrman, Gray played baseball; like Goodwin, she fashioned impromptu playthings. Hers were made out of cardboard boxes and "things like that." When Jane was ten years old, her family moved and she got her own bedroom. There she often played with her dolls, dressing and undressing them and pushing them around in a small buggy. She also owned paper dolls of the Dionne quintuplets and of Shirley Temple, and she cut out clothes for them from catalogs and fashion magazines.[3]

Individuals such as these three, experiencing childhoods in the first half of the twentieth century, were surrounded by myriad adult-directed opportunities for play. Their parents bought them toys—whether construction sets for boys or dolls for girls—herded them into playgrounds and club meetings, celebrated them on their birthday, and strived to shelter and enlighten them in school and out. Adults, like those of previous generations, wanted to be sure that children learned as they played, to guide young imaginations toward functional ends, and to safeguard their kids from harmful influences. But no less so than their forebears, children of the era concocted mischief and courted danger. They just could not help it. As memoirist Janet Gillespie recollected from her 1920s youth:

> We were happy, intoxicated by the obvious havoc we were causing. I knew perfectly well we were being naughty but I also knew with calm certainty that we were naughty only in grownup terms. Since all the really interesting and original things we did were labeled "naughty" by the adult world, I didn't mind being naughty at all. I liked it and so did [my sister]. We were not interested in goodness; it was too boring.[4]

Too boring. There lay the key to a youngster's point of view. To be sure, accounts such as those above are retrospective and sentimentalized, but they almost unconsciously reflect a viewpoint that occupied many a young mind. Whereas adults wanted young people to "grow" emotionally and intellectually as they played, to always do something useful, and to "play nice," children craved fun as they defined it. That definition sometimes included mischief—being "naughty" and "having a fling at the illicit." Young people of preteen ages sought to incorporate the whole world into their own culture, to transform and to control that world. They knew how to occupy themselves with virtually anything. For example, in his humorous but insightful recollection of his pre–World War II childhood, Robert Paul Smith ruminated on how a new technological device like a phonograph could engender consequences that no professional educator might ever foresee:

> I learned that when the records went around slow, the sounds were slow, when they went around fast, the sounds were high. This, I believe, is science, and I found it out for myself. I found out that when

the turntable went around fast, the horse chestnuts flew off. I would like to say that I found out that heavy things flew off faster than light things, but I don't know if that's true. I think it's true. I think that's what I later learned was called centrifugal force.[5]

One can hear a parent chiding a youngster like Smith, "Don't play with that! That's not a toy." But the blending of this kind of childish curiosity with traditional and new play sites, with old and new materials, with conventional and different play partners, and with expanded time for unsupervised activity made the first half of the twentieth century a golden age of children's play.

Using the Environment

Indoors and outdoors, in plain sight and in secret, under adult control and unsupervised, preadolescent children of the early twentieth century adapted a range of environments to their play. For youngsters growing up on farms and in small towns, nature continued to provide ample opportunities for playful pursuits. Born in 1908, small-town Maine resident John Gould wrote that his play revolved around bows and arrows, but implements were not what mattered. "The important thing," he stressed, "was that we went into the woods. We went to the woods in all weather and all seasons, and there wasn't much we didn't know about them." To escape the poverty of the Memphis ghetto, African American author Richard Wright's mother took young Richard and his brother to live with his grandmother in the then small community of Jackson, Mississippi. There the Wright brothers roamed the "wide green fields" where they were free to "play and shout." Young Dorothy Howard regularly wandered through the woods of her East Texas home, though she armed herself with sticks in case she encountered a snake. And future editor Hal Borland, raised in small-town Colorado, often left his father's printing shop to explore the surrounding countryside.[6]

Incorporation had always been the common theme of outdoor play in rural environments, and it remained so in the early twentieth century. Rural writer Louise Dickinson Rich engaged in time-honored amusements with flowers, attempting "to blow every last bit of fluff from the white head of a dandelion-gone-to-seed in one breath," holding "buttercups under each other's chin to see if a golden reflection would prove that we liked butter," plucking petals from daisies and chanting " 'He loves me, he loves me not,' because that's what Big Girls did," and biting off "the ends of honeysuckle and trumpet-vine blossoms and [sucking] out the drop of honey, telling each other how good it was, although it really didn't taste like much." Opal Whiteley, raised in an Oregon lumber camp during the early 1900s, filled her diary with accounts of how she amused herself by looking for animals in the woods and then giving them historical names to match their appearance. And as a child, southern writer Frank Conroy and his friends "spent most of our time in the woods. The first project was a tree house built precariously high in a tall pine." There, the boys whiled away their time "lazing around in the sun, [and] we'd tell stories and pick the black pine tar off our hands and feet." Conroy also related how he "hid caches of canned food and comic books at different places in the woods. We rarely used them; it was the idea that pleased us."[7]

The natural environment also offered backdrops for private reverie and invented drama. Literary critic Samuel Hynes, sent by his father to live on a farm one summer, relished his time spent in nearby woods and pastures. "I went there alone sometimes, to wander and just look at things," he recalled. Like other youngsters, Hynes and some neighbor boys used the fields for a stage on which to play cowboys and Indians, "creeping through the underbrush (Indians) and galloping down the hills (cowboys)." Or, they reenacted other fabled stories from the American past "in a grove that stood in the middle of Mr. Nelson's cornfield. . . . There in the cool shade we were settlers surrounded by Little Crow's warriors, or the U.S. Cavalry planning a raid on an Indian camp."[8]

As urbanization made uninhabited environments increasingly inaccessible, the cityscape took on a more important role in children's play cultures. Instead of forests and fields used by rural kids, city kids appropriated, incorporated, and transformed streets, sidewalks, backyards, alleys, vacant lots, dumps, sewers, fences, rooftops, and buildings for their amusement. Growing up in the Bronx during the 1920s, Kate Simon, eldest daughter of a Polish immigrant shoemaker, found her immediate environs too limited for her roaming.

"The block wasn't enough anymore, even the empty lot," she wrote in her memoir:

> We snooped in the Italian market . . . all the way up on 183rd Street and Arthur Avenue. We skated far along Tremont to stare down the tracks below Park Avenue, peering far downtown as we waited for trains that never seemed to run. But there was good garbage on the tracks, the rare sight of dozens of whiskey bottles along with the more familiar rotten oranges, old shoes, and mice rustling in torn bags of bread crusts and chicken bones.[9]

Catharine Brody, whose childhood was spent in the "unfashioned" West Side of New York City, described how the streets and sidewalks permeated most fully the lives of the children:

> [These places] were the true homes of the small guineas, micks and sheenies, the small Italians and Jews. . . . Sweets tasted better in the streets; a new dress waited for the verdict of the streets; a beating or a scolding faded in the noise of all the beatings and scoldings audible and visible through the many open windows on the streets. . . . We [children] could not go into the woods hunting for the first violets, but on the day that the sidewalks bloomed with the chalked boxes and numbers of "potsies" [hop-scotch], on that day we knew that spring had come.[10]

Through the flexibility of their play culture, urban children of the early twentieth century tried hard to claim the streets as their recreational setting, and they often succeeded. Native-born and immigrant working-class youngsters especially compensated for their lack of resources by using public spaces creatively at all times of the year. Beyond the scrutiny of family and teachers, the streets offered a special opportunity for independence. Sophie Ruskay, daughter of Russian immigrants in New York City, recalled:

> Children owned the streets in a way unthinkable to city children of today. . . . We shared the life of the street unhampered by our parents who were too busy to try to mold us into a more respectable pattern. If we lacked the close supervision of the genteel world of maids and governesses, we gloried all the more in our freedom from restriction.[11]

Outdoor urban spaces showcased children's inventive play skills. Youngsters adapted formal games and created new ones, incorporating the built environment and the objects they found there. Formal games of baseball and football rarely took place because there were not enough players to complete two full sides and because there was not enough open space. But informal ball games with improvised equipment and boundaries abounded. Comedian George Burns perhaps embellished his memory of childhood baseball games, but his humorous description was not far from what was probable:

> When we played baseball we used a broom handle and a rubber ball. A manhole cover was home plate, a fire hydrant was first base, second base was a lamppost, and Mr. Gitletz, who used to bring a kitchen chair down to watch us play, was third base. One time I slid into Mr. Gitletz. He caught the ball and tagged me out.[12]

In summer, youngsters applied their ingenuity by placing a "spanner" —a perforated tin can—over a hydrant that they opened to improvise a spray for myriad water games. Urban structures were an essential and challenging component of hide-and-chase games such as ring-o-levio, hares-and-hounds, and others, and, as author Emily Kimbrough recalled, the streets rang with cries of "Olly, olly out's in free!"[13]

A quality that separated many urban neighborhoods in the first half of the twentieth from those of the latter half was the fact that undeveloped green space, even in the urban core, still existed. Consequently, vacant lots served as informal playgrounds and left many a child with fond memories of make-believe settings for play dramas of all sorts. Robert Paul Smith and friends observed that "the only thing a vacant lot was vacant of was a house." He and his friends imagined one such place as a jungle, where they built rafts and huts in the manner of their hero, Tarzan. Likewise, Kate Simon alluded to an empty lot near her New York City home that was "as full of possibilities as a park. . . . The few girls who managed [to gain access to the lot] were never quite the same again, a little more defiant, a little more impudent." And Michael Gold, an East Side New Yorker, testified:

> My gang seized upon one of these Delancey Street lots, and turned it, with the power of imagination, into a vast western plain. We buried treasure there, and built snow forts. We played football and baseball

through the long beautiful days. We dug caves, and with Peary explored the North Pole. We camped there at night under the stars, roasting sweet potatoes that were sweeter because stolen.[14]

Once the grownup world decided to erect a structure on a formerly vacant plot of land, the area still provided play opportunities, though of a riskier sort. Historian Henry May, raised in Berkeley, California, cherished memories of converting neighborhood lots into "inexhaustible playgrounds." "During the late 1920s," he recalled, "new houses were built on most of these lots and the more daring boys . . . climbed on the scaffolding when the carpenters stopped work." Robert Paul Smith and friends liked to spy on a construction crew during working hours, and when the builders went home, Smith and company filched boards, nails, and other materials to construct their own play hut. Zachary Summers liked to cavort on the construction site of New York's Belt Parkway. "That was one hell of a great time," he testified, "those two or three years when they were building an overpass, because when it snowed we would go all the way to the top of the bridge and with a sled we would go all the way down maybe a quarter of a mile."[15]

Inner-city sidewalks during the 1930s and 1940s spawned one of the most unique child-generated games of the period: the chanting jump-rope game of double Dutch, a game still in vogue today. Combining girls' traditional singing game with call-and-response chants of African and African American cultures, the game employs the cooperative participation of two girls swinging the ends of one or two ropes while the jumper (sometimes more than one) in the middle engages in individualistic and highly competitive jumping routines. Vocal interaction occurs between the rope turners and the jumper in which the turners challenge the jumper to express herself physically while attempting to keep her jump going. A fall or missed beat means disqualification and the opportunity for another jumper to enter the center. One popular version of a chant at the time, for example, highlighted preteen preoccupation with romance. The turners would begin with a rhyme such as, "Strawberry jam, cream of tartum / Give me the 'nitial of your sweet-heartum." They then would chant the alphabet, "A, B, C, D," and so on while the girl in the middle jumped in various styles over the swinging rope or ropes. The letter on which the jumper stumbled signified the name of the man she would marry. By continuing to

DOUBLE DUTCH. A rhyming jump-rope game played frequently by African American girls, double Dutch was easily adaptable to urban streets and sidewalks. *Library of Congress*

jump successfully through the whole alphabet, a jumper could "win" the game. Other rhymes included more bawdy lyrics, such as, "Behind the 'frigerator / There was a piece of glass / Miss Lucy sat upon it / and it went right up her . . ."[16]

Double Dutch was, and is, a game easily adapted to the outdoor urban environment. Not even three players were required because a fence post, door handle, or any inert object on which the end of a rope could be tied could act as one of the turners. In most neighborhoods, clotheslines, purchased, found, or pilfered, were widely available. Because of its competitive quality, the game was co-opted by adult organizers in the late twentieth century, with formation of an American Double Dutch League in 1975. The organization formalized rules, included boys, and sponsored competition, some of which was televised. But for girls in Harlem and other African American neighborhoods, the game provided a popular form of independent, unstructured street play.[17]

While property owners and police constantly harassed children playing on the streets, youngsters' most menacing enemy was traffic. At first, vehicles were only a nuisance, and street play necessitated a theft of time between wagon and trolley traffic. Referring to her experiences with both horse-drawn and motorized conveyances early in the century, Sophie Ruskay wrote, "We looked upon them merely as an unnecessary interference with the progress of our games. Sometimes, to be sure, accidents occurred, but they were rare; either we were very fleet of foot or the drivers obligingly slowed down their horses." Children also incorporated moving wagons, cars, and trucks into their games while continuing to play in traffic, hitching rides and using vehicles as targets for snowballs. But ultimately they lost the battle. The growth in number and speed of cars, trolleys, and trucks made it increasingly difficult for street play to coexist with adult transportation needs.[18] Still, as indicated in the previous chapter, public playgrounds and parks as alternatives to the streets had only limited success; unsupervised outdoor spaces, even if they had to be shared with meddling adults and dangerous traffic, often remained the play sites of choice.

When weather and darkness halted outdoor activity, children proved imaginative in incorporating indoor spaces into their play. At home, for example, attics and cellars offered valued retreats for solitude and fantasy. To Samuel Hynes, "The attic was my private place. Nobody else went there; . . . I spent a lot of time up there by myself, playing elaborate games that I made up, with trucks and tin soldiers, or just looking out the window." Future naturalist Edwin Teale had "a cat-like love of attics. There was always unexpected treasure to be discovered in the mysterious, dim light of the Lone Oak storeroom. It was a repository of history. Attic hours were entrancing journeys into the past." And in his fictional account of childhood, Flannery Lewis admitted, "Like an attic, a basement is a secret place, slightly removed from the world but still within sight of it; the time you spend there is your own and of no relation to your everyday life on the surface."[19]

Youngsters also used other indoor spaces. Susan Mildred Brown and her girlfriend improvised a clubhouse above the elevator shaft in her New York City apartment building. There she "ate Fig Newtons and read comics." Richard Wright treasured playing in the long hallway and under the stairs in his grandmother's Jackson, Mississippi, home. Jade Snow Wong, raised in San Francisco's Chinatown, amused herself in the trouser factory owned by her father. There she "played hide-and-seek around the high bundles of blue denim, rode on the pushcarts used for loading overalls, [and] climbed onto the cutting tables to talk to the women as they worked."[20]

In addition, household common areas and furniture offered play opportunities. Growing up in Maine, Louise Dickinson Rich imagined herself Robinson Crusoe as she played indoors. She recalled that "we constructed [a cave] by moving chairs from all over into proper juxtaposition with the dining room table and draping this framework with blankets stripped from various beds. Then we crouched inside, in the roles of Robinson and Friday, sallying forth only to kill game for the pot or repel cannibals." African American writer Elizabeth Laura Adams used the living-room carpet to inspire her childhood reveries. "There were times," she wrote, "when I imagined it the magic rug upon which the Thief of Baghdad sat; and when no one was nearby to observe, I would ceremoniously seat myself in the center of it and make a wish to be carried up to the moon."[21] Usually settings for solitary or small-group play and seldom visited by adults, remote indoor places were key to children's urge to control their activity.

Toys: Bought and Made

As I noted earlier, commercial child-centered toys began to abound in the first half of the twentieth century as the American toy industry and its marketers prevailed on parents to fill their children's lives with instruments of joy. Kids gave their parents pleasure as they seemed to cherish many of these new objects: bicycles, dolls, erector sets, yo-yos, board games, and many more. But just how and what youngsters played with and the meanings they attached to their playthings remained a more complicated matter than adult toy givers and toy makers presumed. Parents and other kin used toys as means to reward children and secure their affection, particularly on special holidays and celebrations, and children usually accepted the gifts with appreciation. Samuel Hynes, rhapsodizing on the joys of Christmas presents he received as a child in a wealthy family, exemplified the newly available kinds of commercial toys when he wrote,

> In one long tinseled, colored-lighted, tissue-paper-wrapped morning
> I am given: a toy furnace that melts lead and casts toy soldiers, a

chemistry set, Tinkertoys, Lincoln Logs, an Erector set, Big Little Books, Tootsie Toy cars, a dump truck that really dumps, skates, crayons, a magic blackboard that erases itself, a Lionel train, skis.[22]

But children continued to use the toys in a variety of independent ways that adults did not anticipate. And like counterparts in previous eras, youngsters of the first half of the twentieth century fashioned their own playthings and in doing so expressed their quest for autonomy.

Besides all the new additions to the toy box, tried and true playthings from earlier time periods continued to occupy childhood activities. For example, Helen Smith Bevington, born to an adulterous preacher whose family was forced to move from town to town during Helen's New England girlhood, managed to retrieve some pleasure from her disrupted youth when she played with jacks, rode her bicycle, and occupied time with a friend's formal dollhouse.[23] Diarists and autobiographers growing up during the period also made frequent references to traditional playthings such as skates, sleds, and wagons.

The expanded stock of play apparatus in the new consumer society, however, could induce jealousy on the part of youngsters who felt deprived. Nancy Hale, living outside of Boston, envied her neighbor Mimi whose family provided her with an elaborate playhouse equipped with miniature furniture and "real Dresden china made for children's use." In response to her entreaties, Nancy's parents acted as many middle-class parents did. "I had to have a playhouse," she recalled. "I wept. And so the abandoned milkhouse was swept out, some of my nursery furniture was moved into it, and an ornate Victorian knocker was screwed on the weathered board door that would not quite close, and it was officially referred to as my playhouse."[24]

Yet, if memories can be believed—individually they must be read cautiously, but in aggregate they suggest palpable patterns—improvised toys continued to command a dominant position in children's culture. Girls incorporated and transformed a variety of common objects. Barbara Jordan, who became the first African American woman to be elected to the U.S. Congress, recalled from her Houston, Texas, youth: "There were a couple of kids who lived on the block and we played all the childhood games. There were pine needles, and we'd gather them together and make a little house. We'd get a bottle and put a piece of rope in the end and that was your doll." Estha Briscoe

Stowe, growing up in Oklahoma, "improvised whatever became available. We used empty tomato or corn cans along with pieces of bailing wire to make tin-can walkers. With a foot on each can and each hand holding a wire loop, we could 'walk tall' and cut little round circles in the hard dirt." Kate Simon, sitting on the fire escape of her family's New York City apartment, played endlessly with a box of cloth scraps, combining "the pink with the blue; no, the yellow with the blue, the shiny with the dull; two shinys." And Mary Mebane, born in 1933 and raised in a rural black community in North Carolina, liked to capture lightning bugs, grasshoppers, and toads and make up games of house with them. June bugs were especially entertaining. "If you tied one of his legs to a string and attached him to the clothesline," Mebane explained, he would fly in a great circle and sing for you. We didn't mean to be cruel, and after he sang for a while we would let him go." She had to be more careful of toads, however: "Mama told us to stay away from toad frogs. If they peed on you, you would get a wart. But we played with them with sticks."[25]

Boys were equally inventive. Historian Bruce Catton, who spent his childhood in Benzonia in western Michigan, reminisced about the playthings he made for himself:

> Take an old broomstick and to one end nail a slim triangle of wood, suitably whittled; you then have a Kentucky rifle as good as anything Daniel Boone had, and if you can get a fragment of an abandoned cigar box and cut out something vaguely resembling a trigger and hammer, and fasten it loosely to the breech of this weapon with a brad, so much the better.[26]

Humorist Sam Levenson retold a delightful account of how he and his peers transformed common objects into play objects:

> Ashcan covers were converted into Roman shields, oatmeal boxes into telephones, combs covered with tissue paper into kazoos . . . a chicken gullet into Robin Hood's horn, candlesticks into trumpets, orange crates into store counters, peanuts into earrings, hatboxes into drums, clothespins into pistols, and lumps of sugar into dice.[27]

Poor children growing up during the Depression had special need to substitute informal playthings for commercial toys. John Camonelli told his interviewer that he "didn't have no toys, no money, no bicycles—so we had a 'pushmobile,'" which was a scooter made out of an orange crate and a skate.[28]

Radio and motion pictures as well as popular literature now inspired numerous toys and games. Although commercial products derived from the adventures of Little Orphan Annie, Shirley Temple, Popeye, Tom Mix, and Buck Rogers were available on toy shelves, children adapted their own amusements from such characters and stories. Future actress Anne Jackson, born in a small town near Pittsburgh the daughter of a Yugoslavian immigrant, moved to Queens, New York, where "around age ten" radio and movie dramas inspired a game she called "Who's this?" in which she and her friends tried to guess each other's imitations of movie stars. Journalist Caryl Rivers recalled playing "Inner Sanctum," after the "scary radio show" with her two girlfriends. She also drew from comic books to expand her play and "adopted Wonder Woman as my role model."[29]

Though improvised dolls made from straw, cloth, and other materials remained part of girls' play experiences in the first half of the twentieth century, commercially produced dolls from companies such as Effanbee and E. I. Horsman had expanded appeal. Unable to afford the new dolls, Sophie Ruskay still craved them. As she walked past a store window, she could not resist stopping to look. "The dolls were gorgeous," she observed, "blue-eyed bits of perfection dressed in unimaginable splendor. . . . What else could one do with such a doll except look at it in ecstatic wonder."[30] Most girls, however, owned one or more of these dolls and played with them alone and with other girls. Among the plethora of toys, dolls of this era occupied a unique position because of their multiple functions. Some dolls evoked maternal responses, and others fulfilled needs for fantasy and vicarious yearning; still others acted as surrogate companions.

These meanings have been preserved in the Doll Oral History Collection at the Strong National Museum of Play in Rochester, New York. Interviews about doll playing were taken from women whose girlhoods dated from the 1910s to the 1940s.[31] Unlike literate and often famous autobiographers who referred to doll playing in their autobiographies, the interviewees in this collection were mostly undistinguished mothers and their adult daughters. Their testimonies about their play preferences and relationships disclose insights into what playtime meant to ordinary preteen girls of the era. They reveal that girls normally played with dolls in socially prescribed ways but also that they sometimes deviated from expected behavior and that their allegiance to doll play was not as strong as adults might have expected. As doll makers, most of them female, began constructing their products from softer, more pliant material and gave their dolls a more realistic feel than the wood and metal replicas made by male manufacturers, doll playing closely approximated the experiences of handling actual babies and enhanced the mimicking of the maternal functions characteristic of girls' doll play.[32]

Among the contributors to the Doll Oral History Collection, Ann Klos gave a typical response when she stated, "In my mind, a doll is always a baby doll that you handle as a baby." Klos also owned a miniature stove, miniature refrigerator, and miniature sink to supplement her domestic-oriented doll play. References to a doll as "my baby" and "my little girl" were common among several of the interviewed women. They spoke about how they dressed and undressed their dolls, put them to bed, fed them, and wheeled them around in miniature carriages. As Joanne Wasenska recalled, "My mother always allowed me to play with my dolls as though they were real babies. And I did . . . my mother allowed me to get out of bed after I had gone to bed . . . to give my baby a bottle because that is what mothers did."[33]

The subjects of the oral histories referred to the peer-like sociability of other kinds of dolls, however, as frequently as they described the maternal function. Alice Wolpert defined her favorite doll "Anna" as a "companion," an object to "accompany one in dreams and reality . . . to be a friend." Phoebe Watts's dolls also were considered "companions" with "alter egos who could do things I was not able to do." Girls who had no female siblings seemed especially likely to deem their dolls as friends. Barbara Beard, born in 1920, spoke of her dolls as "companions to a little girl [with] no sister." To her, a doll was "a person who stays with you, even all night. It's someone to fantasize with and about." And Georgianna Apolant remembered a special doll "as my confidante, alright, because I was an only child."[34]

Many of the interviewees had used their dolls as psychological crutches, endowing them with qualities that exceeded simple companionship. Thus Ann Reebok, in referring to her dolls, said, "I talked to them. I always supposed that they answered me." Rita Blum, though she had four sisters, spoke of her doll not only as "somebody I could take care of [but] somebody who wouldn't talk back." Lois Greene-Stone was even more introspective: "What a doll did for me is give me definition. Part of what I am is also because of my dolls which may have to with the definition of a young girl . . . the doll becomes a companion and an extension of one self."[35]

It seems plausible to speculate that in this particular time period, the very personal relationship that girls had with their dolls was unique. Before 1900, when most dolls lacked a realistic look and feel, girls gave them more decorative functions than did girls after 1900. After character dolls became common in the 1930s and 1940s, and especially after Barbie and her imitators appeared in the 1950s and beyond, dolls took on more vicarious functions of fantasy rather than those of everyday peer friendship. Thus between the early 1900s and the mid-1950s, a doll that looked and felt like a friend could, in a girl's imagination, be a friend in a realistic way that had not previously existed and would be altered subsequently.

The oral histories also portray a somewhat overlooked dimension of doll play in the early twentieth century: the extensive use that girls made of paper dolls. With a history dating back to Asian cultures of the ninth and tenth centuries A.D., paper dolls were first imported into the United States from Great Britain in the early nineteenth century. Though a few small American companies began printing paper dolls at this time, most such products continued to come from England and Germany.

In 1859, however, the American women's magazine *Godey's Ladies Book* began printing black and white doll figures and colored cut-out clothing for them. Other women's magazines soon followed suit, but the explosion in the appearance of paper dolls and clothing in women's and children's periodicals occurred after 1900. A doll named Lettie Lane and her family made their debut in *Ladies Home Journal* in 1908, Polly Pratt and her friends entered *Good Housekeeping* in 1919, and several other household and fashion publications, such as *McCall's* and the *Delineator*, featured their own characters, often accompanied by story lines. By the 1930s, children's journals such as *Golden Magazine* and *Jack and Jill* also were presenting paper doll characters and clothing. During the Depression, when many families could not afford costly toys, paper dolls associated with comic book characters, such as Brenda Starr, the Katzenjammer Kids, Daisy Mae, and Li'l Abner, and celebrities such as Mary Pickford, Norma Talmadge, Jackie Coogan, and even Rin Tin Tin, could be found in major newspapers. At the same time, comic book racks and toy shelves began to display books of cut-out doll characters, clothing, and accessories. One historian has called the period from the 1930s to the 1950s the "Golden Age of Paper Dolls," when girls—and a few boys—found inexpensive pleasure in collecting doll bodies and then awaiting the next magazine, book, or newspaper publication for a new outfit to cut out for their toys.[36]

Paper dolls dominated the memories of nearly half of subjects of the oral history interviews. Alice Clifford typified the phenomenon when she testified that at age nine, "I loved them [her many paper dolls], especially those that were historical like ladies of the white house [sic] and Gone With the Wind. . . . They were a challenge to cut out perfectly and to play stories with." Sources for the dolls varied. Norma Tetamore cut out her paper dolls from magazines; Shirley Cohen Fagenbaum took hers from catalogs; Jane Yuile got hers from books; Margaret Rohack snipped characters from the Sunday comics. Girls seemed especially to enjoy creating clothing and other paraphernalia for their paper dolls. Phoebe Watts and her friend became so engrossed in designing and coloring paper-doll clothes that they "often never got around to cutting [the dolls] out." Likewise, Virginia Littman designed clothing and colored them with crayons. Lois Green-Stone claimed that she drew her own paper dolls and designed clothing by tracing patterns from magazines, while Roberta Rugg traced then cut out character dolls from newspaper photographs. Saleta Smith and several others constructed furniture for their paper dolls. What appealed about paper dolls to many girls, according to Mrs. James Kern, was that "they didn't come from a store and they didn't take a lot of room to store in my dresser drawers."[37]

Certainly, not all interviewees in the Doll Oral History Collection preferred or played with dolls as girls. Mary Kinsella claimed to like roller skates better than dolls. Mary Weber, "was not much for dolls, really, I wasn't . . . we [Mary and friends] were quite into sports. You know, we liked basketball and hockey. " Helen Becker sometimes played with dolls by herself but was more enthusiastic about participating in baseball games and hide-and-seek with neighborhood children. Jeanne Wenrich admitted to owning dolls and paper dolls, but she cherished more the memories of winter snowball fights and sledding, summertime romping on her backyard bars and swings, and the neighborhood fair that she and her friends organized. Thus, just as it did in the nineteenth century, doll play occupied only a segment— and not always the dominant segment—of early-twentieth-century girl culture.[38]

From the child's perspective, then, a toy was packed with many meanings. To be sure, new commercial toys had appeal, but simple objects transformed into playthings evoked powerful memories. Emily Kimbrough, raised in small-town Indiana, used both formal and informal toys to mimic her elders by re-creating "Mr. McNaughton's store," complete with pretend money and a pulley to convey a basket of money to the cashier. Edwin Way Teale applied his extraordinary inventive aspirations to the creation of a "Dragonette," an elaborate flying contraption that he fashioned from sheet iron, wood, and piano wire. The simple collection of goods, whether from nature or from things adults discarded, or of manufactured items such as trading cards, fulfilled a child's obsession for achievement.[39]

Youngsters also derived their own unintended pleasures from commercial items. A toy as simple as a yo-yo, for example, could stir philosophical contemplation. According to Frank Conroy,

> The greatest pleasure in yo-yoing was an abstract pleasure—watching the dramatization of simple physical laws, . . . the geometric parity of it. . . . I practiced the yo-yo because it pleased me to do so, without the slightest application of will power. . . . The yo-yo represented my first organized attempt to control the outside world.[40]

It is unlikely that a ten year old consciously recognized such deep meaning, but the combination of "abstract pleasure" with the "slightest application of will power" undoubtedly had an important effect that only the child could sense. The new profusion of board games shifted a considerable amount of play indoors, where boys and girls spent more time than their predecessors mastering symbolic information. But most of all, children imparted their own social meaning to toys. Samuel Hynes expressed it best: "On my bike I'm no longer a little kid, I'm a kid."[41]

Playmates, One and All

Though with some exceptions sex-segregated play had been the characteristic mode of play since colonial times, it was in preteen years during the first half of the twentieth century that sex segregation became an especially prominent feature of a young person's life. Sophie Ruskay described the state of affairs: "The separation of boys and girls so rigidly carried out in the public schools also held on the street, boys played with boys, girls with girls." In their play, children followed socially prescribed gender roles. For the most part, boys almost never considered playing with girls; boy culture implicitly would not tolerate such interaction. Richard Wright spoke for his own sex when he commented, "It was degrading to play with girls and in our talk we relegated them to a remote island of life. We had somehow caught the spirit of the role of our sex and we flocked together for common moral schooling." Girls, however, often were aware and resentful of their second-rate status. According to Ruskay, "Occasionally we girls might stand on the sidelines and watch the boys play their games, but usually our presence was ignored. There was no doubt about it, girls were considered inferior creatures." Likewise, ten-year-old Sylvia McNeely complained in her diary entry for March 13, 1929, about having to yield space in the basement to boys who wanted to play marbles there. "That's always the way with boys," she grumbled. Those boys seemed always to be bedeviling her. Later that year, Sylvia disclosed, "The dum boys humed [hummed] with my comb and put their dirty germs on it." Resentment was a common theme. As Louise Dickinson Rich was prompted to observe, "Boys to us were simply more fortunate children who were allowed for some reason we couldn't fathom to wear sensible clothes which gave them an unfair advantage in climbing trees or leaping brooks."[42]

Boy culture seemed to flourish in an independent, alternate world of urban and rural environments where values of loyalty, physicality, and competitiveness prevailed.[43] Diarists and autobiographers whose childhoods occurred during the first half of the twentieth century accentuate these qualities in their play. Even when given opportunities to engage in preferred activities, boys resented outside interference. When progressive reformers and child savers tried to impose supervised athletics on boys of both the lower class and the middle class,

INFORMAL BASEBALL. Throughout the early twentieth century, boys organized their own varieties of baseball games, which they could play without needing enough players for two full teams. *Baseball Hall of Fame*

to teach them cooperation and obedience, boys often expressed a preference for their own self-structured competitions. Playwright Dore Schary, for example, spent his boyhood in a relatively poor section of Newark, New Jersey, where he and his male friends found the attempt by adults to teach them the ideal of fair play "beneath us." They played by their own rules:

We had grown up in a neighborhood where One O'Cat, Red Rover, Pinch and Ouch, Run Chief Run, and Johnny on the Pony were played for keeps. A protest over the rules usually ended the game and started a free-for-all. It wasn't that we were bad losers; it was just that everybody wanted to win.[44]

Likewise, Bruce Catton did not absorb the rules of baseball from some professional instructor; rather, he and his pals learned as they "went along," playing a game called "scrub" which did not need two full teams. "There was no score," Catton related, "and technically the game had no end; only dinner-time or some other interruption ended a game." Samuel Hynes and friends played the very same informal ball game, calling it "Bounce Out." Other boys waged improvised but ruthless athletic competitions, replete with their own strict regulations. For example, Chicago-born working-class writer Albert Halper and his comrades created a game of diving for pennies in a park lagoon. According to Halper's amusing account, "A vague code of ethics grew up. For instance, no kid was allowed to stick his finger into another diver's nostrils or ears while under water. Shoving and kicking were allowed, but no scratching, no gouging." The description might have been embellished; the heap of evidence suggests that the behavior was not.[45]

Richard Wright and other boys might have rebuffed girls, but a number of girls nevertheless did play, and some even preferred to play, with boys. Female autobiographers' recollections of intergender activity were undoubtedly selective and self-congratulatory, but the sum of memories indicates an authentic variation from the norm. Louise Dickinson Rich, owning a good ball and a baseball glove, frequently was able to join neighborhood boys in games of scrub and follow their pact that "if anyone broke a window in the Cushman's house . . . all players were mutually responsible and had to chip in and pay for it." On these occasions, Rich adopted the boys' code of ethics, recalling that sometimes, "a good fight" ensued from a game because "we were very touchy indeed about our honor, our rights, and any real or fancied cheating or discrimination." African American journalist Ellen Tarry, daughter of a Birmingham, Alabama, barber, preferred to join in boys' play because "they could climb higher, run faster, and skate better than girls, and it was fun keeping up with them." Caryl Rivers grew up on "a street full of boys" in suburban Baltimore where she claimed to have played baseball and tackle football, and where she "learned not to have any truck with dolls or house or sissified girls' games. . . . I was convinced that being a girl was on O.K. thing. Could I not do anything boys could do, and do it better? Except, of course, pee on target."[46]

It appears that most of the time girls' interactions with boys were episodic, and sometimes the boys exploited a girl playmate who entered their games. Nature writer Sally Carrighar was raised in Cleveland, where the frequent absence of her railroad-employee father and the stress of living with a mentally ill mother caused her to be a shy child who avoided playing with girls. But she allowed herself to be "taken into a gang of boys to act as their spy" and help them in other activities. Ruby Berkley Goodwin played house with girlfriends, but when she frequented nearby Horn's pasture, she was allowed to join boys in action games of "kick the can, frog in the middle, or chickany, chickany, cranny crow." The recruitment of girls into boys' activities could also be reversed. Sylvia McNeely logged into her diary of July 8, 1929: "Six of us girls had a show in the side-yard. We got six boys to come and watch so of corse we each got one penney. They didn't like the show and wanted their money back. Boys have never liked any of the shows we had. They din't get it." And occasionally, interactions deviated from original intentions. Anne Jackson reported that when she was around ten years old, she and a girlfriend would play jacks and jump rope on her New York City street next to boys playing basketball nearby, and at times the boys would "ask us to play hide-and-seek, whip the lash, or ring-a-levio." The games, Jackson admitted, could include slightly illicit behavior when "we'd hide and kiss the boys in the cellarways. But we both gave up those games as communion drew near, mostly because when we played ring-a-levio the boys got fresh when they caught us."[47]

When girls played with each other, they predictably engaged in gender-prescribed activities. For example, on May 11, 1929, Sylvia McNeely informed her diary, "I took some close [clothes] over to Betty Kean's house and we dressed up." Kate Simon, experiencing what she called "a *Little Women* phase" of her girlhood, joined friends for mutual embroidering. "In for the sociability rather than the craft, a number of us settled for fast cross-stitching," she recalled. Simon also related that when the light grew too dim to sew, she and her companions sat on the stoop steps, gossiped, and sang popular songs. Emily Kimbrough and a comrade collected leaves, grass, and acorns that they then used to mix a "magic concoction" which they tied to a tree.

"This was to attract the fairies," she explained.[48] These were not amusements that would have appealed to boys.

However, references to girlhood pastimes also included a variety of active amusements that resembled those that did appeal to boys. Like boys, but separate from them, girls engaged in chase-and-base games, capture games, and ball games, in addition to simple running, skating, biking, and sledding. Louise Dickinson Rich described a game called "Stealing Eggs," played with a dozen stones and two teams, both of which were usually all girls. "Friendship went by the board when it came to picking teams," she stressed. The game involved two territories with a stone / egg at the back of each territory. The object was to steal an "egg" and return without being tagged— captured—in enemy territory. Rich also described "Duck on a Rock," a game requiring players to throw at and knock an object off a rock and recover it before being tagged by the guard. Mary Mebane liked a game she called "last-one-squats-shall-tell-his-name," in which girls formed a circle, sang a song, then sat after the song's last word: "Last one down was 'it' and had to tell the name of the one she loved."[49] Like black girls who improvised rhymes in their double Dutch competition, white girls also chanted as they jumped rope. Examples of rhymes that Kate Simon said she learned from Rosa, her Italian neighborhood friend, contained themes of violence, such as,

> Bouncy, bouncy ballee
> I let the baby fallee
> My mother came out
> And slapped me in the mouth

and ribaldry,

> My sister had a baby, his name was Sonny Jim.
> She put him in a pisspot, to teach him how to swim.
> He swam to the bottom, he swam to the top,
> My sister got excited, and pulled him by the—[50]

—proving that neither boys nor African American girls had a monopoly on puckishness.

In all these activities, it would be hard to underrate the influence of the peer group. As pointed out earlier, children's time spent with peers had expanded considerably since the late nineteenth century, and by the twentieth century peers had become *a*, if not *the*, major socializing force for many children. The peer group created a social arena in which youngsters subscribed to ideals and assumptions influenced by, but distinct from, those of parents, teachers, police, and clergy. That arena was not always democratic; age, size, sex, class, race, and ethnicity often determined who was included and who held sway.

Few diarists or autobiographers would admit to being bullied or left out, but occasional references do exist. Though she learned American games of hopscotch and hide-and-seek at school recess, Chinese American Jade Snow Wong, for instance, was teased with racial epithets and found herself the object of whispers by Anglo girls. As in earlier periods, black and white children in the South often played together, but only for a limited period of years. In preparing his autobiography, African American educator Benjamin Mays interviewed a number of other blacks of his own age and discovered that while 63.7 percent of them stated that they had had white playmates, the "vast majority admitted that such shared play ceased in pre-teen or early teen years, usually at twelve or thirteen. When play stopped, so did friendship."[51] Ely Green, an African American raised in Sewanee, Tennessee, learned about racial discrimination at age nine, when he tried to join some white boys in a football game:

> When I arrived there were many children playing football. I had been one of the players on one of the teams, and much favored before this day. Just as I started to walk onto the lawn someone kicked the ball, and it landed just in front of me. I picked it up, intending to kick it. A boy named Randolph snatched the ball from me, and said, "This ball belongs to me. I did not buy this ball for a nigger to kick." It seemed that every boy there turned his back to me.[52]

Benjamin Mays, who grew up on a South Carolina tenant farm, expressed the most vital element of youth culture in the South: whether it was in work or play, black children always needed to "be careful and stay out of trouble with white people."[53]

Peers did not monopolize all of a child's free time; solitary amusement took place as well. Whether the private meanderings of city streets and rural countryside, or the sedentary entertainment of in-door games and hobbies, or individual fantasy play with dolls and myriad other playthings, children found ways to occupy themselves. Such play often was dictated by circumstances. A daughter of Bohemian parents who lived just outside Boston, Nancy Hale often sat on the beach and "built sand castles surrounded with moats through which the tide sent surging currents, [and] aqueducts that carried the water from one round dug-out pond to another." She claimed to have "no memory" that other children joined her in these pursuits. Patricia Ziegfeld, daughter of theater impresario Florenz Ziegfeld, traveled extensively with her parents and consequently found that she had to amuse herself most of the time because she was surrounded by adults who indulged her but did not often play with her. Mostly, she played with her pets and dolls. Edwin Teale's solitary time involved a range of distractions, from investigating the habits of insects to pretending he was an Indian. African American fiction writer Chester Himes, whose father moved the family from Pine Bluff, Arkansas, to St. Louis when Chester was a boy, liked to "cut classes and roam alone through the strange big city; spending hours in the railroad station watching trains come and go."[54]

As always, it is important to keep in mind that several factors made playmates inaccessible to many preteen children. Large parts of the country remained rural and isolated in the early twentieth century, preventing some youngsters from a social life rich with peer friends. Children who worked long hours on farms, in factories, and at street trades had little time for playing baseball, jumping rope, or cutting out paper dolls. Nor could families of these young people afford erector sets, Patsy dolls, and tiny tea sets. Authoritarian parents also prevented their children from playing with others. One farmer expressed his opinion about his children's play to a labor investigator, sneering, "There's plenty of work for 'em," he stated, "and no time for foolishness."[55]

Moreover, group play was not always pleasant or peaceful. As several memoirists quoted above testified, playing with friends sometimes resulted in conflict, even fisticuffs. Streets, playgrounds, and vacant lots could become battlegrounds between racial and ethnic groups, or even between bands of youngsters or individuals who simply did not like each other. Gang rivalries became more heated among adolescents, but younger kids recognized social differences and entered into skirmishes that usually remained relatively harmless but could escalate. Ben Swerdowsky, a Jew raised in New York's Spanish Harlem, told of affixing razor blades to a kite tail and manipulating it so that it would cut the line and down a rival's kite. "The Spanish kids were very skillful at this," he marveled. Other conflicts, however, were not so tame. The potential for violence among children, mainly boys, seems to have increased in the early twentieth century. The resulting physical injury and rancor left psychological scars on some while forcing others to learn how to survive.[56]

Perhaps most importantly, the mutual play of peers strengthened the elements of a separate children's culture and widened the gap between generations. Whether in the "sanctified space" above the elevator shaft where Susan Mildred Brown read comics with her girlfriends, the "bottom of a ravine" where Caryl Rivers and her cohort indulged in the "forbidden fruit" of sliding down a sewer pipe, or the "scrub" ball games that Bruce Catton played endlessly with his friends, children helped each other to concoct a separate and sometimes secret world. Here, as Richard Wright declared, "we flocked together for common moral schooling. . . . We spouted excessive profanity as a sign of our coming manhood; pretended callousness toward the injunctions of our parents; and we strove to convince one another that our decisions stemmed from ourselves and ourselves alone."[57]

Joys and Risks of Autonomous Play

As historian Gary Cross has noted, child-study and child-recreation experts of the early twentieth century "danced on a narrow ledge." They believed that children needed to be able to play freely, but with objects selected by their parents or other arbiters; moreover, play must occur in ways and places that sheltered youngsters from the dangers of the adult world. Child authority Luther Gulick, for example, argued that expert leaders needed to manage the group play of boys lest they become "disorderly" and engage in activity inappropriate to their stage of development. Psychologist G. Stanley Hall's model of ideal play included activity initiated by children but managed by adults. The goal was not conscious social control but an "act of scientific management."[58]

Seen from a child's perspective, this logic was often unacceptable. As numerous testimonies from characters presented throughout
this chapter indicate, children challenged adult prescriptions, infusing their independent activity with both creativity and risk. When
unwanted (to adults) consequences ensued, the older generation intervened and the younger generation lost their prerogative. Sophie
Ruskay related what happened when her immigrant, working-class
parents erected a "large wooden swing":

> Mama cautioned us to swing on it very gently. We were content to do
> just that for about a week until the novelty wore off. Then I invented
> a game called "playing gymnasium." I planted my feet on the arms
> of the seat, grasped the spindly rail overhead and, with a mighty
> heave, swung my legs to where my hands were holding the rail. I let
> go my hands and swung just from my knees. Dangling upside down,
> seeing everything topsy-turvy, was great sport, until one of my
> friends spoiled everything by falling and breaking her arm. Mama, to
> placate the girl's angry mother, had the swing carted away.[59]

Dodging the control of parents has long been a part of growing
up, but in the first half of the twentieth century resistance and the
quest for autonomy flourished in ways that previously had not existed
and would fade after mid-century. This is not to say that children were
uncommonly disobedient and that they consistently subverted adult
authority; most kids were "good" much of the time. Rather, between
the early 1900s and about the mid-1950s, the nature of unstructured
play, the places in which it occurred, and the peer-oriented culture of
childhood promoted a type of behavior that, in varying degrees, signified children's freedom of action. Thus, Grace Grimaldi's father could
warn her, "If I catch you walking around, I'll break your neck," but
Grace did what she wanted anyway because she *could* walk around
and had numerous opportunities to do so.[60]

At times, youngsters such as Grace Grimaldi overtly defied parental restrictions. Barbara Jordan, who spent much of her Texas childhood with her grandparents, was warned by her grandfather not to
play with certain neighborhood children, "but sometimes," she admitted, "I would sneak around—I mean literally sneak out" to play with
them. Animal scientist Arthur Goldhaft's Russian immigrant mother
lamented, "Alter, Alter, what will become of you? You will become a

street bum," when he returned from playing ball on the street near his New Jersey home, but such parental misgivings did not stop him. A few youngsters found an ally in one parent against the other. New Yorker Louis Green, forbidden by his father from playing baseball, recalled "I couldn't tell my father I played ball, so my mother would sneak out my baseball gear and put it in the candy store downstairs." Mostly, youngsters simply followed their own customs, aware of adult rules but ignoring them just the same because that was the way to preserve independence. As Robert Paul Smith, describing all the seemingly trivial diversions he and his childhood friends engaged in, explained, "when we were kids, we had the sense to keep these things to ourselves. We didn't go around asking grownups questions about them. They obviously didn't know."[61]

The quest for independence was not always guileless; mischief, more serious wrongdoing, and genuine danger always lurked when children went unsupervised. Youngsters left to their own devices can be annoying, and in the burgeoning consumer society of the early twentieth century opportunities for disruption were rife. City kids patrolled gutters and alleys to collect discarded or temporarily abandoned objects that they could use in their play, but they also mined store shelves and clotheslines in various degrees of petty thievery, much to the consternation of merchants and housewives. Samuel Hynes's friend "Birdy" taught him how to "snitch" from a Minneapolis dime store. "Snitching was easy, [Birdy] said. The toys were out there on the counters in front of you, you just took one. Dickie D. said everybody did it; he's snitched lots of things." A candy store or pushcart also made for tempting targets. Anne Jackson shoplifted from Woolworth's "for the fun of it." And bothersome vandalism, such as Michael Gold's throwing a dead cat into a Chinese laundry, minor acts of arson, and knocking off men's hats with snowballs, were common.[62]

Away from watchful eyes, preteens frequently put themselves at risk: stealing rides on trucks as Michael Gold and Harpo Marx claimed they did, swimming and skating in unsafe ponds as Anne Jackson did, and wading into storm sewers as Caryl Rivers did.[63] Samuel Hynes expressed the kind of audacity common among children in this era, maintaining that, "if you rode [your bicycle] farther off there was danger enough, and plenty of chances to do what you were forbidden to do." As one example, Hynes described,

The Milwaukee railroad tracks down beyond Lake Street were out-side the neighborhood, beyond the limits of what was allowed. Par-ents were afraid of the freight trains. But we went there anyway to hang over the bridge rail above the tracks and watch the trains rum-ble by below. . . . You could climb down the side of the cutting with the other kids (absolutely forbidden, this), and dare each other to stand close to the tracks while a train passed and yell insults at the brakeman in the caboose.[64]

Such precarious acts were a staple of the new boy culture, but girls, too, seemed to have courted danger, trying, in Caryl Rivers's words to be "daring and resourceful." These certainly were not the adult aims of a sheltered childhood. Diaries and autobiographies rarely refer to injuries sustained from mischievous behavior, but there undoubtedly were scrapes, bruises, broken bones, and more severe and tragic con-sequences. It is not clear whether or not childhood injury was more common in this era that predated helmets, pads, and other protective devices, but it is clear that children frequently indulged in hazardous behavior that flouted adult prescriptions.

An entry in seven-year-old Emily Wortis's diary, written on December 4, 1945, previewed how the golden age of unstructured play was to end and what would replace it. Appearing a bit overwhelmed, she griped, "I cant keep track of all the days so maybe I shouldn't right [write] everyday because I have home work and music lessons and guitar lessons and Brownies and many other things."[65] A new, organ-ized world of childhood was dawning. Under its aegis lurked not only all the impositions on time hinted at by Emily Wortis but also an array of mighty forces that included a box with a screen on which charac-ters and scenes could be viewed passively; another kind of screen on which mock battles could be fought and messages exchanged; a series of dolls whose "realistic" anatomical qualities and high-fashion cloth-ing became the stuff of dreams; a multitude of mechanical toys and games usually requiring batteries and derived from child-oriented media and advertisements, and an intensified desire by parents to en-sure their children's success and shield them from any and every po-tential danger.

6

The Commercialization and Co-optation of Children's Play, 1950 to the Present

FEW IF ANY people knew it at the time, but October 3, 1955, was a landmark day in both the history of American television and the history of American childhood. That Monday marked the debut of *The Mickey Mouse Club,* an hour-long children's variety program that aired on ABC in the late afternoon, five days a week. The year 1955 already had been memorable for television because it included the initial broadcasts of such celebrated programs as *The Lawrence Welk Show, The 64,000 Dollar Question,* and *Gunsmoke.* Perhaps more pertinently for the history of childhood, just seven months before *The Mickey Mouse Club* first aired, one-half of all Americans had watched the TV adaptation of the Broadway hit musical, *Peter Pan,* the story of "the boy who never grew up." And in July of that year, Disneyland, a "magical" amusement park for children (and their parents) opened in Anaheim, California.

The Mickey Mouse Club was the first major network show aimed directly at preadolescent children, and its success was impressive— ten million viewers a day. Unlike previously popular programs such as *The Howdy Doody Show,* which catered to a younger audience, and *Kukla, Fran and Ollie,* which amused older viewers as well as children, *The Mickey Mouse Club* featured young performers and tried to connect with the twelve-and-younger age group. Loading productions with moralism, patriotism, and advice, the producers endeavored to carry out Walt Disney's goal of fashioning "a better world of tomorrow" and to create "the leaders of the twenty-first century."[1] Each presentation used a cast of "everyday" kids—"Mouseketeers"—outfitted in clean-cut, black and white clothing and mouse-eared hats, who sang, acted, and danced in various show segments. In addition, each day of the week featured a different theme: Fun and Music; Guest Star; Anything Can Happen; Circus; and Talent Roundup. Reluctant to present

THE MICKEY MOUSE CLUB. The first network children's television show using child performers, *The Mickey Mouse Club* starred only one adult, Jimmie Dodd. *Library of Congress*

youngsters as acting fully on their own, Disney producers cast a sole adult, the cheery, musical Jimmie Dodd, to guide the Mouseketeers throughout the show.

Another unique feature of *The Mickey Mouse Club* was its commercial appeal directly to children. Significantly, one of the program's original and continuous sponsors was the Mattel Toy Company, formerly a manufacturer of plastic ukuleles and jack-in-the-boxes. Before *The Mickey Mouse Club*, very few toy makers had advertised their products on television. Popular "toy king," Louis Marx and Company, with sales in excess of $50 million, spent just 312 dollars on publicity in 1955.[2] In 1952, Hassenfeld Brothers (later renamed Hasbro), a maker of pencil boxes and other school supplies, began advertising its new toy product, Mr. Potato Head, on TV. But most toy manufacturers avoided mass marketing except at Christmas time.

Mattel recast the mold. Daily commercials on *The Mickey Mouse Club* for the Mattel Burp Gun yielded sales that exceeded all expectations. More importantly, because the Burp Gun was not likely to appeal to parents as a "useful" toy—it fired Ping-Pong balls and was not intended to promote learning—and because kids could not afford to buy the product themselves, the company had somehow to sway children into convincing their parents to purchase the gun, as well as other Mattel toys, for them. Company marketers accomplished this goal by producing televised ads, replete with the slogan, "You can tell it's Mattel, it's swell."[3] Soon, Mattel and other toy marketers were applying sophisticated survey techniques in order to discover children's desires and preferences and then to integrate those factors into TV commercials. Their aim was to boost children's consumer influence. As one marketing analyst later asserted, "The trend is for children to get more decision making authority and exercise that authority at a younger and younger age."[4]

Four years after it began advertising its Burp Gun on *The Mickey Mouse Club,* Mattel introduced a product that was to become arguably the most enduring icon of American girlhood: the Barbie doll. Created by Ruth Handler, who with her husband Elliot had founded Mattel in 1945, the first Barbie was a three-dimensional representation of the lifelike adult paper dolls that Handler's daughter Barbara, who inspired Barbie's name, played with. While traveling in Switzerland, Handler had come up with the Barbie concept after noticing a German creation named "Lilli," a doll with a woman's body that included protruding breasts and an hourglass figure. Lilli first functioned as a caricature that was sold mainly to adult males and later became popular among European children. Handler got the idea that a doll more "real" than paper dolls could inspire American girls, in her words, to imagine "their lives as adults" and to use "the dolls to reflect the adult world around them."[5] Rather than represent Barbie as a seductress, Handler hired designers to make over Lilli's look, keeping her voluptuous body but giving her a face of "the girl next door." Dressed in a striped swimsuit and open-toed shoes, Barbie came ready to acquire outfits from a line of fashions and accessories that Mattel sold to fit her. Barbie was an instant sensation. Initially costing $3 apiece, 350,000 dolls were sold during the first year of production.[6] Millions more were to follow. Barbie in no way strayed from female stereotypes, but because in her glamorous consumerism she represented a free-spirited teenager, she enticed girls to emulate her style, a style that was defined by marketers rather than by parents.

BARBIE DOLL. The glamorous Barbie, with her "anatomically correct" (though much exaggerated) physique,
brought the commercialization of girlhood and girls' play
into a new era. *Picture Research Consultants and Archives*

Barbie and *The Mickey Mouse Club* exemplify the two major
themes of adult domestication of children's play since the mid-twentieth century: commercialization and the co-optation of time and activity. Since the mid-nineteenth century, parents and their expert advisors have given high sentimental value to childhood but also have attempted to channel children's play toward specific ends. Anxious to
make play functional and safe, they at first employed various cultural agents to achieve regulation: moral suasion, educational toys,
supervised playgrounds, schools, clubs, and organized sports. More
recently, they have structured youth activities, imposed toy safety

guidelines, and filed liability lawsuits, all with the goal of enriching and protecting vulnerable children. At the same time, commercial entities such as Disney and Mattel have wedged themselves between parents and children. Instead of acting as toy advisors and toy selectors, parents have become chiefly toy financiers—and not always that—while young people, in association with marketers and media, have seized control of toy predilection. In this regard, television took a key role. As business economists Sydney Landensohn Stern and Ted Schoenbaum observed, "Mattel's decision to advertise toys to children on national television fifty-two weeks a year so revolutionized the industry that it is not an exaggeration to divide the history of the American toy business [and, I might add, the history of children's play] into two eras, before and after television."[7]

In this chapter, I explore the interaction between commercialization and new forms of adult co-optation of play in the second half of the twentieth century. In the next chapter, I focus on the attempts by children of this period to subvert adult control, and I examine how successful their attempts have been in their quest for autonomy.

An Outburst of Kids

"A pig in a python." That is how one writer described the image of the baby boom, the demographic explosion of the mid-twentieth century that jostled practically every facet of American society and culture thereafter. In 1946, usually marked as the boom's onset, 3.4 million babies were born in the United States, a record and an increase of 20 percent over the previous year. For the next eighteen years, annual births hovered around four million, totaling some seventy-five million and creating a bulge in the population that, as its members aged, made its presence visibly known in virtually every facet of American life, much like the image of a large animal that is swallowed and makes its way through a snake's body as it is digested.

The boom may have started with babies, but the babies soon became preadolescent youngsters, lots of them. In 1950, when the first baby boomers were still infants and toddlers, the American population counted more than twenty-four million children aged five to fourteen, or 17 percent of the total. But then as the boom kids began to reach school age, their proportions soared. In 1960, when there were more than thirty-three million of them—an increase of 37 percent in just ten years—children aged five to fourteen comprised 18.6 percent of the total population, and in 1970 they accounted for 20.1 percent and they were forty-one million strong. Their numbers had increased by 40 percent in just two decades while the nation's total population had risen by just 34 percent. Thereafter, as the baby boom subsided— it usually is said to have ended in 1964—and as the bulge of boomers began moving through adolescent and postadolescent years, the numbers and percentages of preteens decreased, fluctuating between thirty-five and forty million and dropping to around 15 percent of the total population by the year 2000.[8]

Several new historical factors affected the lives of baby boom children and those who followed them in the second half of the twentieth century. For one thing, the number and proportion of women in the paid labor force rose dramatically, passing a milestone in 1981 when, for the first time, a majority of the country's adult females held jobs outside the home. More importantly for children, an increasing percentage of employed females were married, including married women with children. The number of wage-earning mothers had dropped after World War II, as childbearing and a domestic ideology kept many married women at home. But not for long. By 1987, more than half of women were returning to or taking on paid employment within a year after giving birth. Fewer than a third had done so as recently as the late 1970s.[9]

Moreover, rates of divorce and of babies born outside of marriage escalated. Of white women who married in 1940, at least 14 percent eventually divorced; of those who married in the 1960s and 1970s, at least 50 percent had divorced by 1992. Rates of marital separation rates also climbed. Divorce and separation frequencies among African Americans were even higher. Between 1970 and 1996, the sum of all divorced Americans, male and female, more than quadrupled, from more than four million to more than eighteen million. And between 1970 and 1992, the proportion of children born outside of marriage rose from 11 percent to 30 percent.[10] Since 1992, divorce rates and out-of-marriage births have declined somewhat, but the two phenomena nevertheless have meant that large numbers of children lived, and are living, with just one parent. Between 1970 and 1996, for example, the proportion of children under the age of eighteen who lived with only one parent rose from 12 percent to 28 percent. In every year since 1972, at least a million children have experienced a parental breakup.[11] And, as life expectancy increased, from sixty-eight years in 1950 to seventy-seven in 2000, youngsters of the late twentieth century were far more likely than children of previous generations to have several living grandparents, most of whom were eager to indulge them.

Demographic factors of the postwar years have had numerous consequences for the play lives of children. In some instances, the effects have shifted in diverging ways. In the 1950s and 1960s, when the baby boom bulge was largest in the preteen age category, families were at their peak size. The apex, however, did not always mean that there were lots of sibling playmates. One of the important but overlooked features of the baby boom was not that a given woman bore substantially more children than her ancestors of the nineteenth century did but, rather, that childlessness became rare. Most baby boom mothers had three or four children, usually two to three years apart, while the percentage of childless married women fell dramatically. Before the boom, 22 percent of adult women bore no children; during boom years, the proportion dropped to just 8 percent.[12] As a result of these changes, a family in post–World War II America contained several young people of preadolescent age at some point in time.

By the 1970s and 1980s, however, women in general were having fewer babies, one or two more likely than three or more. Consequently, once a child born in these years reached school age, she or he was more likely to play alone at home than with a brother or sister. Whereas a child with one or more older siblings could receive second-hand toys and instruction in modes of play from someone of the same generation but more experienced, an only child or one lacking a same-sex sibling would be subject to his or her own devices for creating amusement when not in the company of peers. And, the shortage of at-home playmates, combined with prevailing parental norms about protecting children and enriching their lives, meant that adult-structured activities rather than intersibling entertainment increasingly prevailed in a child's out-of-school time.[13]

Furthermore, as more mothers entered the workforce—according to the U.S. Bureau of Labor Statistics, in 1999, some 78 percent of mothers of children ages six to thirteen were employed—direct parental supervision or guidance of family play diminished considerably, further increasing the probability of solo activity, including play, at home. Especially in single-parent households, usually headed by a female whose paid employment was essential, the number of "latch-key" children spending time home alone multiplied. According to the New York University Child Study Center, by the close of the twentieth century between five and seven million youngsters aged five to thirteen were latchkey children for at least a part of each week. Some analysts estimated the number to be much higher. Most of these children —about three-quarters—were on their own after school, but about one in six was alone at home before school and one in eleven at night. Children of the very poor were less likely than those from families above the poverty line to be left unattended, mostly because the poorest families inhabit unsafe neighborhoods and use friends and kin for childcare. At the other end of the socioeconomic spectrum, youngsters from families with means could be deposited with professional caretakers or in formal after-school programs.[14]

The peer socialization that began to dominate children's lives in the late nineteenth century extended into the late twentieth century, but with new variations. Schools continued to be the incubators of peer groups. In the 1950s and 1960s, baby boom children swelled enrollments in elementary schools, where graded classes bolstered same-age associations. By century's end, age-graded schooling still prevailed. Beyond the classroom, school-sponsored activities at recess and after dismissal from formal class time kept youngsters of the same grade—and thus the same age—together. Indeed, age served as a key determinant in children's daily lives as much as gender did. Books and curricula received age and school-grade designations, and packaging on games and toys specified the suggested—implicitly meaning "approved"—age range for users. Children's sections of bookstores, for example, labeled shelves according to the age-appropriateness of the literature, and it was common to find advisories such as "for ages 7 to 11" or "ages 12 and up" on game and toy packaging. Magazines intended as parenting guides commonly printed on their covers teasers such as "Age-By-Age Guide To Play."[15]

Trends in demography and peer association were joined by one other powerful contextual factor. As consumer goods such as clothing, toys, prepared foods, and other products proliferated, a highly commercialized economy increasingly surrounded childhood. For decades, children had been what one analyst has called "bit players" in the marketplace. Parents were the chief objects for advertisers of children's consumer goods; they had the money and, presumably, the control of their offsprings' acquisitions.[16] But from mid-century on, marketers such as Mattel and Hasbro targeted the needs and desires of young people as never before. One journalist observed in 1964, "Children have become a Market—often referred to as the 'subteens' by people who apparently see them mainly as avid little consumers and can't wait for them to become bigger, teen-age consumers."[17] Moreover, as parents rewarded their children with ever-larger cash gifts and allowances, youngsters could flex their own purchasing muscle. One survey found that preteen children themselves bought $6.1 billion worth of goods in 1989, $23.4 billion in 1997, and $30.0 billion in 2002, an increase of 400 percent in thirteen years. Most purchases went for food—sweets, snacks, beverages—but toys were in second place with clothing expenditures growing rapidly.[18]

All of these factors—birthrates, parental employment patterns, family organization and disruption, peer socialization, the consumer economy—enveloped late-twentieth-century children in a world that differed considerably from that of their parents and grandparents. Indeed, it could be argued that at no time in the past did modern childhood contrast so sharply with childhoods of preceding eras than in the past few decades.

The Endangered Childhood

In the second half of the twentieth century, parental attitudes toward their offspring branched well beyond the base established earlier. More than ever, Americans put children at the center of their culture. Leading this ideological movement was pediatrician Benjamin Spock, whose book *Common Sense Guide to Baby and Child Care*, published first in 1946, countered conventional hard-line parenting techniques by countenancing overt affection toward children and promoting pleasure for older and younger generations alike. Parenting should be fun, Dr. Spock insisted, especially if mothers and fathers tried to make their kids happy and secure. Such advice made Spock's guide immensely successful. Since publication, the book has been printed in seven editions and has sold over fifty million copies in thirty-nine different languages. By the 1950s, almost as many families had Spock on their bookshelves as they had a Bible; to many, *Baby and Child Care*, as it became known, *was* a Bible. It not only comforted parents—"Trust yourself," Spock counseled, "you know more than you think you do" —but also translated Freudian psychoanalytic theory on child development into commonsense terms.

As its title indicates, Spock's manual focused mostly on infancy and early childhood, but it did offer some advice for parents of preadolescent children, including a special chapter on "From Six to Eleven." During these years, as in earlier stages, Spock argued, a child's psychological health was of foremost concern. To this end, Spock employed both G. Stanley Hall's recapitulation theory, which posited that human development repeated the history of human culture, and Freud's theory of the latency period (ages five to puberty), in which children learn how to adjust to their social environment. In such a scheme, preteen youngsters relived the stage in which their prehuman ancestors developed close family ties but also began attempting to function independently. According to Spock, a child in this "in between" age category "no longer wants to be loved as a possession or as an appealing child. He's gaining a sense of dignity as an individual person, and he'd like to be treated as such." Spock advised parents to tolerate, at least to some degree, preteen rebelliousness and "bad manners" because these behaviors were only natural.[19]

Expanding from Spock's iconoclastic views, other advice writers went further and asserted that too much discipline could bruise a child's fragile ego, prompting later critics to charge that Spock advocated "permissive" child rearing. In 1953, for example, a writer in *Marriage and Family Living* warned that "permissive parents found their lives more disrupted by their children's behavior" than restrictive parents did. Such conclusions, however, were oversimplified. A parent could overlook some of a child's irritating ways, but, Spock advised, "stick to your guns in matters that are important to you."[20]

Spock's assurances notwithstanding, with so many baby boom young people flooding nurseries, schools, and neighborhoods, anxieties over endangered childhood intensified. The creed of shielding vulnerable children that had taken root in nineteenth-century advice literature and had expanded with the rise of professional child-saving experts in the early twentieth, persisted after 1950, as parents and other adults worried about a perceived—and sometimes real—increase in threats to health and safety. Terrified by the polio epidemic of the early 1950s, parents reacted by keeping their children away from swimming pools, from summer camps, and even from their playmates. Although the Salk vaccine eased the polio outbreak by the mid-1950s, professionals fixated on safeguarding youngsters from every possible hazard. Experts particularly took note of potential injuries to children from accidents resulting from automobile traffic, bicycles, toys, and all varieties of unsupervised activity, with the result that by the 1970s bicycle helmets, pads, street crossing guards, recall of allegedly unsafe products, and tightly controlled play activity—sometimes mandated by legislation—proliferated. A conclusion drawn from dozens of studies of children's deaths and injuries included a typical warning: "Kids are not small adults," stated the University of Michigan Health System. "They see, hear, think, and act differently in traffic than adults." The statement included a long list of dangers to children from biking, skating, riding scooters, riding a school bus, pushing a shopping cart, and even simple walking. The Michigan agency even felt a need to specify such obvious advice as "Children should always walk on the sidewalk" and "Make sure [bicycle] helmets . . . are fitted and worn properly."[21] Additionally, by the 1970s, publicity of and alarm over child abuse and abduction reflected heightened urgency about safeguarding kids from a menacing environment.

Because child experts continued to deem play as vital to the realm of childhood and because play remained, in Spock's words, "serious business,"[22] adults focused particular attention on protecting children at play. The best way to prevent injury to person and property was to impose forms of control that would act, as one writer observed, "like the brakes on a car."[23] Control meant oversight and order, because, according to one observer, "There is no question—from the adult point of view—that unorganized play has its drawbacks. It is usually noisy, often disorderly and sometimes downright destructive."[24] A writer for the *New York Times* in 1966 quoted a doctor as advising that "children should never play unsupervised . . . [they] seem to incur fewer accidents when they are playing organized games."[25]

Assuming that they possessed the technical and moral expertise to design "safe" play as a means of molding young people into orderly, responsible beings who would become orderly, responsible adults, parents, teachers, and recreation experts in the early and mid-twentieth century had transformed play into regimented, managed activity with such agencies as Little Leagues, scouting, and boys' and girls' clubs. By the latter decades of the century, the older generation expanded its endeavors, endorsing such strategies as discouraging war toys, using play for therapeutic purposes, combining supervised play with supervised education to make schools "fun," and opposing gender-typed toys. Also, from its creation in 1972 onward, the U.S. Consumer Product Safety Commission recalled "unsafe" toys from the market and published standards for playground safety. Playground equipment attracted special scrutiny, as the American Society for Testing and Materials issued ever-stronger safety guidelines for playground equipment. Noting that most playground injuries occur when children fall off equipment onto hard surfaces, analysts Joe L. Frost and Irma C. Woods cited several surveys that identified the hazardous quality of contemporary playground equipment, including excessive heights, poor signs, and unsafe mixing of large and small apparatuses. Several writers urged tighter state and local regulation of public play areas. And parents resorted to the courts for redress when their children were injured away from family supervision. One celebrated lawsuit, for example, occurred in 1986 when parents in Burlington, North Carolina, won an out-of-court settlement when their daughter tripped and sprained her wrist because, they claimed, her school's physical education teacher, attempting to improve coordination, forced the girl to run a race backward.[26]

But keeping youngsters safe was not enough for some parents. As historian Steven Mintz has pointed out, in addition to protecting children, many parents by the 1970s began to emphasize a "prepared" childhood, one that would equip young people for success in postmodern society. In 1968, one educator, sounding like an updated Cotton Mather, voiced a common opinion when he wrote, "As the values and goals of success have been switched from acquisition of material things to educational and personal achievement, middle-class parents have become less and less patient with the 'wastefulness of play.'"[27] Upwardly mobile parents wanted their preadolescent kids to be better than average in all things, so they tried to provide them with professionally run activities that would enrich their minds, tone their bodies, inculcate physical skills, and enhance their self-esteem. To these ends, they enrolled their daughters and sons in gymnastics and karate academies, language and drama programs, music lessons, after-school science and math clubs, organized sports leagues—all with the goal of satisfying parents' aspirations for their offspring. Concomitantly, parents and social agencies concerned with the welfare of less advantaged children and with preventing such youngsters from being lured into gangs, drug use, and other antisocial behavior, steered children into organized activities sponsored by churches, schools, YMCAs and YWCAs, and boys' and girls' clubs.[28]

The bête noir that seemed to thwart many a parent's aims was television. As soon as the new medium became widespread in the 1950s, communications analysts observed that children, especially preadolescents, ostensibly were being mesmerized by the combination of visual images and sound coming from broadcasts, and they concluded that TV programming influenced uncritical minds in insidious ways. One of among numerous near-hysterical analyses, the 1961 book *Television in the Lives of Our Children* accused the medium of destroying children's sense of values and causing them to grow up too soon.[29] Equally important, according to the authors of this critique, television replaced active, healthy play with passive, sedentary apathy, and they calculated that by sixth grade, children had spent as much time watching television as they had spent in school. Other critics charged that TV created Saturday morning and after-school "ghettos" where kids' culture was shaped by violent cartoons, fantastic adventures, and ads for frivolous toys and sugary junk food. The ready-made fantasies, they argued, deprived children of the challenge of creating and exploring self-generated fantasy worlds. In addition to the hypnotic effect of television for children, the violent and salacious content of prime-time programs and news broadcasts, viewed by young people as well as by adults, caused some observers to conclude that TV destroyed the value of childhood innocence. Critic Neil Postman, for example, carped in his 1982 polemic *The Disappearance of Childhood,*

> The children of the industrial revolution knew very little beyond the horror of their own lives. Through the miracle of symbols and electricity our own children know everything anyone else knows—the good with the bad. Nothing is mysterious, nothing awesome, nothing is held back from public view. . . . What does it mean that our children are better informed than every before? . . . It means . . . that in having access to the previously hidden fruit of adult information, they are expelled from the garden of childhood.[30]

The history and effects of television's role in the creation of children's culture has been deftly examined elsewhere and need not be reviewed here.[31] Certainly the medium, which by the 1980s consisted of cable channels such as Nickelodeon and Disney, as well as national networks, opened new opportunities for program producers, retailers, manufacturers, and, especially, marketers to shape children's tastes and desires. And after 1984 when the Federal Communications Commission removed the limitation on the content and total minutes of commercials that could be broadcast during children's programs, advertisers had free rein to maneuver young audiences toward specific products. Whether or not there has been a causal relationship between TV violence and children's violent behavior remains a topic of debate, but a large body of studies has made that connection, or at least has concluded that viewing violence on television and in movies desensitizes young people to carnage and cruelty. But, as Stephen Kline has pointed out, children are able to decipher TV content and ads more skillfully than critics have been willing to recognize, and when it came to play and toys, especially those advertised on television, youngsters have exerted both subtle and direct influence on marketers and manufacturers.[32]

Toy Makers and Parents

In 1986 the Television Bureau of Advertising issued a report titled "Target Selling the Children's Market," which included some shrewd insights into the new dynamics of family life and the rise in disposable income resulting from economic progress. Noting the decline in birth rates as baby boomers moved into adulthood, the report concluded that American parents were able to make a bigger spectacle out of fewer children than ever before. The result, said that report, was that people were spending more on their sons and daughters and that they were buying more new childhood products because hand-me-downs had become scarce. In addition, because more than half of all mothers with children at home had become members of the employed workforce, both parents "may have more money, but they have less time to spend with their children. To compensate, they may buy more things for their children." The things being bought with what has been called "guilt money" often were toys.[33]

Other demographic and economic shifts also caught the attention of the authors of "Target Selling the Children's Market." With divorce and remarriage rates on the rise, many children have dual sets of parents and several sets of grandparents. Because divorced parents often see even less of their children than do working parents, observed the bureau, spending for children's products often helps "ease the pain" of separation to both children and parents. Moreover, as noted earlier in the chapter, adults were living longer, with the result that grandparents had become more prevalent. But because grandparents often reside at some distance from their families, they do not always know a grandchild's practical needs in terms of clothing, school supplies, and the like. Consequently, grandparents, as well as aunts and uncles, are more likely than ever to treat and seek affection from grandchildren by buying them toys.[34]

As all of the foregoing trends suggest, in the past half century, commercially produced toys have come to occupy a much more central position in the concept of children's play than ever before. In earlier eras, children amused themselves simply by "roaming," or by playing with informal objects, often improvised at home rather than fashioned by artisans and manufacturers. But from the 1950s onward, the extraordinary multitude of mass-produced and mass-marketed playthings narrowed the concept of play so that in the minds of adults and children alike toys came to be equated with play.

Sales figures of commercially marketed toys reinforce the point, as they soared from $4.2 billion in 1978 to $17.5 billion in 1993 and to $25 billion in 2001. These numbers do not include amounts spent on video and computer games, which reached $10 billion by 2003. By the 1990s, American toy makers were unveiling between three thousand and six thousand new products each year, and expenditures on toy advertisements to children ranked second only to ads for food. Media commercials from Mattel, Hasbro, Kenner, and other firms not only announced the availability of a particular toy but also showed young viewers how to use it—in other words, how to play. Even though the Children's Advertising Review Unit of the Council of Better Business Bureaus developed self-regulatory guidelines requiring that toy ads present products in truthful ways—for example, stating whether batteries or other accessories are needed and avoiding suggesting unsafe ways to use the item (ads rarely mention how difficult it is to assemble a toy, however)—the visual representations prescribe the mode of play because they specify in glowing language explicitly what the toy can and should do.[35]

Moreover, toy makers learned that they could bypass parents and cater directly to children's desires. Before the 1950s, companies such as A. C. Gilbert and Effanbee Doll Company prevailed on parents to enhance their children's pleasure by buying them an erector set or a companion doll, or makers of so-called educational toys such as Playskool and Lego could reinforce parents' desire to provide their children with useful "tools of play." By contrast, in the latter half of the twentieth century, corporations such as Disney and Mattel, aided by superstores such as Toys "R" Us and Walmart, oriented their marketing toward creating and responding to children's fantasies. They employed researchers and bought media time to create demand so that children would then nag their parents to acquire specific products, a practice that has been called "pester power." Psychologist Susan Linn, in her book *Consuming Kids*, reported on a survey taken by a marketing newsletter that asked 150 mothers of three to eight year olds to record their children's purchasing requests over a two-week period. The survey counted over ten thousand nags, almost five per child per day. In this new scenario, then, adults became providers and onlookers more than selectors and players.[36]

To a large extent, the imposition of commercial interests between parents and children resulted not just from television advertising but also from the cultural notion that proper parenting included fulfilling a child's need for pleasure, self-expression, and social interaction. As one of countless examples of how experts prescribed the path to healthy emotional growth, psychologist Helen Boehm in 1989 urged that youngsters in the six-to-eight-year-old range be given "toys and games that foster friendships and promote sharing, cooperation, and teamwork."[37] The nation's economic growth in the quarter century after World War II had created an attitude that everyone, especially a child, was entitled to a good life, and thus parents, eager to see their offspring happy and well-adjusted, found it difficult to resist the profusion of commercial playthings that their kids said they wanted. What they wanted were toys.

At first, the new toys that were marketed after World War II were fairly traditional and comprehensible. Recalling their own childhoods, parents understood the popularity of tried-and-true items such as baby dolls, trains and trucks, and BB guns, and they found mild amusement in new novelty toys such as Slinky (first marketed in 1945), Mr. Potato Head (patented in 1952), and hula hoops (introduced in 1958). Soon, however, character toys such as Barbie and G.I. Joe (which were more elaborate than the Shirley Temple doll and the miniature soldiers of the previous era), superheroes and their paraphernalia from TV cartoons, and a host of playthings licensed from movies took over. The kinds of toys being marketed differed considerably from the traditional playthings that had been bought in earlier eras. Advertisers quickly learned that they could merge a "backstory" of fantasy with a product to create a meaningful relationship between toy and child. The licensing from movies, television programs, and sports gave toys very explicit significance. Whether the item was a Barbie doll, a set of Transformers, a Star Wars light saber, or My Little Pony, children understood the history and personality of the item in a way that most adults did not. As Stephen Kline has suggested with regard to one popular plaything, "Barbie's attraction as a doll was that children identified with her character [a fashion-conscious teenager] rather than with her 'role' as a toy."[38]

In addition, the dramas inherent in character and related toys that were built around fashion (for girls) and action (for boys) diverged from toys of the previous era in that they no longer previewed the child's future adult roles, nor were they intended to bring parents and children together in mutual play.[39] Formerly popular playthings such as Lincoln Logs, miniature tea sets, baby dolls, and erector sets declined in popularity after the late 1960s, diminishing the importance of toys intended to prepare children for adult roles, whether through small-scale engineering or simulated housekeeping. Instead, fantasy toys conquered the market, giving youngsters much different views of the world. Boys' futuristic and military toys, inspired by the movie *Star Wars* (1977), for example, related to a simplified, violent tale of good versus evil. In such a realm of agile, muscular characters, aggressiveness meant control and freedom; in fantasy toys for preteens, at least, qualities of foresight, perseverance, and practice were subordinated to the goal of immediate dominance, a behavior that troubled many critics. Barbie and her clones proved to be problematic in another way because they fostered a desire to indulge in "carefree buying," a consumerism that was unattainable to girls from low-income households. Yet Barbie also represented a new kind of role model, not a nurturing big sister or mother-in-training that previously had portended a girl's future but, rather, a liberated teenager with her own wardrobe whose parents had faded far into the background. The objective in the story line in girls' fantasy toys thus was "popularity," achieved mainly through grooming and acquisitiveness.[40]

Though fantasy and character toys certainly were not the only playthings being marketed—over the closing decades of the twentieth century, fad toys such as hula hoops, Frisbees, and pet rocks rose and fell in popularity—these kinds of toys became dominant because they merged narrative into play. In Kline's words, they achieved "a kind of synergy between a child's fascination with TV programmes and their intense engagement in imaginative play."[41] In an earlier era, fantasy drama presented in radio, film, and comics had spawned some successful playthings, such as Dick Tracy detective paraphernalia and Shirley Temple dolls, but entertainment media in the late twentieth century seemed to assume even more decisive importance in children's imaginations. While children playing time-honored forms of play such as jumping rope or building a snow fort needed only simple instructions on procedure, which they could learn directly from each other, playing with licensed commercial toys from the *Star Wars* films or the TV series about Teenage Ninja Turtles required special knowledge that only those exposed to these media phenomena would understand. Even the recent Harry Potter craze has impinged on children in new ways. Though the Potter novels hark back to a time when the printed word sparked a child's imagination, the film series and licensed products construct images that give youngsters entry into a fantasy world that is packaged for them without their having to read the books.[42]

Also, fantasy and character toys, especially as depicted in their ads, were, and remain, loaded with gender stereotyping. Increasingly in the closing years of the twentieth century, marketing consultants, perhaps reflecting preconceived points of view, concluded from their surveys that because boys and girls were attracted to dissimilar products, advertisers should separate their campaigns by sex. Boys were said to desire power and thus needed to be represented as playing with action toys that emphasized success—meaning victory in combat and competition. By contrast, consultants assumed that girls craved glamour and were more likely than boys to sit indoors where they quietly played with dolls and games. They thus adjusted their commercials accordingly. Feminists challenged these conclusions and tried to advance the notion that gender representations of toys should be ambiguous and evoke similar responses in all children. Academic researchers sympathetic to this point of view asserted that the sex

typing of toys in ads and TV programs has the effect of creating artificial gender differences in children's behavior. But in contrast, researchers employed by toy companies insisted that girls and boys play
very differently, even with the same toy. Boys, they argued, tend to
transform their environment to fit their imaginary worlds and engage
in taunting each other in ways that represent a kind of male affection.
Girls, alternatively, accommodate their activities and their play spaces
to what already exists and direct their antagonisms toward those outside the group through gossip.[43]

While gender distinctions in toys have remained powerful, to
a certain extent, the mass marketing of character and fantasy toys
through television has had a homogenizing effect on play that has
blurred social differences. Though market-wise toy makers have tried
to cater to special consumer identities, creating an African American
Barbie and an American Indian Barbie, for example, nevertheless, the
characters, story lines, and "rules" of play that were derived from
mass media reached all regions and all population groups with similar
effects. To use these toys as they were presented in TV programs and
ads, youngsters were not supposed to improvise—or, at least, they
were discouraged from doing so. They supposedly have been familiar with the standardized script and followed its lead, whether it involved combat or dress up. In actuality, children adhered to these
scripts less frequently than is sometimes assumed; still, many of the
new toys exerted a constraining effect.[44]

That constraining quality was embedded deeply in children's
video games, an explosive phenomenon of the late twentieth century.
Electronic toys, such as mechanized trains and miniature sewing
machines, had existed since the early 1900s, as had battery-powered
cars and novelties. Just after mid-century, electric games using lights,
noises, and vibrating boards became popular. But by the 1970s, com-
puter-chip-driven toys began to flood the market. A nation that was
child centered and steeped in prosperity began spending millions of
dollars on expensive electronic games (especially sports and battle
games), talking dolls, and even child-sized cameras and music-play-
ing devices.

But it was the animated games that could be played on a video
screen that most captured kids' fancy. The first video games were sim-
plistic adaptations of larger arcade attractions, consisting of a Ping-
Pong game ("Pong") or a disc with a mouth that swallowed objects

moving around the screen ("Pac-Man"). By 1982 the appeal of such games for home use seemed to be running its course, but the industry soon revived when advances in semiconductor technology made games much more artistic, realistic, and complex. In the mid-1980s, Nintendo, a Japanese company that originated in 1887 as a manufacturer of playing cards, began marketing computer games, some of which were handheld and self-contained and others that plugged into a television. These early games found hundreds of thousands of buyers, even with price tags on some products well above $100. By 1987, Nintendo sales reached $650 million, triple those of the previous year. Nintendo video games, most of which involved combat and required hand-eye coordination (for example, Blast Master and Super Mario), inspired numerous copycat companies, such as Sega, a Japanese company that originally made arcade machines, to produce ever-more sophisticated electronic games, including ones for older consumers. As evidence of the extraordinary popularity of such items, by 1992 total sales of video games surpassed all ticket sales at movie theaters.[45]

Until recently, many video games, because of their electronic bases and unsophisticated software, had an inflexible quality. A programmed game contained specific goals and required set strategies that made it difficult for a player to deviate into unintended ways of playing. Surveying the field in the 1980s, educator Eugene Provenzo Jr. complained that video games discouraged originality and the creation of alternative scenarios. Neighborhood kids who played their own informal outdoor game of war, Provenzo observed,

> made up the game as they went along. Defections to the other side were frequent and modifications of weapons were an ongoing and complex process; strategy and negotiations were important components of the game. This simply cannot happen in the physically impoverished and tightly rule-bound universe of video games. . . . Players must follow a complex series of instructions according to very a carefully defined set of rules. If they do not, they lose the game.[46]

In other words, a child could not use the electronic devices in ways other than those directly required by the game itself. Also, though it was possible to play chess against a computer or engage in an on-screen football game, the player could not "cheat." Though Provenzo admitted that the newest wave of video games have become more interactive through virtual reality, enabling new types of play in a re-defined playscape, he agreed with technology expert Sherry Turkle that "when you play a video game you are a player in a game pro-grammed by someone else."[47]

The latest video games, however, are more accommodating to al-ternative styles of use. Various simulation games, such as the SimCity series, offer children opportunities for applying their own concepts and strategies for both entertainment and edification. Moreover, a host of fantasy, adventure, and sports games offer the player more choices and entail more complex strategies. Many games can be played on the internet, and numerous independent websites have been created to offer players advice on how to compete and win.[48]

A long line of critics has decried video games as unhealthy and dangerous. An updated edition of Dr. Spock's guide warned,

> The best that can be said of them [computer games] is that they may help promote eye-hand coordination in children. The worst that can be said is that they sanction, and even promote, aggression and vio-lent responses to conflict. But what can be said with much greater certainty is this: most computer games are a colossal waste of time.[49]

Boys more than girls—especially boys over ten years of age—have be-come heavy consumers of video games, perhaps because of fantasy themes of battle, killing, and destruction, though computerized games that facilitate learning seem to have piqued girls' interest no less than boys'. Detractors such as Spock's followers charge that the intense mayhem, dismemberment, and sexism inherent in the most popular games cannot help but promote violent confrontation and numbness to brutality in real life, not to mention the celebration of criminality and objectification of women. In recent years, among the top-selling video game has been the series Grand Theft Auto, one version of which has a character who kills a prostitute after having sex with her. Though rated in a manner that supposedly proscribes sales to young consumers, evidence exists that its sales include thousands of pre-teens. Furthermore, recent technological developments not only have made on-screen game violence more graphic and realistic looking but also enable players to scan in and incorporate into games personal fac-tors such as photos of friends and enemies or of their own neighbor-hood. A few studies have suggested that users—again, mostly boys—

find video games more exciting and desirable than human contact, causing some critics to lament that the games prevent children from cultivating friendships, as well as undermining parent-child communication.[50]

In the past few years, computer games for girls have also stirred some controversy, though objections have not been as rife as those focused on games played by boys. One girls' game, for example, the free—meaning that it can be played at no cost—website paperdoll heaven.com is an updated version of the paper doll play that was so popular in the first half of the twentieth century. It is just one of many doll-dress-up games now available on the internet. Visitors to paper dollheaven.com can select an online paper doll from a list of more than three hundred celebrities, then "dress" the character from online collections of outfits and jewelry, just as their grandmothers and great-grandmothers cut out characters and outfitted them from newspapers and other printed sources years ago. A player could choose an underwear-clad figure of, for example, Julia Roberts, Madonna, or even Elvis Presley and drag pieces of clothing with which to adorn the character from an adjacent wardrobe on the screen, then vary the outfits according to the player's whim. Though it revives a once-popular and innocent amusement and presents girls with a multitude of choices, paperdollheaven.com has detractors. Many of the doll characters in their undressed state are presented in skimpy underwear, provoking moralists to warn parents about the website's subliminal sexuality. In addition, the website nourishes the fascination—or overfascination—with media celebrities that some culture critics deplore. And girls who register to become a member of the site and acquire access to special dolls can create personal profiles and instant message each other, which, as one detractor points out, "is often an invitation for trouble."[51]

Another seemingly innocuous and extremely popular (mostly) girls' online virtual simulation game, Neopets, also has evoked criticism. Neopets, first posted in 1999 and currently owned by media giant Viacom, enables players ("Neopians") to adopt and care from one to four species of artificial pets by earning "neopoints" awarded from participating in over two-hundred website-sponsored games, puzzles, and battles, which take place in a fictional planet with varying environments. In addition to the games and pet care, the phenomenon includes trading cards, merchandise, and several independent websites offering advice on how to win the contests. There also are subtle advertisements in the form of references to commercial products put out by companies such as McDonald's and Disney. (Unlike other very popular game sites, such as Millsberry.com and Postopia.com, which are created and supported by consumer companies General Mills and Post cereals, Neopets.com is independent.) Criticisms arise from the game's alleged manipulative features: commercialism, the gambling component involved in obtaining neopoints, incentive to cheat by using internet guides, and addictive quality. In addition, some parents object to the creeping commercialism that requires players to purchase entry into parts of the website even though the game ostensibly is free. As one parent carped about Neopets, "I don't know why (the game) was even created because you can't even do anything with your points except buy stuff for your pets, which by the way, don't die and can't do anything except battle."[52]

While writers and parents have been paying attention, previously and presently, to the content and effects of computer and video games, a different phenomenon was absorbing preteen girls: American Girl. Created in 1986 for girls aged seven to twelve, American Girl initially marketed a series of eight eighteen-inch dolls, each of which was designed to represent a nine-year-old girl who might have lived at a specific point in American history. The dolls are ethnically as well as temporally diverse. For example, according to American Girl marketing, Kaya is "an adventurous Nez Perce [American Indian] girl growing up in 1764, before America became a country"; Josefina is "an Hispanic girl living in colonial New Mexico in 1824, during the opening of the Santa Fe Trail"; Addy is "a courageous [African American] girl determined to be free in 1864 during the Civil War"; and Kit is "a clever, resourceful [white] girl growing up in 1934 during America's Great Depression." Unlike glamorous Barbie, American Girl dolls look almost ordinary. As one observer recently wrote, "They are girls, with plastic bodies that show off appropriately chubby thighs; they wear children's clothes, not outfits that Beyoncé could wear to the Grammys."[53] Each doll is accompanied by her own set of six books that involve the character in historically relevant stories related to family, school, celebrations, and adventures. According to the company's promotional literature,

> Gentle life lessons throughout the stories remind girls of such lasting values as the importance of family and friends, compassion, respon-

sibility, and forgiveness. Full of wisdom and encouragement, the stories both protect and prepare girls, showing them how to meet their
own challenges with strength and courage.[54]

In addition, the company claims, "All the products in the American
Girl Collection are extensively researched at museums and historical
societies throughout the United States, and are manufactured to exact-
ing standards of historical accuracy, aesthetics, and quality."[55]

American Girl's founder, Pleasant Rowland, was a middle-aged
author and former teacher who believed that girls needed an alternative to Barbie's sexual connotations. After visiting the living history museum at Colonial Williamsburg, Rowland decided to create a
"miniature version" of historical life using "the very playthings—
dolls and books—that girls have always loved."[56] Through direct
mail and catalog sales rather than TV advertising, Rowland expanded
her business dramatically, with annual sales reaching $300 million by
the early 1990s. The Pleasant Company, as American Doll's producer
was known, added more books, a doll for younger girls, a line of contemporary American Girl Today dolls, and retail and entertainment
sites called the American Girl Place in Chicago and New York City.
The advertising-free *American Girl* magazine, which began publication
in 1992, presents content "designed to affirm self-esteem, celebrate
achievements, and foster creativity," and it now boasts more than
650,000 subscribers.[57] In 1998, Rowland's company was acquired by
Mattel for $700 million, but American Girl products have retained the
trademark name.

The unique play qualities of American Girl are especially evident
in the company's catalog and in the *American Girl* magazine. Though
conceived to elicit parental approval, American Girl, like other marketers to children, also focuses directly on its preadolescent consumers. The catalog, which advertises the dolls and all manner of items related to their stories, uses as its slogan "Where will her INNER STAR
take her?" It emphasizes a girl's journey of self-discovery that can be
achieved by acquiring American Girl products. But the intent is not
disingenuous. The ads imply that by playing with American Girl dolls
and reading their associated books a girl can immerse herself in the
past yet still learn universal lessons. For example, "Kit," the Depres-
sion-era doll, does not have a set of fashionable clothes and accessories; her possessions include a plain, plaid school outfit and an ordi-

nary metal-framed bed. One of the books featuring her character, *Kit Learns a Lesson*, relates her trip to a soup kitchen and a "lesson about being thankful" amid her poverty. This is not a Barbie-like fantasy.

The *American Girl* magazine features no music or movie celebrities but instead presents games, crafts, fiction, and advice on family, friendship, and money. The letters submitted by young readers reveal ways that American Girl fosters independence in parent-approved but, significantly, not parent-involved ways. For example, in an article titled "Money Matters," Sylvia, age thirteen from Minnesota, described how she prevailed on her parents to raise her allowance by typing "a report stating why I wanted more money and what I would do to earn it." In the letters section at the beginning of one issue, Mandy, age twelve from Missouri, expressed her appreciation for an article on friendship. "You're right about needing all kinds of friends," she wrote, "and I think *all* friends should be trustworthy." And in an "Advice" section, an eleven-year-old girl, complaining that she and her mother fought over having her own cell phone, was told how she could act maturely and convince her mother to buy her one.[58]

Not as objectionable as Grand Theft Auto, Neopets, or Cheerleader Barbie, American Girl has occupied a unique niche in girls' play culture. The dolls, books, paraphernalia, and magazine are marketed with a message that is supportive of preteen self-reliance while at the same time including academically edifying qualities. The effect can be powerful. As one former collector rhapsodized,

> I LIVED for [American Girl]. . . . I think I loved the dolls so much because they provided insight to . . . new cultures. I read every single [book], re-read them many times, and I went through different periods of who my favorite one was. I ended up loving Molly, the WWII girl, the most. I remember wanting to see what Kirsten (the Swede) lived like so badly that I wished I could go to Sweden, where I thought the women still dressed in petticoats and lived in an old fashion way.[59]

No surveys, by American Girl or by independent interests, have determined whether or not the phenomenon has reached low-income children. Such an effect is unlikely, given that, in 2005, an initial purchase combination of doll, book, and accessories for just one character sold for around $100 ; additional clothing outfits cost $20 and more, and an item such as Kit's no-frills bed sold for $54. (Books were less expensive, usually $6.95 for a 175-page paperback.) But for girls with means, American Girl provides a nexus of fantasy and history that can become an important component of a girl's free time.

Computer games were certainly not the only toys that made adults nervous. With safety, both physical and emotional, so much a concern of parents and child advocates, virtually every new plaything now comes under close scrutiny. During the 1960s and 1970s, parents worried about allowing children to play with guns, toy or otherwise. As this concern (partly) ebbed, other concerns became prominent. The U.S. Consumer Product Safety Commission (CPSC), created by Congress in 1972, to protect the public "from products that pose a fire, electrical, chemical, or mechanical hazard or can injure children," has since its inception applied safety standards to thousands of toys and removed many from the market. In 1999 alone, the CPSC required that manufacturers recall ninety-five toys, children's products, bicycles, and bicycle components. The seventeen toy products recalled for failure to meet CPSC safety requirements, mainly pertaining to flammability and sharp points, included 1.7 million units.[60]

Even unregulated toys provoked objection, including moral complaints. For example, as Barbie and her retinue became ever-more elaborate, some adults feared that girls would take the dolls' sexuality too seriously. Brian Sutton-Smith alluded to the fears expressed over a 1975 version of Barbie's sister called Growing Up Skipper. This doll could be made to mature from a prepubescent, flat-chested girl into a teenager with modest bust, slimmer waist, and taller torso by rotating her left arm. Sutton-Smith, with a flair of whimsy, quoted a writer in *Ms. Magazine* who grumbled,

> The mind reels at the possibility for "creative play"—eight-year-old girls trying to grow their own (breasts) and thereby twisting one another's arms into a mess of torn ligaments, small boys staging porno exhibits. . . . One wonders whether men would tolerate a comparable male toy. Can't you see it: Growing Up Buster—twist his leg, his penis grows and his testicles descend.[61]

Other adults fretted that anatomically correct dolls would make children grow up too quickly and "rush out of childhood, finding boyfriends and girlfriends at the age of six."[62]

Detractors also griped about the ways manufacturers altered cherished toys of the past in ways that stifled creativity. In her 2005 anti-commercialism book *Consuming Kids,* aptly subtitled *The Hostile Take-over of Childhood,* Susan Linn charged that traditional construction toys such as Legos and Lincoln Logs no longer come boxed as collections of materials that would encourage a child to use them freely. Rather, she observes, they are packaged in "kits," complete with explicit instructions that specify the "right way" and, implicitly, the "wrong way" for putting the blocks together. Play-Doh, the baby-boomers' favorite now manufactured by Hasbro, also is packaged in kits that frequently have resulted from partnerships (what the professionals call "cross-marketing") with other companies such as McDonald's and contain "recipes" for fashioning Big Macs, french fries, and Chicken McNuggets from Play-Doh clay. By discouraging imaginative play, Linn claims, toys marketed in these ways quickly become boring because of their built-in "planned obsolescence."[63]

Many more examples could be presented, but perhaps more importantly, writers and researchers came to believe that *too many* toys had become available. As early as 1960, one journalist remarked that parents were obsessed with giving their children some kind of material stimulation every moment of the day, with the result that "gratification piled upon gratification no longer suffices." Children had so much stuff, said the author, that they had become bored with themselves.[64] Several years later, Dixie Oliver, a writer for *Life* magazine, observed that children were so deluged with playthings that they had lost the ability to invent a toy or game. "After all," she noted, "why should they bother? Daytime TV with its violent and raucous cartoons and the toy industry with its year-round Santa Claus have just about rendered self-amusement alien to the American way of life."[65] In 1957, social critic Roland Barthes feared that the abundance of toys alienated children and destroyed their creative abilities. The child, Barthes declared, "can only identify himself as owner, never as creator . . . [toys] are supplied to him ready-made; he has only to help himself, he is never allowed to discover anything from start to finish."[66] More recently, Juliet Schor charged that children have become so deeply enmeshed in American materialistic culture that they cannot cope. The result, she concluded, is that they "are beset by anxiety, headaches, stomachaches, and boredom."[67] No doubt that by the late twentieth century the American child's toy box could never have been big enough to hold what toy makers were trying to cram into it. But whether or not their imaginations were dulled by this abundance is questionable.

During the 1950s, American children's play culture crossed a watershed. The commercial culture that had matured in the first half of the twentieth century expanded so broadly that children were subjected to what business consultant Lisa Morgan has labeled "over-the-top experiences."[68] Moreover, the swift and pervasive rise of electronic media, particularly television, movies, and video games, after 1950 enveloped childhood with new meanings. Opportunities for fantasy play mushroomed, but at the same time character and story lines shaped children's amusements in a way that, at least in some fashion, overrode independent imagination. Moreover, TV and computers ironically accomplished what parents and educators had been trying to do for a century: the electronic revolution did more than playgrounds, clubs, schools, and educational toys to divert many children from street games and undirected neighborhood play.

At the same time, many parents' desire to safeguard, enrich, and entertain their children intruded on free play time. Families with two employed parents who could afford to do so deposited their kids in after-school and weekend activities and lessons, supervised by adult surrogate parents. Many who lacked the means to finance formal activities did not try to prevent their children from watching television; studies of youngsters' TV viewing habits found that hours in front of the tube were higher among lower socioeconomic groups than among more advantaged children. Safety regulations and fear, real and imagined, kept many boys and girls away from environments that previous generations had fully utilized because their parents were either unaware of or unconcerned about the potential risks and hazards. In spite of infringements on their previous prerogatives in determining and filling their informal time, however, American preadolescent children proved remarkably resilient. As I discuss in the next chapter, children's creativity as nurtured in the underground of their independent play culture continued to manifest itself in both familiar and new ways.

7

Children's Play Goes Underground, 1950 to the Present

EACH YEAR, 80 percent of the thousands of new toys that are introduced into the American market fail to capture a significant share of what now amounts to more than $12 billion in sales. This means that neither marketers, who try to persuade kids to buy certain toys, nor parents, who assume that they know what their daughters and sons like, are as perceptive as they think they are. Rather, preadolescent children continue to express a kind of independence in their play and in doing so subtly influence the commercial world by determining how and with what they amuse themselves. Getting to understand children's culture poses the biggest challenge to marketers because it is only by letting youngsters speak for themselves—exerting at least some power over the adult world—and then acclimating to those young needs that toy makers can succeed. As analysts Sydney Landensohn Stern and Ted Schoenbaum noted more than fifteen years ago,

> The secret to success lies inside the head of an eight-year-old child. That is the eternal paradox of the toy industry. Adults running multi-million dollar toy companies are always trying to climb back inside that eight-year-old head. Creative people in the industry love to boast that they have not grown up, that they have retained enough youthful enthusiasm to know what children consider fun.[1]

As the children's consumer economy and its handmaidens in the advertising industry expanded in the latter half of the twentieth century, toy makers and retailers increasingly applied the concept of "play value" as a means of reckoning the success of a product. But defining play value meant carrying out research, and to marketers research meant finding out directly what young people liked—in other words, what "value" they attached to the toy. How children themselves acted toward a toy, rather than how some adult *assumed* they would react, became the most important factor in determining how and whether the toy would be marketed. As the product-testing manager at game maker Milton Bradley Company declared, "Our management philosophy maintains that contact with children through the product development cycle is the best way to ensure that we make toys that children will enjoy."[2] Thus, at the same time that they were being bombarded on television and in print with exhortations to play with one product or another, children, through their expressed preferences as measured by researchers, were exerting influence over what was being marketed to them. They were, in a sense, empowered by the very forces that critics said were manipulating them.[3]

Girls and boys in this era have exercised influence—"agency"—in other ways as well. For one thing, as noted in the previous chapter, children quickly have learned how to express their desires in a way that induces parents, relatives, and other gift givers to purchase particular items. In contemporary America, "pester power" reaches fullest force during preteen years and when combined with a new ideology that grants kids greater say in family decision making, it enables children to acquire goods as never before. Moreover, children in their preteen years now have more discretionary cash from gifts and allowances to spend on themselves. Thus they have their own means to satisfy their wants by participating directly, as well as indirectly, in consumption.

As has always been the case, commercial toys are not the only components of children's play. With parents ever present in their lives, children nevertheless still have reveled in the activities they devise to amuse themselves independently. Writer Annie Dillard, growing up in Pittsburgh in the 1950s and 1960s, recollected a dual quality of her childhood that exemplifies the experiences of many children in the late twentieth century. She described the attention her parents gave to her drawings and poetry, their willingness to buy art supplies and sports equipment for her, their readiness to listen to her problems and "supervise my time." But Annie also had "days and nights [that] were my own to plan and fill," times when adults did not

> get involved with my detective work, nor hear about my reading, nor inquire about my homework . . . , nor visit the salamanders I

caught, nor listen to me play the piano, nor attend my field hockey games, nor fuss over my insect collection with me, or my poetry collection or stamp collection or rock collection.[4]

Annie's parents may have been more indulgent than most—in recent times mothers and fathers normally feel obligated to attend their children's performances and sporting events—but her freedom to pursue her own curiosity was undoubtedly achieved by escaping the "supervised hours" as much as it was permitted by her parents.

Annie Dillard and countless other children of the late twentieth century demonstrated impressive resourcefulness in creating an underground play culture away from adult auspices. Like Annie, youngsters can be compliant and confiding in the company of adults, yet also be sly and mischievous when alone and with peers.[5] They still have exerted at least some power over their play environments, their playthings, their play companions, and their freedom to take risks. But perhaps more than in any previous era, their autonomy within these features of play has become increasingly constrained, with results that reflect both positively and negatively on today's juvenile culture.

Finding a Place to Play

In 1981 a study by the U.S. Consumer Product Safety Commission reported, with some dismay, that American children were not using playgrounds in the intended manner. According to the commission's study, "Walking up and down a slide, climbing onto any aspect of playground apparatus that allowed a grip or foothold, and roughhousing were evident in the in-depth investigation."[6] The youngsters who were under observation by the commission's investigators were doing more than defying the safety precautions of their elders; they, like generations of boys and girls who preceded them, were incorporating and transforming spaces and objects for their own purposes. Though these spaces and objects were increasingly becoming off limits, children still tried hard to retain their long-accustomed autonomous use of them.

A well-known catalog of factors constricted the outdoor, informal places where children could play in the late twentieth century. As noted in this book, since the early 1900s, mechanized vehicles had increasingly overwhelmed city, suburban, and even rural streets, while commercial interests, local governments, and watchful adult protectors worked to remove children from sidewalks and other public spaces. Burgeoning amusements, from board games to television to computers, lured children indoors, and protective parents discouraged their offspring from roaming neighborhoods and woods. The built environment of many a community, including both housing developments and commercial and industrial structures, filled open spaces such as vacant lots and fields, pushing youngsters into formal play sites and organized activities.

In the latter half of the twentieth century and into the twenty-first, children had less inclination and less capacity to resist these impositions than their forebears had. Whereas in earlier periods young people waged guerrilla warfare against adult co-optation of public places by incorporating objects and environments into their informal play, they now have found that the large-scale forces of modern society are more difficult to contest. More and more, as one observer at mid-century contended, young children suffered from "shortages of play spaces," and those playing on streets and sidewalks were considered by adults to be "just in the way."[7] Forced removal has teamed with a multitude of contrived, organized activities especially to curtail large-group outdoor play. Folklorists Amanda Dargan and Steven Zeitlin observed in their research on city play that instead of choosing up sides for group games carried out on the streets and in playgrounds, children now tend to play in twos and threes, because open spaces have disappeared and fewer kids are available.[8]

Still, children have replicated the playtime ways of previous generations by appropriating places and objects of the adult-controlled environment. Dargan and Zeitlin observed children transforming park benches, alleys, and other ordinary scenes into settings for games and imaginary dramas. In New York City, youngsters designed their own "version of Fifth Avenue: the children hail taxis and merrily mimic St. Patrick's and Macy's Thanksgiving parades. In other neighborhoods, children play priest, gas station attendant, pet store owner, baby, doctor, and even drug dealer."[9] Kate Simon, daughter of immigrant parents, made the rooftop of her apartment building "my second kingdom" (her first was the street), "snooped in the Italian market," and peered down train tracks for imaginary trains.[10] Annie Dillard and her friends took over Pittsburgh's Richland Lane and its backyards, where they engaged in ball games and mock war battles amid "a limitless wilderness of trees, garbage cans, thickets, back porches, and gardens, where no one knew where the two sides' territories ended."[11]

Youngsters also have adjusted to new environments by altering old amusements into new competition. The formerly timeless pastime of marbles, which best could be played on smooth dirt surfaces, became difficult to undertake on asphalt and concrete, whose hard surfaces made the marbles roll too far. But the boys' street game of skelly (also known as "skully," "kilsies," and "caps") has survived in some places because paved surfaces can be adapted to the game, which involves flicking bottle caps toward a target outlined with scoring boundaries drawn along sidewalks and curbs. Skelly also reflects the ways boys can incorporate ordinary objects as well as paved areas into their play. Like shuffleboard, the game's strategy includes knocking an opponent's caps off the board. This can best be accomplished by weighting one's own bottle caps with tar, cork, wax, melted crayons, orange peel, or other substances. Competitors take special pride in crafting their skelly caps. Don Fellman recalled his special way of weighting his: "At my window, I would take different color crayons, and affix the beam of light so they would melt and move and flow around—it was almost like a chemical experiment."[12]

Simon, Dillard, and Fellman alluded to activities that remained possible in the 1950s and 1960s. By the later years of the twentieth century, however, such playscapes were harder for children to create, and so many of the treasured street games had disappeared that some nostalgic adults tried to revive them. In 1999, two baby boomers, Marc Pesner and Mick Greene, established Streetplay.com, a website to celebrate and revive urban street play as a response to the "more organized and less organic" forms of play common to current children's amusements. Their game roster lists twenty-one entries, including familiar ones such as marbles, jacks, and stickball, and more arcane pastimes such as fivebox, halfball, and Hit the Stick. The last game's rules are representative of how youngsters used to, and still can, transform and incorporate objects and environments for play:

> Neither speed, strength, nor agility matter here; careful aim and a light touch are the important skills. Hit the Coin and Hit the Stick require two players, a relatively level, uncracked two-square stretch of

sidewalk, and a coin (usually a penny) or a Good Humor ice cream stick.

The players stand at either end of two concrete squares with a coin or stick placed directly in the center seam. The object is to hit the coin or stick with the ball and, even better, attempt to flip it over. Each hit brings one point, each flip is worth two, with play ending once a player reaches 11 or 21.[13]

The website also describes variations in rules for skelly, stickball, handball, and spaldeen (a high-bouncing rubber ball common in the early twentieth century) games, a special section on street games that characterize "girl power," and advice on how to use stoops, streets, and walls.

The existence of a website that nostalgically explains obsolete improvised games to readers who most likely are adults underlines the fact that modern environments have become hostile to such outdoor play for children. Moreover, formal play sites of the past—namely, public playgrounds with their equipment fixed in concrete or resting on gravel—have provoked adult concern for child safety. During the 1990s, approximately 150,000 children were treated at hospitals annually for injuries sustained on playgrounds.[14] It is impossible to determine how many of these injuries were minor abrasions or contusions that cautious parents thought should be examined by medical professionals, and how many were serious enough actually to require professional treatment. Nevertheless, play advocates have argued for new kinds of play spaces that are safe and planned but flexible.

Examples from abroad have offered models. After World War II, for example, Denmark developed what were called "adventure playgrounds," sites where children were encouraged to manipulate materials and equipment in their own way, such as build huts, forts, dens, and tree houses and undertake cooking projects—play activities that crowded urban areas and safety-conscious parents previously had inhibited. But adventure playgrounds, noted one study, failed to catch on in the United States because they were "unsightly" and lacked adult supervision. Another alternative was the "creative" playground, a space that combined traditional swings and slides with informal objects such as spools, tires, and building materials. A few such places were built in the United States in the 1970s and 1980s, but most were short-lived, as were "vest-pocket playgrounds" that occupied small, unused spaces between city buildings. Again, concerns for safety and supervision intervened.[15]

Recently "pay-for-play" sites, sometimes called "child entertainment centers," have come to replace playgrounds in many cities and suburbs. These are colorful outdoor and indoor spaces, often existing at fast-food outlets and designed mostly for children below age ten or so. They provide "soft contained play equipment," such as large plastic enclosures full of brightly colored balls, tunnels, slides, and arches, all designed to maximize safe activities and prevent lawsuits over injuries. (The Consumer Product Safety Commission has even drawn up a "Soft Contained Play Equipment Check List" for businesses and parents.) Indoor pay-for-play centers also have multiplied and, like the outdoor facilities, are designed to protect against injury and offer an alternative to inner-city playgrounds where drugs, kidnapping, and violence are threats.

Pay-for-play centers have not yielded desired results and have provoked their share of critics. One chain of indoor "edutainment" centers, Discovery Zone, grew rapidly in the 1980s but failed to provide sufficient variety for improvised play because its soft, contained play equipment was too stationary, and it also acquired a reputation for poor management. Some cynics scoffed that the centers' initials, DZ, actually stood for "disease zone" and "dirt zone." The chain filed for bankruptcy twice in the 1990s. Generally, Discovery Zone and other pay-for-play places, which range from Chuck E. Cheese Pizza Time Theatres and Discovery Zone outlets to theme parks, have provided what two critics have called "guilt-reduction devices" for fathers to become "Disney Dads," fulfilling their paternal responsibilities by taking their children in tow for a few hours of purchased entertainment.[16] It is perhaps unfair to expect commercial play centers to serve larger purposes, but their existence does reflect a new kind of adult-constructed substitution for disappearing outdoor sites for children's free play.

A major trend in the location of children's play of late is that much of it has moved indoors. According to Brian Sutton-Smith, "Whereas our mothers used to say, 'Don't bother me, go and play outside,' often they no longer make that suggestion because they feel that streets are unsafe or that their [children's] companions are undesirable. Instead they take their children to some public organizations or places."[17] Though Sutton-Smith may be exaggerating the newness of indoor play—diaries and autobiographies from earlier eras suggest a considerable amount of indoor play—his point about the relative decline of informal outdoor play is valid. With access to privacy in their own bedrooms and, among middle-class and wealthier kids at least, other areas of the home that adults seldom frequent, children can control indoor space to an extent that they no longer can even approximate on the streets and in yards. The increasing primacy of television and computers in children's lives over the past fifty years has affected their environments in a way that, as Sutton-Smith has contended, has shifted their activities from a "manual" involvement with objects and places to a "symbolic" relationship with information and amusement.[18]

Thus the most identifiable shifts in patterns of play have occurred in the realm of play environment. A recent survey of the ways children spend discretionary time found that of the fifty-one nonschool, nonwork hours kids had available to them each week, only about one-half hour was spent in unstructured outdoor activities, while fourteen and a half hours were spent in indoor unstructured play and more than twelve separate hours were spent watching television.[19] The fields and woods where rural youngsters once roamed, the streets and sidewalks where urban kids invented amusements, and even the parks and playgrounds where children cavorted away from adult eyes no longer constitute the cherished playscapes that they once provided. Indoor play and structured outdoor play, such as adult-organized baseball, basketball, and soccer leagues, are single-interest activities that do not enable preteen children, inhabiting an age range where creating social relationships is a major function of their culture, to explore ways of sharing space and building bonds with a community of peers.[20] In previous eras and in some places currently, those communities have not always been beneficial, as the antisocial behavior of youth gangs and the vulnerability of unsupervised children to unsavory teen and adult influences have demonstrated. But children who historically interacted on a sustained basis, whether in urban neighborhoods or rural open spaces, did have opportunities for building relationships in environments that are less available to young people at present.

The Play Value of Toys

Critics of modern children's culture have concluded that commercial toys, with their specific links to media and fantasy characters and the restrictive quality imposed by their mechanization, have dulled the creativity that once had been stimulated by homemade playthings. While there can be no doubt that commercial toys of recent vintage impose some inflexibility on play, if for no other reason than that kids more easily grow out of them than in previous times, children nevertheless have shown remarkable resourcefulness in using their toys in ways adults had not foreseen. Brian Sutton-Smith, a critic of the critics, has observed that nay-sayers "seem to assume that one can simply look at the character of [modern] toys and make predictions as to how they will be used and what their effects will be on human creativity."[21] Furthermore, as suggested at the opening of this chapter, youngsters have exerted considerable but unheralded influence over the kinds of toys that are marketed to them by expressing their impressions of a product's "play value."

Fantasy characters and fantasy stories have played a very important part in the independent material culture of recent childhoods, and comic books marched in the vanguard of this phenomenon. Among the first child-oriented, mass-produced goods that children could purchase by and for themselves, comic books enabled girls and (mainly) boys to express their preferences and define a market separate from what adults wanted for them.[22] Comic books have roots in newspaper comic strips that had begun to occupy a segment of popular literature at the turn of the nineteenth century. Though not initially intended for young readers, newspaper comic strips nevertheless presented satire from the perspective of a child's world, including prankish humor such as that of the Katzenjammer Kids and human-interest dilemmas such as those of Little Orphan Annie. Early comic strips were often referred to as "funnies," symbolizing an amusing and nonutilitarian quality that linked them to childish emotion.[23] With the popularization of movie cartoons and radio, newspaper comics began incorporating heroes and their adventures from these media, enhancing the appeal of Donald Duck, Popeye, Flash Gordon, and others.

A few collections of popular comic strips were compiled in the 1920s, but the critical step occurred in the late 1930s, when a publisher known as DC (for Detective Comics) began marketing comic book series in pamphlet-length publications using cheap newsprint and, significantly, sold to children at prices (usually five and ten cents) that they could afford. In a format longer than an individual comic strip but shorter than an ordinary book, comic book producers presented serialized stories with well-developed characters that could appeal to juvenile readers. By the 1950s, these publications had become, both by their content and by their affordability, not only a common component of children's literature but also a symbol of an alternative, even oppositional, children's amusement culture. In this way, comic books, as Stephen Kline has stated, "changed the face of children's fiction."[24]

The history of this genre is well told elsewhere and can be briefly summarized here. Comic books flourished during and after World War II, first with the appearance of dozens of superheroes such as Superman, Batman, and Captain Marvel, and then with the development of "romance" and "western" comics such as the Young Romance series and Hopalong Cassidy serials. With the publication of crime and horror tales in the late 1940s, however, adults began to get nervous because the content and characters of these stories were far more sinister and threatening than those of previous comics and because kids seemed so spellbound by them. In 1950, a U.S. Senate committee charged that comic books contributed to juvenile delinquency; subsequently, parent and teacher groups such as the Cincinnati Parents Committee organized to ban them. In 1953, Frederick Wertham, a psychiatrist who worked to reform juvenile delinquents, published a book titled *The Seduction of the Innocent,* in which he likened comics to crime-inducing drugs. Wertham claimed that the visual and textual depictions of mayhem and horror not only lured formerly wholesome children into paths of crime and violence but also caused reading disorders and youthful sex offenses. He even went so far as to conclude that Superman was a fascist vigilante and that Batman and Robin were a homosexual couple because they lived together in sumptuous quarters filled with flowers and were devoted to each other in unmanly ways.[25]

Wertham's exposé prompted another Senate investigation the next year which in turn induced the Comic Magazine Association of America to create a list of standards, sanctioned by a stamp of approval, that virtually eliminated battle scenes and other violence, as well as steamy romance, from comic books. At the same time, thirteen states and several cities passed laws restricting the sale and content of comic books. As a result, numerous publishers were forced out of business. In spite of these efforts, however, children continued to buy comics, and a few companies and their series survived the code, including Marvel Comics, the successful producer of superhero adventures

COMIC BOOK HEROES. A leading superhero of the Marvel Comics stable, the patriotic Captain America battled Nazis, Communists, and other enemies in numerous comic book stories, giving children—in this case, boys—a type of literature that was all their own. *Picture Research Consultants and Archives*

featuring Spiderman, Incredible Hulk, and Captain America. Eventually, rising production costs, television, new action toys such as Barbie and G.I. Joe, and multiple other diversions reduced the popularity of comic books. Nevertheless, by the late twentieth century, they had left a legacy of countless characters and story lines that influenced the toys that hit the market.[26]

The incursion of comic book publishers into the imaginations of young people had provoked parents, politicians, and psychologists to take an adversarial relationship with the genre. But children themselves expressed their tastes and independence when instead of traveling to the library to find "wholesome" reading material they carried their dimes down to the corner drugstore and bought a cheap literary product intentionally designed with them, not their parents, in mind. Revealingly, Frederick Wertham's diatribe against comic books included the conclusion that their danger was especially pervasive because even the poorest children could—and did—buy them without parental permission. What the success of comic book consumption re-flected, then, was not only that they provided youngsters with new ways to challenge adult authority but also that they signified an in-creasingly powerful alliance between children and commercial inter-ests intent on profiting from youth culture.

This alliance proved to be an overlooked but vital component of children's play culture in the late twentieth century because, as noted, toy producers learned to bypass the parental point of view and go di-rectly to young consumers for assessments of a product's marketabil-ity. Like any rationalized business, toy makers strived to reduce risk, and so they needed to undertake research. Their research deviated from what educators and psychologists were studying in that it un-dervalued what parents wanted for their kids; instead, the experts hired by the toy industry surveyed reactions and preferences of chil-dren themselves. While social scientists directed their research toward issues of cognition and growth, in which playthings were supple-ments, toy marketers were more interested in directly observing how and with what children played to determine how to market a toy.

Beginning in the 1980s, marketers of toys, snack foods, and chil-dren's clothing, tried to discern what Kline has called "the secret inner world of children's culture." They studied toy preferences by filming and listening to girls and boys at play. By the end of the century, mar-keters were organizing child-focus group testing, telephone surveys to children, and even in-school interviews—all intended to determine young people's tastes. For-profit consulting firms such as Just Kid Inc. and the Strottman Group were formed to conduct research, mostly on food preferences but also on play behavior. According to sociologist Juliet Schor, many new products reach the market today only after "kid brainstorming" sessions that create "feedback loops" in which young consumers are observed by marketers to find out what trends are "in." From studying these loops, marketers advertise products to both match and manipulate kids' tastes. With specific regard to toys, the object of this process has been to determine "play value," a meas-ure of the product's appeal as defined by the duration and intensity with which a tested child plays with a new toy.[27]

Once marketers have determined a toy's play value, they need to get it off the store shelf and into a child's home. In accomplishing this, marketers have shown keen understanding of the linkages between children and consumer society. Surveys from the 1960s onward have shown that children frequently have accompanied parents on shopping trips, usually to malls, and either have been granted or independently exert influence on the family purchasing process. The result has been that children have learned how to control what toys they acquire. The feedback loop between children and producers/marketers that determines play value creates a second loop when marketers focus advertising campaigns based on youngsters' preferences, and then the youngsters, responding to televised and other ads, express their wants to adult toy buyers and gift givers, either subtly or through nagging. As an executive from Kenner Products remarked without excessive exaggeration in 1983, "Kids are the determining factor in toy purchases 90% of the time."[28]

By the end of the twentieth century, according to a study by the Geppetto Group, a New York–based consulting firm specializing in marketing to children, those in the six-to-twelve age range visited stores two to three times a week and they added six items to the family shopping cart on each visit.[29] According to marketing consultant Cheryl Idell in a 1999 article in the journal *Selling to Kids* (just the existence of such a periodical signifies a lot about current marketing), the success of this "pester power" depends on the type of parents being pestered. The "Bare Necessities" parents are usually affluent but also conservative; they are most likely to resist nagging. "Indulgers" constitute about one-third of all parents and are found in all social classes; they are impulse buyers who can't say no to their children's requests. Many single or divorced parents are in the third, or "Conflicted" category; they accede to nagging because they are driven by guilt. And those in the fourth type, "Kids' Pals," like to play with their offspring, so they are easy targets also.[30] Furthermore, as more mothers have entered the workforce, taking their children shopping has become a way to combine the meeting of household needs with a family outing; thus the Geppetto survey found that 80 percent of children in this age range regularly accompanied their parents—usually mothers—on shopping trips.[31]

But many children, especially those of ages ten to twelve, have cultivated habits of shopping by themselves, especially because they flash more discretionary cash to spend than previous generations had. In post–World War II America, the weekly allowance took on new meaning. "Whereas parents once gave out an allowance in return for work or regular achievement, or to help teach children to save and plan for the future," Kline has written, "they now [give] money to children as a reward for good behaviour, as a gift or as a way to teach children the skill of buying for themselves."[32] James U. McNeal, a Texas A&M professor and oft-consulted expert on selling to children, has claimed that in 1989 children aged four to twelve, alone or in the company of adults, accounted for $6.1 billion in purchases; the total ballooned to $23.4 billion in 1997 and stood at an estimated $30.0 billion in 2002, an increase of 400 percent in less than a decade and a half. Food in the form of sweets, snacks, and beverages comprised the major spending category, but toys claimed second place.[33]

One of the most distinctive features of children's toy culture of the late twentieth century was the surfeit of playthings that any individual child possessed. To be sure, a family's economic resources affects how much a youngster actually owns, but even low-income children often have lots of toys that they select for themselves. Among preadolescents, many of these playthings have involved characters and stories that once were defined by comic books but now are derived from television and movies. These dolls, games, and paraphernalia reflect the influence of media promotion, but they also represent a kind of defiance that previously had not existed in children's culture. Whether it is a Barbie doll whose representation of an "autonomous teenager" is more important to a girl than her anatomical correctness, a Nintendo game involving grotesque monsters and a story line from a movie or a Saturday morning television cartoon show that no adult would deign to watch, or playthings related to Bart Simpson and his dysfunctional family, modern toys separate the younger generation from the older.[34]

Children make sense of the avalanche of available toys and play opportunities in several ways. They watch television and interact with peers and, as a result, acquire and play with toys in a standardized fashion. They also apply their imaginations and use playthings in ways that toy makers have not anticipated. They use money from Monopoly games as currency for playing store, they substitute a toy car for a ship or plane, and they ignore the printed rules of a board game and instead create their own game using the pieces.[35] And they show stronger preferences for informal playthings than for commercial toys. In the late 1970s, educational psychologist Janice Beran conducted a study of 295 Midwestern children ages ten to twelve, asking them to rank eighteen different types of play on a one-to-five point scale, five representing the most positive reaction, one the least positive. Significantly, the subjects' rating for "playing with dolls and battery toys," that is, manufactured playthings that had quite specific functions, averaged out at 3.13, well below the mean of 3.40 for all eighteen categories. By contrast, the surveyed children gave "playing with homemade things" a rating of 3.67, well above the mean.[36] Analogous surveys for the early twenty-first century have not been undertaken, but it is probable that similar results would occur. For example, some research has suggested that girls now simultaneously express longing for dolls, especially those depicted in TV commercials, and then spurn them for play activities that they feel are more exciting. One journalist even recalled from her own childhood that instead of fantasizing about Malibu Barbie's indulgent life, she maliciously dismembered her doll and chopped off her hair to simulate some kind of accident.[37]

Some psychologists have concluded that different children view TV in different ways and are not completely captivated by what they see. Several studies have agreed with the mainstream criticism that children are easily manipulated by television commercials but also note that the most vulnerable youngsters are those under the age of six and that as they grow older children become increasingly cynical about the content of advertisements. The effect of television ads, according to one such analyst, is "pervasive" but not necessarily "decisive." That is, commercials have indeed created an "orthodoxy" of what play is all about, but particular commercials are not as influential as critics believe. Most youngsters in the preteen category know enough not to believe all programming and commercials, they learn to distinguish what is fictional and what is not, they do not identify with every hero or heroine, and they comprehend that it is unrealistic to imitate a character's behavior. There is no disputing that the fantasies that they see on TV are the dominant themes that children integrate into their play, but they can adapt the themes to their own emotional needs.[38]

Just as some analysts view television in a less-jaundiced way, others are less willing to pronounce a negative verdict on video and computer games. They have concluded that such game play empowers preadolescent youngsters with a sense of control and relieves some of the tensions of childhood. Other observers have determined that increased, rather than lessened, conviviality has resulted because the games motivate kids to exchange information with each other, including communicating over the internet. These game-oriented chat rooms and other forms of interaction create cyberspace communities that often are overlooked and have a far more benign quality than the blogging that has captured the attention of news media.

As early as 1979, enthusiasts were arguing that the gaming and learning taking place on computers were, according to one writer for *Time* magazine, "solitary activities that do not seem solitary" because of the intense interaction between "one person and one computer." The result, ostensibly, was "not only a new kind of thinking, but what amounts to a strange new way of socializing."[39] Such hyperbole may have been a bit overstated; still, later studies have also suggested that many video games sharpen skills in inductive reasoning, memory, and planning, all of which prepare a youngster for the challenges of the adult world.[40] In his provocative book, *Everything Bad Is Good for You,* technology writer Steven Johnson argues that

> far more than books or movies or music, games force you [in this case, children] to make *decisions*. . . . All the intellectual benefits of gaming derive from this fundamental virtue, because learning how to think is ultimately about learning how to make the right decisions: weighing evidence, analyzing situations, consulting your long-term goals, and then deciding. . . . From the outside, the primary activity of a gamer looks like a fury of clicking and shooting, which is why so much of the conventional wisdom about games focuses on hand-eye coordination. But if you peer inside the gamer's mind, the primary activity turns out to be another creature altogether: making decisions, some of them snap judgments, some long-term strategies.[41]

A few analyses have even surmised, arguably, that grades in schoolwork do not seem to suffer from video game playing at home and that, at least among school-age children (not adolescents), there is no direct relationship between video games and psychopathology — though, like war toys, violent games may increase short-term aggressive behavior.[42]

The ways that children have used, and continue to use, toys rather than how grownups *want* toys to be used remains the most vital quality of children's autonomous play. "Approved" play is that which follows beliefs, customs, and rules established by adult authority. But children's manipulation of objects for their own purposes creates true play value. Kids of the present era may be no less creative than those of past times. According to Sutton-Smith,

> [Critics of modern toys] seem to assume that one cam simply look at the character of toys and make predictions as to how they will be used and what their effects will be on human creativity. It is very doubtful if that is possible. . . .
>
> Play's excitement derives from both following the cultural rules for behavior [that is, acquiring toys and playing with them as sanctioned by the adult world and the media] and defying the cultural rules [autonomously finding alternative uses and methods].[43]

Toys, then, can and do have dual function, one in the minds of adults and another in the culture of children.

Playing Alone and Together

Along with alterations in play environments, the electrification of play, whether it has involved battery-operated toys, computer and video games, or youth versions of adult playthings such as cameras and iPods, has signified one landmark change in preadolescent children's culture of the last half of the twentieth century. A shift in the composition of playmates has marked another. Early in the period, from about the 1950s to the early 1970s, elements of previous peer play culture remained strong. The makeup of play groups consisted of neighborhood friends and schoolmates who frequently and intimately associated with each other. For example, Susan Robben, born in 1955, started a diary when she was eight, and in one of her entries she referred to an intimate bonding with a girlfriend that is probably much less likely to occur today because protective parents would be more vigilant than Sarah's parents were to prevent it. "Today for the first time," Susan wrote on June 19, 1963, "Gail Greenfield and I had a cut and we made blood sisters. This is how we did it. Paula Greenfield got some of my blood and put it on Gail's cut and got some of that blood and put it on my cut. And that's how we got to be blood sisters."[44] Boys, too, had a constant cast of close male friends with whom, as New Yorker Brian Sullivan experienced in the early 1970s, they daily explored city spaces, raced on roller skates, and rode the subway to escape "the apron-strings feeling of being driven somewhere in Mom's station wagon."[45]

While some of these qualities have endured, to a large extent play groups and activities for the subsequent kid generations of the 1980s onward have revealed quite different characteristics. For many pre-teens, especially from middle-class and wealthy families, a schedule of adult-structured, formal activities has at least partially precluded im-provised pastimes such as becoming blood sisters or roaming a nearby park. As a result, though they retain peer-oriented relationships, con-temporary children experience multiple and sometimes differently combined groups, depending on the activity. A nine-year-old might be involved with one assemblage on a soccer team, another group in an art class, and another on the school bus. The pervasiveness of planned activities has meant that even if a child wishes to play informally with comrades, as Susan Robben and Brian Sullivan did, few of such poten-tial friends would be available because they are engaged in their own formal commitments. When informal group play does occur, it more likely involves assemblages of twos and threes rather than the choos-ing up of sides for large-group games. Low-income children might have more opportunities for informal and continuous associations than youngsters with more resources, but unsafe neighborhoods and the lure of television could curtail the use of streets and backyards that once had occupied previous generations. For many youngsters, then, the neighborhood has declined as a source for playmates, as well as an environment for play, leaving the school as the main site of continuous peer association but mostly in a controlled setting.

The waning in what might be called camaraderie play has been re-placed to a considerable extent by an increase in solitary play. Care must be taken in concluding that over time there has been a linear rise from very little solo play to extensive solo play. Evidence from previ-ous chapters shows that throughout American history children have amused themselves alone, perhaps more than scholars and contempo-rary observers believed. Whether they went out "rambling" through fields and woods as Catherine Maria Sedgwick did in the eighteenth century or pretending to be a "teamster, a gun-playing, bronco-bust-ing vaquero, or a hearty steamboat man" on his dining room floor as Theodore Dreiser did in the nineteenth century, youngsters have al-ways found ways to play by themselves. But by the late twentieth cen-tury, the number of hours children spent in isolated, sedentary activity has occupied a considerable portion of their waking, nonschool time. In their study of almost three thousand children in the early 1990s, sociologists Sandra Hofferth and John Sandberg determined that television viewing occupied one-fourth of an average youngster's free time. Children aged six to nine watched TV around twelve and one-half hours per week, and those aged nine to twelve watched almost thirteen and one-half hours. Notably, older elementary schoolkids spent almost five hours per week reading and studying and younger elementary schoolchildren also spent more than three hours per week at these activities, suggesting that for some at least, schoolwork outside of class occupies a significant segment of time. Hofferth and Sandberg also found that youngsters devoted more than two hours per week to hobbies and "other passive leisure," presumably including video or computer games and internet surfing.[46] As of this writing, comprehensive tallies of hours spent on Myspace.com and similar websites are scarce, but there can be no doubt that this activity now consumes considerable time of many preteens.

As traditionally has been the case, unstructured play of preadolescent boys and girls has been mostly sex-segregated, though, as in the past, gender-integrated activity has also been evident. Also, youngsters playing together have followed distinct, gender-typed styles. Anthropologist Helen Schwartzman cites a study of middle-class New England children that confirmed boys' persistent predilection when playing together to modify play sites and build things, whereas girls tended more to embellish existing places and materials. Another study of the group play activities in which ten year olds liked and disliked to engage concluded that boys consciously shunned activity associated with the opposite sex or that had "intellectual" implications, and girls avoided aggressive play that they associated with boys. Kate Simon's father reinforced these distinctions when he scolded her for playing with boys, warning that if she continued to do so, "I would surely become a street girl, a prostitute." Maria Cuca, daughter of Yugoslav immigrants, confided to her diary when she was ten that she enjoyed her friend's birthday celebration because it was a "hen's party. No roosters." And on some days, Annie Dillard, at age ten, viewed boys as some kind of fascinating but alien species:

> They walked clumsily but assuredly through the world, kicking things for the hell of it. By way of conversation, they slugged each

other on their interesting shoulders. . . . They moved in violent jerks from which we [girls] hung back, impressed and appalled, as if from horses slamming the slats of their stalls.[47]

African American girls have continued to engage in their all-girl singing, clapping, and jump-rope games, such as double Dutch, that combine collaboration with individual competitiveness. Dargan and Zeitlin observed that in urban neighborhoods such as Harlem and Bedford-Stuyvesant,

Half a dozen ropes still turn on a hot day. Groups of five or six girls perform cheers, a chanted dance ensemble piece with hand clapping and improvised (often sexual) verses. Groups of girls rehearse in private so that rival groups will not "steal" their cheers, and sometimes they try out their chants on a roaring subway where they can sing at the top of their lungs and hardly disturb their fellow riders.[48]

Beginning in the 1970s, African American boys became increasingly involved in the game of playground basketball, or "street" basketball, that attracted teenage and older black males of the inner city. (White youths of the suburbs have adopted some aspects of playground basketball in their informal games, but the game itself remains closely identified with inner-city playgrounds.) Though preadolescent African American boys are not able to execute the athletic and acrobatic styles that older youths perform, their styles do mimic the individualism, taunting, and intimidation ("trash talk") that distinguish the urban playground game from the more organized, team-oriented style that is taught in schools and gymnasiums.[49]

By the time children reach preteen years, many sedentary activities that occupy them, such as board games, are created for one sex or the other. Action-type video games involving sports or battle often require two competing players, usually boys, each of whom operates a "joystick" or control box. Boys and girls also play sex-typed games on internet sites Millsberry.com and Postopia.com, both of which offer games that appeal typically to one sex or the other, though girls may more likely also play boys' games. (Significantly, both Millsberry and Postopia are designed by children's cereal companies, General Mills and Post, and evince the current powerful bond between commercial interests and play.)

PARALLEL PLAY. Eleven-year-old girls Caroline Bell and Kayleigh Frampton each play their own game on the Millsberry game website, but simultaneously converse about each other's game. *Al Mallette/Lightstream*

The internet also has spawned a new, modified type of "parallel play," a form of play previously characterized by very young children who play together with the same objects in the same place but without communicating. Such an occurrence can exist among older kids when a pair of children, usually of the same sex, each of whom has access to a separate computer, either her or his own or at a place such as a library, sit side by-side and play on a website such as paperdoll heaven.com, Neopets.com, or Millsberry.com. On the paper doll site, for example, each girl dresses up a celebrity in her own style, but at intervals during the process the two girls, who might not have been paying attention to each other, discuss their choices.[50]

Marketers have both incorporated and reinforced children's same-sex play preferences. Researchers who tested products by watching how children played in groups concluded that peer influence was vital but that it acted in particular ways that prompted them to tailor TV commercials accordingly. They found, for example, that boys reacted negatively when girls appeared in ads for products that boys considered their exclusive toys, and, conversely, girls objected to boys' presence in ads for what they considered to be "their" items. According to Kline, only 23 percent of children's commercials in the late 1980s and early 1990s showed boys and girls playing together. At the same time, advertisers normally target their youth audience with special effects designed to attract one sex or the other, using, for example, driving music and comic-book action to tempt boys and pastel colors and magic to appeal to girls.[51]

Like their forebears, preadolescent girls and boys sometimes join together in active play, but when they do they engage more frequently in boys' games than in girls' games. Kate Simon, for example, joined neighborhood boys for games such as ring-o-levio and stoopball. She also tried to attain what she called "masculine freedoms" by swiping sweets from a candy store but lamented that "I lost my chance to be a 'tomboy'" when she slipped off a ledge she was climbing with some boys, who then ridiculed her.[52] Annie Dillard played sports with boys, delighting especially in football, where "you thought up a new strategy for every play" and "you got to throw yourself mightily at someone's running legs." Also, when alone, she devised her own baseball game, pretending she was a pitcher and throwing a rubber ball against a target on her garage wall.[53] More recently, no factor illustrates the melding of girls into what were formerly boys' domains than the effect of Title IX directives, the 1972 legislation prohibiting sexual discrimination in educational programs at institutions receiving federal funds. Though the law has applied mainly to high schools and, especially, colleges and universities, and though the number of varsity teams that combine both sexes on their rosters is tiny, its effects have created enhanced opportunities for girls of all ages to participate in sports, formerly a much more exclusive boys' pastime.

Psychologists continue to maintain that play provides an important context in which children learn appropriate sex-role behavior, and thus the games and playmates they choose reflect their perceptions of conduct acceptable to their own sex. But during the past fifty years, as a result of the women's movement and other social changes, sex roles in play are in a fluid state. As early as 1960, a survey showed that boys in the fourth, fifth, and sixth grades tended to express preference for fewer playthings that differentiated them from girls than boys of an earlier era did.[54] Almost twenty years later, Brian Sutton-Smith observed from his studies that "there are many more forms of play that the sexes share than used to be the case." Still, it is likely that sex-segregated play, especially outside of school, will remain the norm for preteen youngsters.[55]

Throughout American history—and, indeed, most cultures' histories—the most salient feature of children's play has been play with others rather than just with toys.[56] Adults have long believed that interactive play provides children with opportunities to develop skills in cooperation, task orientation, adherence to rules, empathy, and other qualities necessary later in life. French philosopher Jean Piaget, one of the twentieth century's most influential theorists of child development, believed that the reciprocal nature of peer relationships in childhood encourages children to negotiate their roles with others and to take more varied roles, whereas their complementary relationship with adults is more unilateral: adults order, kids comply. Such a model does not always fit. A unilateral relationship exists when one child teaches another the rules of a game or how to manipulate a game, and a reciprocal interaction occurs when parents engage with children in games where both generations are familiar with the rules.[57] Nevertheless, there is no doubting the ways playmates influence a child's development.

As in the past, parents and educators of the present are anxious that this development not be cultivated on "the street," so they have created more and more formal activities where, presumably, youngsters can learn in a controlled setting, just as they are supposed to learn in school. To some extent, children, mainly of the middle class, have accepted these structured activities because they generally prefer to play with peers. But ironically, the desire of parents, in concert with toy manufacturers and marketers, to keep children amused has also included material inducements to play alone. The higher the household income, the more likely a child is to spend hours in her or his own bedroom, playing a video game, creating a drama using American Doll or Star Wars characters, engaging with the internet, or watching a private television set.[58] (In 2004, an estimated two-thirds of all children between ages eight and eighteen had their own TV set.[59]) In their seclusion, children are partaking of a kind of autonomy, one that consumer society has expanded for them. But there also are other ways that youngsters of the late twentieth century have pursued independence, and the risks that it entails, beyond the purview of the older generation.

Negotiating Freedom and Risk

In 1954, Frances Horwich, better known as "Miss Frances," hostess of the popular early-morning children's TV program, *Ding-Dong School,* wrote in *Today's Education,* "A few weeks ago a wise young father said, 'Yesterday when I checked my seven-year-old daughter's schedule of activities, I became frightened. It left little time for herself, to think and to play with her own thoughts and ideas. From seven on in the morning until eight o'clock at night, she is a child on the go.'" All his daughter's social and academic burdens, protested Horwich's interviewee, were "robbing her of her childhood." Horwich, who held a doctorate from Northwestern University and headed the education department at Roosevelt University in Chicago, used this complaint to fuel her argument in favor of a child's need to play independently which, she claimed, would provide the youngster with "ample opportunity to live and grow . . . to enjoy what he is doing on his own."[60]

Like Horwich, several child advocates began to complain that young people should have more opportunity to learn through unstructured play without adult interference. Stressing a child's need for privacy, the author of a 1961 *New York Times* article pointedly titled "Children's Hour—Adults Keep Out," carped that anxious parents tried too hard to "communicate" with their children and "to monitor not only the child's activities but also the child's thoughts and feelings as well."[61] (Journalists recently have labeled such overseers as "helicopter parents," who perpetually hover over their kids.) By the 1970s, concerns over safety, education, and emotional security had increased, and a number of writers were lamenting that traditional games that children once could claim as their own had disappeared because parents overemphasized the amount of time a child should spend on learning and individual achievement.[62] In their landmark publication, *Children's Games in Street and Playground* (1969), British folklorists Peter and Ilona Opie conclude that adult involvement in children's play was not as welcome or essential as the older generation presumed. Adults always tried to control play, but, the Opies contended, "in the long run, nothing extinguishes self-organized play more effectively than does action to promote it. It is not only natural but beneficial that there should be a gulf between the generations in [children's] choice of recreation." More pointedly, the Opies rebuked modern adults for

exercising too much control over play, arguing that restricting children's freedom too much could be damaging to society. They wrote:

> If children's games are tamed and made part of the school curricu-
> lum, if wastelands are turned into playing fields for the benefit of
> those who conform and ape their elders, if children are given the
> idea that they cannot enjoy themselves without being provided with
> "proper" equipment, we need blame only ourselves when we pro-
> duce a generation who have lost their ability, who are ever dissatis-
> fied, and who descend for their sport to the easy excitement of riot-
> ing, or pilfering, or vandalism.[63]

Other advocates for independent play also argued that adults had
become too controlling. Organized activity such as Little Leagues,
scouting, and park playgrounds had become so highly structured that
some child psychologists fretted that, as one put it, "Our society . . . is
moving rapidly toward a complete takeover of [the] traditional fran-
chise of childhood."[64] Another, after observing sixth-grade boys in two
settings, one in free play without adult direction and the other under
supervision from a trained recreation expert, concluded that when
left to their own means children successfully made their own rules of
play, while they reacted more dully and did not consider it play when
the teacher directed them.[65] About the same time, an educator wrote,
"When a parent [takes a child's play too seriously], when she comes
to regard play as 'good' for her child and self-consciously proceeds to
make a project of it, somehow it loses its spontaneity and the parent
discourages what she is determined to encourage."[66]

Over the past few decades, organized out-of-school activities,
whether instructional or recreational, have replaced much of the time
preteen children previously had for free play. But other, sometimes
overlooked, factors have contributed to the decrease as well. For example, the time spent on a bus or automobile traveling to and from
school has become a significant curb on many kids' independent play
time. Rural children have been riding buses to school for many years,
but by the last third of the twentieth century the busing of urban
schoolchildren to private and public schools located far from home increased dramatically. As a result, tens of thousands of children, many
of them children of color, sit for a considerable stretch, sometimes
for hours each day, being transported to and from school rather than

playing in schoolyards, backyards, and indoors. Between 1949–50 and 1999–2000, the proportion of schoolchildren (elementary and high school) bused at public expense between home and school increased from 31.2 percent to 57.0 percent.[67] The largest boost in percentage of kids transported to school occurred during the 1970s, when suburbanization and busing to achieve racial desegregation of public schools—and the transportation of children to private schools by families wishing to escape racial desegregation—expanded dramatically. In 1969–70, 43.4 percent of schoolchildren were bused at public expense, and in 1984–85 the rate peaked at 61.3 percent.[68]

Time spent riding to school affects a broad range of children. In 1999–2000, there were 586 elementary charter schools in the United States with a total enrollment of 159,000 children (a relatively small but growing number), many of whom rode buses.[69] Thousands—probably millions—more children, mostly white, are driven to private school on privately funded buses and in automobiles. In 1975, 3.7 million children in grades K through 8, or 10.8 percent of all children in those grades, attended a religious or secular private school, defined as "controlled and supported mainly by religious organizations or by private persons or organizations." In 2000, some 4.9 million children in these grades, or 12.7 percent of the total, were enrolled in private schools.[70] Additionally, in 1999, about 521,000 children in grades 1 through 8, about 2 percent of the total, were homeschooled; their playtime may not have been restricted by travel, but they had less contact with peers than those attending formal schools.[71] To be sure, walking to school did—and does—take time. But this form of travel usually is not carried out in the company of adults and often involves peer accompaniment and playful interaction that is less available in a bus or automobile, where adult monitors are in charge.

While a wide range of adult-created activities occupies their time, children of the present era nevertheless have been engaged, as they always have been engaged, in a skirmish with adults over the content of their play. More than ever, adults provide youngsters with means and places for play, yet children continue at times to create an amusement underground in which they challenge, if not subvert, efforts to control them. Occasionally, kids have overtly confronted meddling adults, as when Susan Robben reported to her diary that she and her friends demonstrated against a Mr. Greenfield who had confiscated their tennis ball. "We were piceding [picketing]," she proudly wrote, "and yelled WE-WANT-THE-BALL. The newspaper men came and took a picture."[72] But more often, the defiance has taken place away from adult scrutiny. Much of this independent activity is innocent, creative, harmless; but some of it can involve danger and malfeasance, even malice. There is no denying the tendency of young people to be obstinate. Dargan and Zeitlin cited an instance, for example, in which a player in a child's ball game earned extra points for hitting the "No Ball Playing" sign. The Opies observed children defying known rules of public propriety by being boisterous, scribbling on the pavement, and intentionally getting in the way. Brian Sullivan, playing in his apartment building, knew that the noise he made annoyed the neighbors, but he often ignored their complaints.[73]

Susan Robben's public boldness may have been exceptional because girls seem to be more subtle in dealing with adult rules than boys, whose actions tend to be more impulsive. Kate Simon described her brother as an "adventuresome explorer and breaker" who often got into trouble—and physically punished—when he impulsively played with and then broke a fragile household decoration. In contrast, Kate admitted, "I was already practiced in the hypocrisies of being a good girl."[74] And unlike Brian Sullivan and Kate Simon's brother, who simply ignored parental proscription, Annie Dillard slyly manipulated her mother into allowing her to ride her bike to a local park "if I never mentioned it" to her father, who forbade such a foray because he claimed that "bums lived there under bridges."[75]

The quest for autonomy in what can be termed "illicit" play among both boys and girls typically involves taking risks.[76] As discussed, , parents and other adults have endeavored with increasing intensity to shelter children from danger, yet young people are naturally curious, and a part of their development involves experimentation and testing their abilities. With immature sensibilities, youngsters at times create amusements in which they unintentionally put themselves in jeopardy. Marilyn Bell, growing up in Oklahoma during the early days of television, incorporated a media fantasy into her play in a precarious way that may have distressed her protective parents but gave her no second thoughts. She wrote in her diary when she was twelve that she and a friend "decided to get one of Kueta's dad's coffin crates from his undertaker business and wrap ourselves up in it and send it special delivery to Liberace."[77] Other children guilelessly accepted dares that augured myriad hazards, and more recently they have innocently entered objectionable and unprotected realms of the cyberworld. Independent acts reflecting childhood naiveté about risk, such as climbing, balancing, and other tests of physical capability, may result in newfound confidence and skinned knees or nasty bruises. Still other components of illicit play may end in more serious consequences, such as when kids misuse parents' power tools, medications, or firearms.

The quandary for parents, teachers, and child advocates has been, and remains, how much risk should youngsters be allowed to take—how to make a distinction between trying to avoid but accepting minor hurts and emotional setbacks on one hand and preventing serious injury and psychological distress on the other. Tom Jambor, a child-development scholar and specialist in the design of outdoor play environments, believes that eliminating risk in play is not only impossible but a "disservice to children's needs." He and others have argued that youngsters continually seek new challenges and that once they master a skill they naturally seek new levels of excitement. Inevitably, bumps and scratches occur along the way. Jambor would reconcile children's precarious behavior with adult anxiety by distinguishing between risk and hazard. *Risk* may occur when a player applies her or his own judgment, which may be flawed, to an act and, as a result, experiences positive or negative consequences. *Hazard* is something external that presents unnecessary danger, such as worn or unsafe playground equipment, real and accessible guns, or unsafe substances.[78] Kate Simon took a risk when she climbed and fell off a ledge. Marilyn Bell played with a hazard when she wrapped herself up in a coffin.

Jambor and others believe, then, that "children need to take risks to explore their physical selves in the social context of their peers to find out what they can and cannot do," and they regret that such opportunities have been narrowed in recent years.[79] For example, a survey by the National Association of Elementary School Principals revealed that as recently as 1989 some 90 percent of reporting school districts maintained recess for fifteen or twenty minutes once or twice a day. Since that time, pressures to improve academic performance have combined with fears of lawsuits to prompt 40 percent of the nation's forty thousand school districts to cut back, eliminate, or consider eliminating recess and lunchtime free periods from their daily schedule.[80]

On one hand, preteen children who tempt risk in their play must negotiate with adults whose attitudes sprawl across a spectrum with

210 Children's Play Goes Underground

trust in a child's judgment at one end and a desire to strictly program activities at the other. But also, adult positions often blend points of view in a contradictory way. Parents and their advisers wring their hands and impose restrictions on what youngsters see and do, while almost simultaneously agreeing that their kids need to learn from being exposed to the realities of the world, including its troubling and nasty elements. Adults have colonized childhood because they thought they understood what it should mean to be young, but in their intention to build and reinforce self-esteem they also have given children leeway to act as they (the children) pleased. Amid the inconsistency, what does seem consistent—and what some adults came to fear—is that children have more wisdom than they are given credit for having.

Jambor and others charge that in attempting to remove all challenge and risk taking, adults force children into unnecessarily dangerous ways of finding thrills and play value on their own. The critics contend that children should be able to engage in activity away from adult supervision where they can "explore and play with their environment by touching, manipulating objects and materials to test their developing cognitive constructs against reality." The answer, they say, is to create open spaces, "natural play preserves," where youngsters can run, explore, and create as they always have done. "Children have not changed," write Jambor, Marcy Guddemi, and Robin Moore. Kids want just to "be children and do childlike things."[81]

Brian Sutton-Smith has perceived children's historical quest for autonomy, which persists to the present, in a more nuanced way. As modern American society has created more amusement opportunities for adults, he has observed, the culture has developed a "disjunction" between what children do (play) and what adults do (recreation, entertainment):

> This disjuncture apparently permits us to attempt to control and domesticate children's play on behalf of their future. We rationalize our own quite irrational play behavior by calling it only entertainment, and we then prevent children from exhibiting such irrationality by saying that they will grow through their play if we keep it sanitized. We can play irrationally, . . . but they must not. By making play a rational series of steps . . . toward wisdom and understanding, we keep them under our control, and we keep out of their lives any elements

of common human irrationality that make us uncomfortable about our own systems of belief, morality, and sexuality. In these systems of belief, it is not that play prepares the future; it is rather that play, or control of it, guarantees that we can control the future of our children on our own rather narrow behalf.[82]

When Annie Dillard played detective or engaged in mock battles with her friends, when Brian Sullivan escaped his mother's apron strings to explore the city, when Kate Simon made the rooftops her "secret garden," and when children were viewed by various observers as just "goofing around," they were acting on their own to make the present tolerable, not to implement their parents' values in preparation for what to them was a distant and still vague future.

In 1994, a group of marketers of children's goods created "Kid Power" conferences and a "Kid Power Xchange" to facilitate the exchange of "youth marketing information." The organization's goal is to keep "a pulse on the kid and teen markets" and develop "strategies for successfully tapping the buying power of children, teens and families."[83] The name "Kid Power" reflects an appreciation of how children have come to exert influence over consumer choices and the commercialization of play. Most makers of consumer goods now have a "tween" strategy aimed at the preadolescent age group who have come to express passionate, well-informed desires for products such as food, toys, and electronics. Thus Kid Power's emphasis on youth marketing also represents the tightened bond between children and commercial interests, a bond that originated over a century ago and that now omits parents, except as providers. At a recent Kid Power conference, Chris McKee, a partner in the Geppetto Group marketing firm, which claims to be "dedicated to the thoughtful, responsible and catalyzing communication to kids and teens" (note the exclusion of parents), observed that "children are becoming far more sophisticated about products and entertainment" than they ever have been. Disputing the charge that children are easily manipulated in consumer society, McKee asserted, "Despite our [marketers'] best and worst intentions, we cannot get kids to buy things they don't want."[84]

Others, however, believe marketers have been disingenuously heralding the sophistication of kids when in fact they, the market-ers, exploit impressionable children and even turn them against their parents. Just as self-appointed protectors of the young wanted to rescue children from dangers of the streets in the early twentieth century, by the end of the century there was what Gary Cross has called a new "moral panic" to shield children from the violence, sexism, and overheated acquisitiveness of the consumer market.[85] Youngsters need parental wisdom, argue the critics of Kid Power and other commercial efforts, to empower children. By substituting packaged fantasy, media hucksters, according to this view, have undermined children's imaginative powers. No longer does a kid picture a fantasy world by looking at clouds or indulge in mundane contemplation such as what one's thumb is supposed to do; instead, he or she obsesses over the life of some teen pop idol or focuses on destroying objects in a computer game. Taking a cue from Piaget, who argued that learning involves a balance between discovery (what he called "assimilation") and imitation (internalizing meanings acquired from outside the self) critics assert that consumer interests have narrowed the creative range of play by defining an orthodoxy that is imposed by television programs and commercials. Advertising on TV thus tells a child what a toy—and through it, play—"means" and prescribes correct actions for particular toys and games.[86]

The diarists and other spokespersons cited in this and previous chapters did not always know what they wanted as children, and they did not always rebuff parental direction. But by the beginning of the twenty-first century, children's attempts to control their play had assumed different elements from those that had prevailed in earlier eras. Both the influence of marketers and the decline of parental influence probably have been less influential than observers from both sides have assumed. Children have been granted more freedom than their forebears had to make consumer choices, but they still depend on their parents for direction, and they adopt models from adult society. Their playthings and their own culture still are conditioned by traditional sex and family roles, but their imaginative abilities continue to flourish.[87]

Thus, while media critics and child advocates have fretted about the hypnotic, sedentary quality that television has inflicted on children, there always is the possibility that kids can convert an object as mundane as a TV box into their own plaything. Isabel Alvarez, growing up in the Bronx, spent Saturday mornings with the television turned on, but instead of being mesmerized by cartoons and adventure stories that were broadcast, she applied her imagination in a way adults never would have contemplated. A new world opened up to Isabel when her sister told her, "You know, there's a city behind the television." Isabel explained,

> See, these old televisions used to have the cardboard [backs] with holes in them. The television was on and we could see all of the lights on in the back. I remembered the structure: there were big tubes on the left and big tubes on the right and these tiny tubes in the middle. So we took the cardboard off and put our dolls in there and played that it was the city of Manhattan. It was our own doll's house.[88]

Kids still find ways to be kids.

Conclusion

TODAY, CHILDREN'S PLAY in the United States is a multibillion-dollar industry consisting of much more than the mass of toys, games, gadgets, and characters stacked on the shelves at Toys "R" Us and Walmart. The business of keeping kids happy also includes for-profit entertainment centers, media, organized sports, party planners, athletic coaches, and more. Yet the same society that has taken such great pains to enrich children's play seems also to be making children unfit, dull, and even violent. According to figures compiled by the National Center for Health Statistics, as recently as the 1960s, doctors classified about 4 percent of American children between ages six and eleven as overweight; by 2002, the percentage had quadrupled to 16 percent, and childhood obesity—not to mention childhood diabetes—had become a matter of serious national concern.[1] Much of the explanation for this trend accuses fat-filled foods and beverages that youngsters consume, but, more relevantly to this book, commentators also link a sedentary lifestyle to the apparent slack physical condition of one in six American preteens.[2] Flabbiness of mind as well as body, say critics, also results from sitting for hours on end in front of a TV or computer screen, where mass-produced story lines of violence, sex, and avarice allegedly divert young people from healthier endeavors.[3] Some even assert that the undermining of traditional active play styles, combined with mass media and a desire to treat and dress children as adults, has destroyed the entire concept of childhood.[4]

The long view of history suggests that things are never as bad, or as good, as they may seem. A survey of children's play and children's culture over the course of American history reveals several themes of continuity and change. Shifts have been both subtle and dramatic; continuities have been both obvious and overlooked. Over time, three basic changes have altered the play of American preadolescents: those involving place, those involving things, and those involving uses of time.

Major Shifts in Play

Place

From the colonial era to the present, natural play sites have diminished while constructed settings have multiplied. There is nothing surprising about the fact that, as the United States became more urban (and suburban), more families lived remote from the natural landscape, and fewer children had access to forests and fields where they could indulge in "roving" and "roaming" and where they could integrate waterways and wildlife into their play. And as informal neighborhood play has declined, many preadolescents now express their autonomy at the mall, where they "roam" either after a parent has driven them there or when they arrive by their own devices.

But simple changes in habitation do not fully account for changes in play environments; shifting cultural views of childhood have mattered, also. Parents and social arbiters always have tried to protect children from the dangers of their surroundings, but they have applied different strategies at different times. In a general sense, before the nineteenth century, parents worried less about the places where children played—as long as they did not stray too far afield—than they fretted about whether or not play accorded with God's and society's designs. As the nineteenth century advanced and built environments expanded, youngsters appropriated new sites for exploration and amusement. But their trespass onto adult-oriented spaces provoked concern over, and restriction of, their uses of those spaces. Thus an early-nineteenth-century book on *Youthful Sports* warned readers that blindman's bluff should not be played indoors, and at around the same time the city of New York banned kite flying in certain sections of town.[5]

The hazards and temptations lurking in modern urban society of the late nineteenth and early twentieth centuries intensified efforts by adults to divert children from unsafe environments into protected spaces. The playground movement and rise of Little League, clubs, scouting, and other organized activities provided settings that adults could supervise, though children did not always use those sites in hoped-for ways. By the end of the twentieth century, parents' desires to shelter and entertain youngsters resulted in expanded formal play sites, but those same desires also enlarged home-based play activity.[6] Thus, a general, though not total, shift to formal rather than ad hoc play sites has constituted one of the most salient trends in play over the past three centuries.

Things

Also, a major revolution has occurred in the matériel of play. The explosive increase of mass-produced, commercially marketed toys has come to occupy an important segment of both American consumer society and of children's culture.[7] Evolving from a society that once considered toys as insignificant baubles or ornamental objects for the amusement of adults as well as young people, to a society in which manufacturers flood the market with several thousand new toys each year, American culture has linked toys so closely with childhood that in the minds of many people toys define play itself.

Not only has the volume of commercial toys expanded, but also there have been critical changes in the nature of toys and in the ways that children have used playthings. First, as childhood came to be appreciated as a separate and special stage of life in the early nineteenth century, toys became more closely related to childhood. They were "children's tools." In addition, formal—meaning manufactured—toys assumed ever-larger functions of entertaining and educating children and as rewards for desired behavior. Later in the century, the number of mass-produced toys increased dramatically, as American manufacturers of dolls and other play goods came into their own. Still, from the seventeenth century through the nineteenth, homemade and improvised playthings continued to define some of children's most favored possessions.

By the early twentieth century, many of the toys that current parents and grandparents fondly remember—baby dolls, Lincoln Logs, erector and chemistry sets, and board games—became common, thereby reinforcing gender roles and providing gift ideas for parents and relatives hoping to secure their children's affection. After 1950, however, a significant shift occurred. The rise of television and marketing directly to children kindled demands for fantasy and character toys that are understood best by children without adult mediation. In many cases, children's preferences, measured by scientific surveys, determines a toy's "play value" and, therefore, its role in the marketplace. As well, the extraordinary effect of electronic and computer-based entertainment plus the internet have given children diversions that some observers have decried and others have applauded.

The recent nexus between play objects, mass media, and electronics has produced another noteworthy effect. That is, media-based computer and video games in particular have helped create a play culture in which age identities have become compressed: preteens prefer to think of themselves as older youths, and many adults adopt the playthings and clothing styles of adolescents—or, at least of college students. Whereas a few decades ago, eight- and nine-year-old girls and boys found gratifying amusement by playing with Barbie, G.I. Joe, tea sets, and dump trucks, many preteens now reject these toys as "babyish" and instead favor action-oriented computer games, high-intensity sports such as skiing and skateboarding, "real" fashion obtainable at the mall (as opposed to "dressing up" in parents' clothing), and other pastimes that also amuse older age groups. What formerly had been adolescent culture now finds patronage among preadolescents. Currently, marketers who once sought to sell toys to fourteen year olds have lowered their age target to ten, and *Seventeen* magazine now aims much of its content at preteens.[8] Simultaneously, adults, in their clothing, television, and movie tastes, as well as their objects of amusement, have manifested choices that formerly related to adolescence and college age. In other words, children's "aspirational age" has risen, while that of adults has fallen.[9] An eleven year old no longer asks for a stuffed animal or fire truck and instead desires a Madden NFL football game, a cell phone, an iPod, or a Beyoncé Knowles CD, while a thirty-five year old may also indulge by buying a Madden football game, a cell phone, an iPod, or a Beyoncé Knowles CD.[10]

Time

In every era, a catalog of constraints has impinged on the time children have had to play. The limitations have operated in complex ways. Social class has always determined how young people use their time. In most eras, youngsters from farm and urban working-class families have had to labor in the family economy: toiling in the fields and the household, serving in the waged workforce, and caring for younger siblings. They had to steal time for play, or, as was often the case, they blended playful activity into their work. As middle-class culture came to value and romanticize childhood in the nineteenth century, parents were more willing to grant their offspring more time for toys, games, and hobbies, as long as time was not spent "idling" and that these pastimes cultivated obedience and "habits of reflection." By the end of the century, playtime had received full affirmation, but more than ever, professional child workers believed that during that time, children, in the words of Maria Kraus-Boelte, "must be taught how to play."[11]

In the twentieth century, two related forces converged to alter the playtime of preadolescents in significant ways. First, the extension of compulsory schooling filled much of all children's daytime hours, regardless of social class, incidentally strengthening peer cultures that increasingly socialized young people in play choices. A partial reduction in a child's family responsibilities, resulting in part from smaller family size and the spread of labor-saving electric appliances, helped create time after school and in the evening during which youngsters could interact with their peer group or play alone with a new cornucopia of commercial playthings. And during the first half of the century, at least, this playtime often took place away from adult supervision in private bedrooms and other secluded areas of the home.

But increasingly, the second factor, parental anxieties over child safety and child achievement, has intensified to the point that parents, supported by all types of public and private interests, have imposed formal activities on children's formerly unstructured and "free" playtime.[12] For underprivileged children, this movement—which some have called an "invasion"—has meant after-school recreational and sports programs in boys' and girls' clubs, neighborhood clubs, YMCAs and YWCAs, and other such agencies. Among middle-class youngsters, karate and gymnastics lessons, computer and foreign-language instruction, soccer and basketball leagues, and school homework have replaced the informal "scrub" baseball that the young Bruce Catton and Louise Dickinson Rich played and the "side-yard" shows that Sylvia McNeely liked to organize.[13] Among all classes, many of today's parents tolerate extensive television viewing and video game playing by their children as alternatives to unsupervised activity on city streets where, if the media could be believed, perils of abuse, abduction, and assault stalk every corner. Even in supposedly "secure" suburbs, many parents prevent their children from straying away from the house to play unobserved in the neighborhood. Thus, although precise data are difficult to come by, there are powerful indications that youngsters at present spend far more time indoors—mostly occupied by TV, the computer, and formal activity—than their predecessors did.[14]

The Quest for Independent Play

Nevertheless, kids still want to be kids in their own way, and although they are generally willing to follow adult prescriptions, they also inhabit an independent, underground culture of self-devised play. And thus the two main continuities in children's play are the quest for autonomy and the demonstration of creativity.

Throughout American history, children often have inhabited two cultural realms, one that abides the expectations of parents and one that sustains children's alternative and sometimes contrary inclinations. That second realm has constituted children's independent play culture. The "Boy's Town" that the young William Dean Howells inhabited, for example, represented a secret place—there were "Girls' Towns," too—that many preadolescent children kept secret from adults, a place, perhaps just a state of mind, where they did things on their own. This special world, this private culture, offered a refuge in which children could amuse themselves at those times when, as Catherine Havens complained to her diary, "grownup people [did not] understand what children liked."[15] Sometimes, youngsters acted alone in this retreat, founding what John Updike labeled "a solitary one-person tribe."[16] Chester Himes constituted such a tribe when he skipped school to roam the streets of St. Louis, and Alice Clifford created a private realm of fantasy for herself when she cut out paper dolls and made up stories for them.[17] On other occasions, a troop of youngsters reveled in the "gang-forming spirit" that James Langdon Hill found so rewarding, when Pierrepont Noyes and his pals created a hidden clubhouse above his community's sugar storehouse, or when Emily Kimbrough and her friends prepared a "magic concoction" to attract fairies.[18]

Children might not have considered adults to be the "natural enemies of kids," as Robert Paul Smith wryly averred, but they often might have agreed with Frances Parkinson Keyes that in matters of their own, "We did not seek . . . advice from any of our elders."[19] Seeking and protecting autonomy were vital preoccupations of youngsters throughout all eras. Whether they pursued their freedom guiltily, as Devereux Jarratt did when he confessed the "depraved nature" of his play in the eighteenth century; impishly, as Adeline Atwater did when she flaunted her "dare-devil spirit" in the nineteenth century; or slyly, as when Barbara Jordan would "literally sneak out" of her house to play in forbidden ways in the twentieth century, children constantly rebelled against the controls that adults wished to impose on their play.

One qualification to this constancy is in order, however. Several factors at work presently have altered the quality of many a child's quest for independence. Preteens like Adeline Atwater may still exhibit a "dare-devil spirit," and inner-city youngsters like Barbara Jordan might still "sneak out" to play in the neighborhood, but suburbanized, media-crazed society confronts children with constraints that differ from those of the past. Children of today take risks, as evidenced by the 150,000 youngsters treated annually for playground injuries.[20] But parental anxieties over real and imagined dangers have expanded indoor playtime and, especially for middle-class youngsters, have made it harder to "sneak out."[21] Instead, children sometimes conspire against parental control by taking risks in cyberworld —either by innocently entering websites where danger lurks or by defiantly viewing or interacting with scenes and people that are inappropriate for their age. Moreover, as suggested previously, by spending so many hours in structured (safety-conscious), adult-supervised activities or in front of a TV screen, youngsters simply have less time to be daredevils.

Nevertheless, the many reflections conveyed by diarists, autobiographers, and child observers presented in the chapters of this book should serve as testament to the impressive creativity that children have demonstrated throughout American history. It is amusing to picture Emily Wilson in the early nineteenth century gleefully whirling around on the rotary top of her family's stove while her sister turned the crank that spun her,[22] to imagine oneself at the end of the nineteenth century playing the complicated street game of "kick-the-wicket" invented by the boys whom folklorist Stuart Culin witnessed,[23] or to marvel at the flying "Dragonnette" that Edwin Teale fashioned in the early twentieth century from discarded materials that he was able to collect.[24] There seems no limit to children's imaginations.

A number of observers strongly believe that today's youngsters lack the kinds of originality described above. Critics such as Neil Postman charge that the media, with their packaged images and outlandish characters, dull children's imaginations, shrink their attention spans, and induce them to expect rather than create stimulation.

JOYS OF FREE PLAY. Playing on their own, taking risks, testing themselves, children always have—and, it is hoped, always will—discover the joys of independent play. *Library of Congress*

According to Susan L. Rechhia from Columbia University Teachers College, "There is a passivity that comes from having toys that entertain you."[25] Electronic toys allegedly discourage children from inventing play on their own. All a player supposedly needs to do is push a button, and after the toy has performed its functions, a child becomes bored and wants something else for amusement. And unlike dolls of the past, fantasy play characters of the present come with their own personalities and story lines that supposedly discourage a child from inventing an original play world.[26]

There seems to be at least some substance to these charges. As I argue in this volume, children always had places, things, and opportunities for unstructured, child-created play, especially in the "golden age" of the early twentieth century when the concept of joyous childhood converged with American consumer society. But these have diminished in recent times. The result has been a new style of play, one that indeed, though not always, can stifle creativity. Moreover, among middle-class children—and among working-class youngsters as well

—the profusion of formal, adult-regulated activities has generated somewhat of a reversion to the notion of play as the child's "work," with youngsters' time outside of school occupied by "useful" pastimes intended to enhance their physical, social, and intellectual skills.

Still, it is hard to conclude that adults have taken the fun out of childhood. Anyone who has witnessed a group of girls creating their own musical or dramatic performance, or a group of boys reproducing a baseball or basketball game in which they mimic their favorite players, would be impressed by how much such children know and how much imagination has gone into their efforts. Adults who fret that multiple hours in front of a television set marinate children's brains with useless drivel and divert them from more constructive pursuits may forget that, like their parents, kids can multitask. Even though the TV may appear to isolate them, youngsters can simultaneously play a game, talk on the phone, work on a hobby, read, eat, and even do their homework while images flash on the screen before them. This talent may not make all these activities pleasurable, but it does challenge conclusions by those such as children's book author Marie Winn who has complained that children "are always watching television . . . rather than having any other experience."[27] Moreover, some observers believe that the real appeal of playing with current action and fashion toys derives from the way that kids integrate both their *knowledge* of expected drama and their *application* of imagined drama. Children do have ability to twist packaged fantasy to fit their own purposes.[28]

I do not wish to advocate that adults refrain from guiding those purposes; history shows that parents always have given, and always will give, useful meaning to children's play. But American culture in the early twenty-first century has constricted the play of young people as never before. We earnestly believe that our open, technological society has made children increasingly vulnerable to all kinds of dangers. So we legitimately take every precaution to insulate them from accidents, from faulty equipment, from predators, from pornography, from drugs, and more. Most of all, we try not to leave them unsupervised, and as a result they either play indoors or they fill their time with activities that have left them overorganized. Yet also, modern child-indulgent culture thrusts preteen children into adulthood by dressing them (or allowing them to dress) in adult clothing, exposing them to mature themes in the media, and forcing them to confront the

stresses of divorce, poverty, war, prejudice, and more.[29] Thus preadolescent youngsters stand at a crossroads, with one foot in childhood
and the other planted in the adult world, and adults are ambiguous
about what should happen at that crossroads.[30]

The ambiguity over children's role—playful kids or serious
achievers—has infected some modes of structured play, particularly
organized sports competition, where of late ugly incidents have occurred. The troublemakers have been parents far more frequently than
they have been children. Numerous incidents of assaults, and even a
murder, have taken place when an overinvolved parent has attacked
an official, parent of a child on an opposing team, a member of the opposing team, or his or her own child. In addition, intense, year-round
involvement by preteens in a single sport activity rather than "playing" in a variety of sports, abetted by parents who crave that their
child achieve utmost excellence, has led to an increase in stress injuries
caused by overtraining and has drained the finances of many families
hoping for a college scholarship or a professional contract.[31] No wonder twelve-year-old swimmers and gymnasts burn out and leave their
sport. This is not play.

It has become fashionable for analysts to recommend that parents devote more time to their children. Parents somehow have come
to believe that they *must* "support" their child by attending every
game, event, and performance in which a son or daughter is involved.
Otherwise, their child might feel abandoned, unloved. But, for preadolescents at least, we need to think more carefully about how *play*—
in Tom Sawyer's meaning of something one is not obliged to do—
should be the private domain of childhood. Perhaps we should consider how and when to give kids more independence to explore their
environment, create playthings, interact with other kids, and simply
enjoy being young. Once again, I return to the wisdom of Robert Paul
Smith on this matter. At the end of *"Where Did You Go?" "Out" "What
Did You Do?" "Nothing,"* Smith protested,

> My fear now is that all of us grownups have become so childish that
> we don't leave the kids much room to move around in, that we fool-
> ishly believe that we understand them so well because we share
> things with them.
>
> This is not only folly, it is not fair. At somebody's house one night,
> a harassed father who was trying to talk to grownups with his brood

around, finally spoke a simple sentence of despair, "For Gossakes, go upstairs or downstairs."

He was, I believe, asking for privacy. He was, I believe, entitled to it.

I think kids are too.[32]

Yes, I think kids are too.

Notes

All citations to Rawick, Suppl. 1, refer to interviews and narratives collected between 1936 and 1938 under the auspices of the Work Projects Administration (and known as the WPA Slave Narratives), published in George P. Rawick, ed., *The American Slave: A Composite Autobiography*, supplement series 1, 12 vols. (Westport, Conn.: Greenwood, 1978). *Mississippi Narratives* encompass vols. 6–10; *Georgia Narratives* encompass vols. 3–4. There is also a supplement series 2 of 10 vols. The full set includes almost four thousand WPA slave narratives, organized by state.

Notes to the Preface

1. Harvey Graff, *Conflicting Paths: Growing Up in America* (Cambridge, Mass.: Harvard University Press, 1995), p. 23.

2. For example, Timothy Dow Adams, *Telling Lies in Modern American Autobiography* (Chapel Hill: University of North Carolina Press, 1990); Kathleen Ashley, Leigh Gilmore, and Gerald Peters, eds., *Autobiography and Post-Modernism* (Amherst: University of Massachusetts Press, 1994); Sidonie Smith and Julia Watson, eds., *Getting a Life: Everyday Uses of Autobiography* (Minneapolis: University of Minnesota Press, 1996).

3. Graff, *Conflicting Paths*, p. 24.

4. A large body of critical scholarship exists on how to read and evaluate autobiography. Among the most useful are Sidonie Smith and Julia Watson, *Reading Autobiography: A Guide for Interpreting Life Narratives* (Minneapolis: University of Minnesota Press, 2001); Timothy Dow Adams, *Telling Lies in Modern Autobiography* (Chapel Hill: University of North Carolina Press, 1990); and Liahna Babener, "Bitter Nostalgia: Recollections of Childhood on the Midwestern Frontier," in Elliott West and Paula Petrik, eds., *Small World: Children and Adolescents in America, 1850–1950* (Lawrence: University Press of Kansas, 1992).

5. Burness E. Moore and Bernard D. Fine, eds., *Psychoanalytic Terms and Concepts* (New Haven, Conn.: Yale University Press, 1990).

6. Erik Erikson, *Childhood and Society* (New York: Norton, 1950).

7. For example, Judith Rich Harris, *The Nurture Assumption: Why Children*

Turn Out the Way They Do (New York: Free Press, 1998), pp. 91–92, 160–65, 179–80; and Beatrice Blyth Whiting and Carolyn Pope Edwards, *Children of Different Worlds: The Formation of Social Behavior* (Cambridge, Mass.: Harvard University Press, 1988), pp. 85–132

8. For example, Media Awareness Network, "Special Issues for Tweens and Teens," 2004, http://www.media-awareness.ca/english/parents/marketing/issues_teens_marketing.cfm (accessed October 10, 2005).

9. Linda Perlstein, *Not Much, Just Chillin': The Hidden Lives of Middle Schoolers* (New York: Ballantine, 2003), p. 55.

Notes to the Introduction

1. Mark Twain, *The Adventures of Tom Sawyer* (New York: Harper and Brothers, 1875), p. 33.

2. Neil J. Smeltzer and Paul B. Baltes, eds., *International Encyclopedia of the Social and Behavioral Sciences*, 1st ed. (Amsterdam: Elsevier, 2001), vol. 17, pp. 11,501, 11,503.

3. Brian Sutton-Smith, the foremost scholar of children's play, has summarized most of the important theories in *The Ambiguity of Play* (Cambridge, Mass.: Harvard University Press, 1997). See also Sutton-Smith's *Toys as Culture* (New York: Gardner, 1986). Some recent theory on the psychological functions of play can be found in Catherine Garvey, *Play*, enl. ed. (Cambridge, Mass.: Harvard University Press, 1990), and Jeffrey H. Goldstein, ed., *Toys, Play, and Child Development* (New York: Cambridge University Press, 1994).

4. Much of the most important theorizing on play derives from the French philosopher and writer Roger Caillois and the Dutch historian Johan Huizinga. Caillois elaborated his theory of play in *Man, Play, and Games*, translated by Meyer Barash (New York: Free Press, 1961). Huizinga's major work in this field is *Homo Ludens: A Study of the Play Element in Culture* (Boston: Beacon, 1955).

5. These distinctions of play are derived from Marcy Guddemi, Tom Jambor, and Robin Moore, "Advocacy for the Child's Right to Play," in Doris Fromberg and Doris Bergen, eds., *Play from Birth to Twelve and Beyond* (New York: Garland, 1998), esp. pp. 519–20.

6. An early finding of this sort is Harvey C. Lehman and Paul A. Witty, *The Psychology of Play Activities* (New York: A. S. Barnes, 1927), pp. 189–90. See also Sutton-Smith, *Ambiguity of Play*, p. 46.

7. Caillois, *Man, Play, and Games*, p. 28

8. Sutton-Smith, *Ambiguity of Play*, pp. 46–47, 231–32.

9. The label of play as children's work has been attributed to Susan S. F. Isaacs in her work, *Social Development in Young Children* (1933), quoted in P. K. Smith, "Play, Ethology, and Education: A Personal Account," in T. A. Pelle-

grini, ed., *The Future of Play Theory* (Albany: SUNY Press, 1995), pp. 1–22. On play as the "business of childhood," see Jerome Bruner, Alison Jolly, and Kathy Silva, *Play: Its Role in Development and Evolution* (New York: Penguin, 1976), p. 26.

10. Gary Cross, *Kids' Stuff: Toys and the Changing World of American Childhood* (Cambridge, Mass.: Harvard University Press, 1997), p. 144.

11. Garvey, *Play*, pp. 6–7. See also Steven M. Gelber's definition of leisure, which applies to play as well, in *Hobbies: Leisure and the Culture of Work in America* (New York: Columbia University Press), p. 7.

12. Sutton-Smith, *Ambiguity of Play*, p. 49.

13. David Nasaw, *Children of the City: At Work and at Play* (Garden City, N.Y.: Anchor/Doubleday, 1985), p. viii.

14. Rena L. Vassar, "The Life or Biography of Silas Felton, Written by Himself," *American Antiquarian Society Proceedings* 69 (1959), p. 127; R. L. Duffus, *Williamstown Branch: Impersonal Memories of a Vermont Boyhood* (New York: W. W. Norton, 1958), pp. 45–46.

15. Amanda Dargan and Steven Zeitlin, *City Play* (New Brunswick, N.J.: Rutgers University Press, 1990), pp. 10–12.

16. Bellamy Partridge, *Country Lawyer* (New York: McGraw-Hill, 1939), p. 97; Sarah Bixby Smith, *Adobe Days* (Cedar Rapids, Iowa: Torch, 1925), p. 35; Henry May, *Coming to Terms: A Study in Memory and History* (Berkeley: University of California Press, 1987), p. 4. Details of city play are in Chapters 4 and 6.

17. Dargan and Zeitlin, *City Play*, pp. 10–11, 23, 40.

18. Details on child/adult boundaries and control are in Chapters 4, 5, and 6.

19. Dargan and Zeitlin, *City Play*, p. 146.

20. Barbara Kirschenblatt-Gimblett, "The Aesthetics of Everyday Life," quoted in Amanda Dargan and Steven Zeitlin, "City Play," in Doris Fromberg and Doris Bergen, eds., *Play from Birth to Twelve and Beyond* (New York: Garland, 1998), p. 223.

21. Sutton-Smith, *Toys as Culture*, pp. 26, 64.

22. Sutton-Smith, *Ambiguity of Play*, pp. 2–3, 247; Cross, *Kids' Stuff*, p. 12.

23. Dargan and Zeitlin, *City Play*, p. 106; Bernard Mergen, "Made, Bought, and Stolen: Toys and the Culture of Childhood," in Elliott West and Paula Petrik, eds., *Small World: Children and Adolescents in America, 1850–1950* (Lawrence: University Press of Kansas, 1992), p. 89.

24. Mergen, *Play and Playthings*, pp. 103–4. See also Karin Calvert, *Children in the House: The Material Culture of Early Childhood, 1600–1900* (Boston: Northeastern University Press, 1992), pp. 5–6.

25. Bruce Catton, *Waiting for the Morning Train: An American Boyhood* (Garden City, N.Y.: Doubleday, 1972), p. 41; Estha Brisco Stowe, *Oil Field Child* (Fort Worth: Texas Christian University Press, 1989), p. 108; Ruby Berkley

Goodwin, *It's Good to Be Black* (Garden City, N.Y.: Doubleday, 1953); Elizabeth Laura Adams, *Dark Symphony, and Other Works* (New York: G. K. Hall, 1996).

26. Television is discussed in Chapters 7 and 8.

27. Mergen, "Made, Bought, and Sold," p. 88; Dargan and Zeitlin, *City Play*, p. 220.

28. Recent safety and production cost concerns have caused the replacement of wood by plastic in most of these toys. The safety issue will become an important theme in later chapters.

29. Cross, *Kids' Stuff*, pp. 139–44.

30. Birgitta Almqvist, "Educational Toys, Creative Toys," in Jeffrey H. Goldstein, ed., *Toys, Play, and Child Development* (Cambridge: Cambridge University Press, 1994), p. 65.

31. Jerome Singer, "Imaginative Play and Adoptive Development," in Jeffrey H. Goldstein, ed., *Toys, Play, and Child Development* (Cambridge: Cambridge University Press, 1994), p. 21; Dargan and Zeitlin, *City Play*, p. 162; Mergen, *Play and Playthings*, p. 98; Tom Jambor, "Challenge and Risk-Taking in Play," in Doris Fromberg and Doris Bergen, eds., *Play from Birth to Twelve and Beyond* (New York: Garland, 1998), p. 320.

32. Brian Sutton-Smith, "Does Play Prepare the Future?" in Jeffrey H. Goldstein, ed., *Toys, Play, and Child Development* (Cambridge: Cambridge University Press, 1994), p. 145.

33. The relationship between toys and media in the current era, however, contradicts this conclusion because children play with a character-related object in ways that are strictly defined within the storyline or personality presented in a movie or TV show. Thus, a child would insist on using a Batmobile only in imitation of how Batman would use it, or build a drama around Rapunzel Barbie only within the fairy tale of the character. For more on this, see Chapter 6.

34. Anthony D. Pellegrini and Ithel Jones, "Play, Toys, and Language," in Jeffrey H. Goldstein, ed., *Toys, Play, and Child Development* (Cambridge: Cambridge University Press, 1994), pp. 28–30; Brian Sutton-Smith, "The Play of Girls," in Claire B. Kopp, ed., *Becoming Female: Perspectives on Development* (New York: Plenum Press, 1979), pp. 236–37; Jeffrey Goldstein, "Sex Differences in Toy Play and Use of Video Games," in Jeffrey H. Goldstein, ed., *Toys, Play, and Child Development* (Cambridge: Cambridge University Press, 1994), pp. 114–16, 125–28; Almqvist, "Educational Toys, Creative Toys," p. 65; Steven Kline, *Out of the Garden: Toys, TV, and Children's Culture in the Age of Marketing* (London: Verso, 1993), pp. 247–49.

35. Sutton-Smith, *Toys as Culture*, pp. 2–3, 5; Singer, "Imaginative Play and Adoptive Development," pp. 22–25; Eugene Provenzano Jr., "Electronically Mediated Playscapes," in Doris Fromberg and Doris Bergen, eds., *Play*

from Birth to Twelve and Beyond (New York: Garland, 1998), p. 513; Kline, *Out of the Garden,* p. 50.

36. Sutton-Smith, *Toys as Culture,* p. 247.

37. Solitary play is discussed in Chapters 6 and 8.

38. Shlomo Ariel and Irene Sever, "Play in the Desert and Play in the Town: On Play Activities of Bedouin Arab Children," in Helen Schwartzman, ed., *Play and Culture* (West Point, N.Y.: Leisure Press, 1980), pp. 164–74. See also Sutton-Smith, *Ambiguity of Play,* pp. 42–43; and William A. Corsaro and Katherine Schwarz, "Peer Play and Socialization in Two Cultures," in Barbara Scales, Millie Almy, Agelki Nicolopoulou, and Susan Erwin-Tripp, *Play and the Social Context of Development in Early Care and Education* (New York: Teachers College, Columbia University, 1991), pp. 234–35. Douglas Newton is quoted in Iona Opie and Peter Opie, *Children's Games in Street and Playground* (Oxford: Clarendon, 1969), p. 2.

39. L. Joseph Stone and Joseph Church, *Childhood and Adolescence: A Psychology of the Growing Person,* 2nd ed. (New York: Random House, 1968), p. 370.

40. Elliott West and Paula Petrik, eds., "Introduction," *Small World: Children and Adolescents in America, 1850–1950* (Lawrence: University Press of Kansas, 1992), p. 11.

41. Fritz Redl, *When We Deal with Children: Selected Writings* (New York: Free Press, 1967), p. 395, quoted in Gary Alan Fine, *With the Boys: Little League Baseball and Preadolescent Culture* (Chicago: University of Chicago Press, 1987), p. 7.

42. Louise Dickinson Rich, *We Took to the Woods* (New York: J. B. Lippincott, 1942), p. 118; Caryl Rivers, *Aphrodite at Mid-Century: Growing Up Catholic and Female in Post-war America* (Garden City, N.Y.: Doubleday, 1973), p. 20.

43. Robert Paul Smith, *"Where Did You Go?" "Out" "What Did You Do?" "Nothing"* (New York: W. W. Norton, 1957), pp. 8–9.

44. Bernard Mergen, "The Discovery of Children's Play," *American Quarterly* 27 (October 1975), p. 399.

45. Dargan and Zeitlin, *City Play,* pp. 136, 162; Joseph E. Illick, *American Childhood* (Philadelphia: University of Pennsylvania Press, 2002), p. x.

46. Harvey Graff, *Conflicting Paths: Growing Up in America* (Cambridge, Mass.: Harvard University Press, 1995), p. x.

47. Sutton-Smith, *Toys as Culture,* pp. 230–32; Kline, *Out of the Garden,* pp. 247–48.

48. Graff, *Conflicting Paths,* p. 11; Kline, *Out of the Garden,* pp. 44–45; Sutton-Smith, *Ambiguity of Play,* p. 42.

49. Piaget's and Vygotsky's theories on this topic are succinctly summarized in Pellegrini and Jones, "Play, Toys, and Language," pp. 38–39. See also

Erving Goffman, *Encounters: Two Studies in the Sociology of Interaction* (Indianapolis: Bobbs-Merrill, 1961), p. 17.

50. Fine, *With the Boys,* p. 60.

51. Ibid., p. 101.

52. William Wells Newell, *Games and Songs of American Children* (New York: Dover, 1963), p. 22; emphasis added. This is a reprint of the 2nd edition from 1903; first published in 1883.

53. "Prince Johnson," in Rawick, Suppl. 1, *Mississippi Narratives,* vol. 7, p. 1169; Kate Simon, *Bronx Primitive: Portraits in a Childhood* (New York: Viking, 1982), pp. 4–5.

54. Frances Parkinson Keyes, *Roses in December* (New York: Liveright, 1960), p. 32.

55. Opie and Opie, *Children's Games in Street and Playground,* p. 16; Schwartzman, *Play and Culture,* pp. 210–11.

56. Schwartzman, *Play and Culture,* p. 202; Sutton-Smith, "Does Play Prepare the Future," p. 146; Jambor, "Challenge and Risk-Taking in Play," p. 322.

Notes to Chapter I

1. Rena L. Vassar, "The Life or Biography of Silas Felton Written by Himself," *American Antiquarian Society Proceedings* 69 (1959), p. 127.

2. Premarital pregnancy rates increased notably from the seventeenth century to the eighteenth; nevertheless, the vast majority of children were born to married women.

3. Steven Mintz, *Huck's Raft: A History of American Childhood* (Cambridge, Mass.: Harvard University Press, 2004), p. 43; George Francis Dow, *Slave Ships and Slaving* (Salem, Mass.: Marine Research Society, 1927), pp. 172–73.

4. Gary B. Nash, *Red, White, and Black: The Peoples of Early America,* 2nd ed. (Englewood Cliffs, N.J.: Prentice Hall, 1982), pp. 16–22; William N. Fenton, "The Iroquois in History," in Eleanor Burke Leacock and Nancy Oestreich Lurie, eds., *North American Indians in Historical Perspective* (New York: Random House, 1971), p. 139.

5. Mintz, *Huck's Raft,* pp. 15–17, 20, 37–38; Harvey Graff, *Conflicting Paths: Growing Up in America* (Cambridge, Mass.: Harvard University Press, 1995), p. 66; Mary Ann Mason, *From Father's Property to Children's Rights: The History of Child Custody in the United States* (New York: Columbia University Press, 1994), p. 30.

6. Graff, *Conflicting Paths,* p. 66; John Demos, *A Little Commonwealth: Family Life in Plymouth Colony* (New York: Oxford University Press, 1970), pp. 100–106; Ross W. Beals, "In Search of the Historical Child: Miniature Adulthood

and Youth in Colonial New England," *American Quarterly* 27 (October 1975), pp. 381–84; Mintz, *Huck's Raft*, pp. 11–23, 39–41.

7. Quoted in Demos, *Little Commonwealth*, pp. 134–35.

8. For example, Linda Pollock, *Forgotten Children: Parent-Child Relations from 1500 to 1900* (Cambridge: Cambridge University Press, 1983); Peter Petschauer, "The Childrearing Modes in Flux: An Historian's Reflections," *Journal of Psychohistory* 17 (Summer 1989), 1–34.

9. Karin Calvert, *Children in the House: The Material Culture of Early Childhood, 1600–1900* (Boston: Northeastern University Press, 1992), p. 6; Demos, *Little Commonwealth*, pp. 100–103.

10. The most useful study of native and white child-raising in colonial times is Gloria L. Main, *Peoples of a Spacious Land: Families and Culture in Colonial New England* (Cambridge, Mass.: Harvard University Press, 2001), esp. pp. 117–55. See also Joseph Ilick, *American Childhood* (Philadelphia: University of Pennsylvania Press, 2002), pp. 9–11; and Nash, *Red, White, and Black*, p. 22. The summary of David Zeisberger's diary is in Mintz, *Huck's Raft*, pp. 34–35, and James Axtell, *The Indian Peoples of Eastern America: A Documentary History of the Sexes* (New York: Oxford University Press, 1981), pp. 23–25.

11. Mintz, *Huck's Raft*, pp. 42–47; Philip Morgan, *Slave Counterpoint: Black Culture in Eighteenth-Century Chesapeake and Lowcountry* (Chapel Hill: University of North Carolina Press, 1998), pp. 501–2, 507, 540–47.

12. Cotton Mather, quoted in Mintz, *Huck's Raft*, p. 46. See also Pollock, *Forgotten Children*, pp. 97–123, and Main, *Peoples of a Spacious Land*, pp. 117–19, 131–35.

13. Douglas Adair, ed., "The Autobiography of the Reverend Devereux Jarratt, 1732–1763," *William and Mary Quarterly* 9, no. 3 (3rd ser., July 1952), 346–93.

14. Ilick, *American Childhood*, p. 30. See also Bernard Mergen, *Play and Playthings: A Reference Guide* (Westport, Conn.: Greenwood, 1982), pp. 6–8; Calvert, *Children in the House*, p. 50.

15. Quoted in Harvey C. Lehman and Paul A. Witty, *The Psychology of Play Activities* (New York: A. S. Barnes, 1927), p. 2.

16. Calvert, *Children in the House*, p. 47; Gary Cross, *Kids' Stuff: Toys and the Changing World of American Childhood* (Cambridge, Mass.: Harvard University Press, 1997), p. 20; and Stephen Kline, *Out of the Garden: Toys, TV, and Children's Culture in the Age of Marketing* (London: Verso, 1993), p. 145.

17. John Locke, *Some Thoughts on Education* (Cambridge, Mass.: Cambridge University Press, 1968), pp. 211–12.

18. Mergen, *Play and Playthings*, pp. 7–8; Brian Sutton-Smith, *Toys as Culture* (New York: Gardner, 1986), pp. 116, 120.

19. John Cotton, quoted in Edmund Morgan, *The Puritan Family: Essays*

on Religion and Domestic Relations in Seventeenth-Century New England (Boston: Trustees of the Public Library, 1944), p. 66.

20. Philip Greven, *The Protestant Temperament: Patterns of Child-Rearing, Religious Experience, and Self in Early America* (New York: Knopf, 1977), pp. 9–16.

21. Main, *Peoples of a Spacious Land*, pp. 137–38, 152; Axtell, *Indian Peoples of Eastern America*, pp. 25–27; Mintz, *Huck's Raft*, p. 35.

22. Vassar, "Life or Biography of Silas Felton," p. 127; Mary E. Dewey, ed., *Life and Letters of Catharine Sedgwick* (New York: Harper and Row, 1871), p. 46; Daniel Drake, *Pioneer Life in Kentucky* (New York: Henry Schuman, 1948), p. 119; Levi Beardsley, "Reminiscences," in Louis C. Jones, ed., *Growing Up in the Cooper Country* (Syracuse, N.Y.: Syracuse University Press, 1965), p. 39.

23. Beardsley, "Reminiscences," p. 43.

24. Calvert, *Children in the House*, pp. 49, 81–82; Main, *Peoples of a Spacious Land*, pp. 152–53; Ilick, *American Childhood*, p. 9.

25. Vasser, "Life or Biography of Silas Felton," pp. 126–27; John Bailhache, "Autobiography," manuscript collections of the American Antiquarian Society, Worcester, Massachusetts, n.d.; Ann Green Winslow, "Laughterre Is Apt to Seize Me," in Josef Berger and Dorothy Berger, eds., *Small Voices* (New York: Paul S. Ericksson, 1966), p. 228; Drake, *Pioneer Life in Kentucky*, p. 120.

26. Calvert, *Children in the House*, p. 50; Winslow, "Laughterre Is Apt to Seize Me," p. 228.

27. Cross, *Kids' Stuff*, p. 20; Calvert, *Children in the House*, p. 47; Bernard Barenhoz and Inex McClintock, *American Antique Toys, 1830–1900* (New York: Harry N. Abrams, 1980), p. 27; Birgitta Almqvist, "Educational Toys, Creative Toys," in Jeffrey H. Goldstein, ed., *Toys, Play, and Child Development* (New York: Cambridge University Press, 1994), pp. 46–48.

28. Cross, *Kids' Stuff*, p. 20; Antonia Fraser, *A History of Toys* (New York: Delacorte, 1966), p. 63; Katherine McClinton, *Antiques of American Childhood* (New York: Bramhall House, 1970), pp. 250–88; Inez McClintock and Marshall McClintock, *Toys in America* (Washington, D.C.: Public Affairs Press, 1961), pp. 22, 67, 78–84; Samuel G. Goodrich, *Recollections of a Lifetime*, 2 vols. (New York: Miller, Orton, and Mulligan, 1856), vol. 1, pp. 92–93.

29. Philip Vickers Fithian, quoted in Calvert, *Children in the House*, p. 31.

30. Almqvist, "Educational Toys, Creative Toys," pp. 46–48; Sutton-Smith, *Toys as Culture*, pp. 119, 225; Calvert, *Children in the House*, pp. 80–81.

31. Esther Edwards, ". . . The Useful Sweetness of Walking with God," in Josef Berger and Dorothy Berger, eds., *Small Voices* (New York: Paul S. Ericksson, 1966), pp. 20–21.

32. Lucy Larcom, quoted in Calvert, *Children in the House*, p. 81; Dewey, *Life and Letters of Sedgwick*, p. 58; Graff, *Conflicting Paths*, p. 57.

33. Samuel West, "Memoirs," manuscript collections of the American Antiquarian Society, Worcester, Massachusetts, 1807; Samuel Moody, quoted in John Walzer, "A Period of Ambivalence: Eighteenth-Century American Childhood," in Lloyd De Mause, ed., *The History of Childhood* (New York: Psychohistory Press, 1974), p. 373.

34. Greven, *Protestant Temperament,* p. 16.

35. Peter Cartwright, *The Autobiography of Peter Cartwright, the Backwoods Preacher,* ed. W. P. Strickland (Cincinnati: L. Swoomstedt and A. Poe, 1856). p. 31.

36. Mergen, *Play and Playthings,* p. 138; Graff, *Conflicting Paths,* p. 11.

37. "Diary of Nahum Jones," manuscript collections of the American Antiquarian Society, Worcester, Massachusetts, 1938.

38. Calvert, *Children in the House,* pp. 44–46, 83–84.

39. Ibid., pp. 83–84, 92.

40. John Barnard, quoted in James Axtell, *The School upon a Hill: Education and Society in Colonial New England* (New York: Yale University Press, 1974), p. 196.

41. Mergen, *Play and Playthings,* p. 14.

Notes to Chapter 2

1. Fanny Newell, *Memoirs of Fanny Newell, Written by Herself* (Kennebec, Me.: Hallowell, 1824); Joshua Evans, quoted in Bernard Mergen, *Play and Playthings: A Reference Guide* (Westport, Conn.: Greenwood, 1982), p. 14; Branson L. Harris, *Some Recollections of My Boyhood* (Indianapolis: Hollenbeck, 1908), pp. 56–57.

2. Caroline Clapp Briggs, *Reminiscences and Letters* (Boston: Houghton Mifflin, 1897), pp. 19, 48; "Ebenezer Brown," in Rawick, Suppl. 1, *Mississippi Narratives,* vol. 6, p. 241.

3. Karin Calvert, *Children in the House: The Material Culture of Early Childhood, 1600–1900* (Boston: Northeastern University Press, 1992), p. 80. See also Gary Cross, *Kids' Stuff: Toys and the Changing World of American Childhood* (Cambridge, Mass.: Harvard University Press, 1997), p. 122.

4. *Historical Statistics of the United States: Colonial Times to 1957* (Washington, D.C.: Government Printing Office, 1960), vol. 1, p. 23. Proportions of children in the five-to-fourteen age group were somewhat higher in newer areas of the North Central and Southern states because, as areas of high in-migration, they had lower proportions of older persons—over the age of forty-five—than did states of the Northeast.

5. Steven Mintz, *Huck's Raft: A History of American Childhood* (Cambridge, Mass.: Harvard University Press, 2004), pp. 75–79; Jacqueline S. Reinier, *From*

Virtue to Character: American Childhood, 1775–1850 (New York: Twayne, 1996), pp. 61, 90; Howard P. Chudacoff, *How Old Are You? Age Consciousness in American Culture* (Princeton, N.J.: Princeton University Press, 1989), pp. 93–94, 97.

6. Thomas Wildcat Alford, *Civilization, as Told to Florence Drake* (Norman: University of Oklahoma Press, 1936), p. 23.

7. "Jim Allen," in Rawick, Suppl. 1, *Mississippi Narratives*, vol. 6, p. 55.

8. Mintz, *Huck's Raft*, pp. 94–117.

9. Mary Lynn Stevens Heininger, "Children, Childhood, and Change in America, 1820–1920," in Heininger, ed., *A Century of Childhood, 1820–1920* (Rochester, N.Y.: Strong National Museum of Play, 1984), pp. 6–8; Cross, *Kids' Stuff*, p. 35.

10. Harvey Newcomb, *How to Be a Man: A Book for Boys* (Boston: Gould, Kendall, and Lincoln, 1847), pp. 10–11, 182–83.

11. B. F. Moulton, *Present from Philadelphia* (Philadelphia: Benjamin Johnson, 1803), n.p.

12. *Boys and Girls Illustrated Primer* (publisher unknown, ca. 1840).

13. Horace Mann, *Lectures on Education* (Boston: L. N. Ide, 1845); Lydia Maria Child, *The Mother's Book* (Boston: Carter, Hendee, and Babcock, 1831).

14. Samuel G. Goodrich, *Recollections of a Lifetime* (New York: Miller, Orton and Mulligan, 1857), p. 52.

15. Maria Edgeworth, *Works* (Boston: Samuel Parker, 1825), vol. 1, pp. 19–20.

16. *Youthful Sports* (Philadelphia: Jacob Johnson, 1802), n.p.

17. *A Present for a Good Boy* (Newburyport, Mass.: W. and J. Gilman, 1821), n.p.

18. Sarah Josepha Hale, ed., *A Gift to Young Friends* (New York: Edward Dunigan, 1837), n.p.

19. For insights into the new role of children's literature, see Stephen Kline, *Out of the Garden: Toys, TV, and Children's Culture in the Age of Marketing* (London: Verso, 1993), pp. 93–95. Nathaniel Willis, quoted in Heininger, "Children, Childhood, and Change in America," p. 2.

20. William Dean Howells, *A Boy's Town* (New York: Harper and Brothers, 1890), p. 177.

21. Catherine Elizabeth Havens, "When I Am Old and in a Remembering Mood . . . ," in Josef Berger and Dorothy Berger, eds., *Small Voices* (New York: Paul S. Ericksson, 1966), p. 219.

22. Edward Everett Hale, *A New England Boyhood* (New York: Cassell, 1893), pp. 94–95.

23. Emily Wilson, *The Forgotten Girl* (New York: Alphabet, 1937), p. 13.

24. Brown Thurston, "Journal, 1834–1893," manuscript collections of the American Antiquarian Society, Worcester, Massachusetts.

25. Henry Clark Wright, "Human Life," in Louis C. Jones, ed., *Growing*

Up in Cooper Country: Boyhood Recollections of the New York Frontier (Syracuse, N.Y.: Syracuse University Press, 1965), p. 107.

26. Emily Inez Denny, *Blazing the Way; or True Stories, Songs and Sketches of Puget Sound and Other Pioneers* (Seattle: Seattle Rainier, 1909), p. 114.

27. Rachel Q. Butz, *A Hoosier Girlhood* (Boston: Gorham, 1924), p. 29.

28. "Laura Ford," in Rawick, Suppl. 1, *Mississippi Narratives*, vol. 7, p. 756; "William Flannagan," in Rawick, Suppl. 1, *Mississippi Narratives*, vol. 7, p. 733; "Tony Cox," in Rawick, Suppl. 1, *Mississippi Narratives*, vol. 7, pp. 522–23; "Hannah Chapman," in Rawick, Suppl. 1, *Mississippi Narratives*, vol. 7, p. 381; "Emily Dixon," in Rawick, Suppl. 1, *Mississippi Narratives*, vol. 7, pp. 621–22; "Isaac Potter," in Rawick, Suppl. 1, *Mississippi Narratives*, vol. 9, p. 1740; "Minerva Grubbs," in Rawick, Suppl. 1, *Mississippi Narratives*, vol. 8, p. 892. See also Mergen, *Play and Playthings*, p. 411; and Mintz, *Huck's Raft*, pp. 94–117.

29. Charles A. Eastman (Ohiyesa), *Indian Boyhood* (New York: McClude, Phillips, 1902), p. 63.

30. James Langdon Hill, *My First Years as a Boy* (Andover, Mass.: Andover, 1928), pp. 1–2, 57–58.

31. Hale, *New England Boyhood*, p. 23; Henrietta Dana Skinner, *An Echo from Parnassus: Being Girlhood Memories of Longfellow and His Friends* (New York: J. H. Sears, 1928), p. 102; Caroline Cowles Richards Clarke, quoted in Harvey Graff, *Conflicting Paths: Growing Up in America* (Cambridge, Mass.: Harvard University Press, 1995), p. 160; Thurston, "Journal," n.p.

32. Hale, *New England Boyhood*, p. 37.

33. "Salem Powell," in Rawick, Suppl. 1, *Mississippi Narratives*, vol. 9, pp. 1747–48; "Sam Broach," in Rawick, Suppl. 1, *Mississippi Narratives*, vol. 6, pp. 223–24; "Manda Boggan," in Rawick, Suppl. 1, *Mississippi Narratives*, vol. 6, p. 156; "Minerva Grubbs," in Rawick, Suppl. 1, *Mississippi Narratives*, vol. 8, p. 892; "Melvina Roberts," in Rawick, Suppl. 1, *Georgia Narratives*, vol. 9, p. 539; "Barney Alford," in Rawick, Suppl. 1, *Mississippi Narratives*, vol. 6, p. 23.

34. Thurston, "Journal," n.p.; Jeannette Leonard Gilder, *The Autobiography of a Tomboy* (New York: Doubleday Page, 1901), p. 96.

35. John Albee, *Confessions of Boyhood* (Boston: Richard G. Badger, 1910), p. 42; Cornelia Gray Lunt, *Sketches of Childhood and Girlhood, 1847–1864* (Evanston, Ill.: n.p., 1925), p. 68; Caroline A. Stickney Crevey, *A Daughter of the Puritans: An Autobiography* (New York: Knickerbocker Press, 1916), p. 8; Hale, *New England Boyhood*, p. 45; John Muir, *The Story of My Boyhood and Youth* (Boston: Houghton Mifflin, 1913), p. 39.

36. Mary Crosby, quoted in Amanda Dargan and Steven Zeitlin, *City Play* (New Brunswick, N.J.: Rutgers University Press, 1990), p. 122; "Ann Drake," in Rawick, Suppl. 1, *Mississippi Narratives*, vol. 7, pp. 644–45.

37. David Clapp, "Journal, 1820–1824," manuscript collections of the American Antiquarian Society, Worcester, Massachusetts; Louisa May Alcott,

"I Had a Pleasant Time with My Mind," in Josef Berger and Dorothy Berger, eds., *Small Voices* (New York: Paul S. Ericksson, 1966), p. 111.

38. These juvenile newspapers are in the manuscript collections of the American Antiquarian Society, Worcester, Massachusetts.

39. Hale, *New England Boyhood*, pp. 122–26; [anon.], "Diary," manuscript collections of the American Antiquarian Society, Worcester, Massachusetts, n.d.

40. William G. Johnston, *Life and Reminiscences from Birth to Manhood* (Pittsburgh, n.p., 1901), p. 110; Elizabeth Buffum Chase, "Reminiscences of Childhood," in Lucille Salitan and Eve Lewis Perera, eds., *Virtuous Lives: Four Quaker Sisters Remember Family Life, Abolitionism and Women's Suffrage* (New York: Continuum, 1994), p. 29; Wright, "Human Life," p. 113.

41. Sabrina Ann (Loomis) Hills, *Memories* (Cleveland, 1899), quoted in Graff, *Conflicting Paths*, p. 14; Butz, *Hoosier Girlhood*, p. 28; Margaret DeLand, *If This Be I (As I Suppose It Be)* (New York: D. Appleton-Century, 1935), p. 142.

42. John Burroughs, *My Boyhood* (Garden City, N.Y.: Doubleday, Page, 1922), p. 43; Crevey, *Daughter of the Puritans*, p. 19; Alford, *Civilization*, pp. 22–23.

43. Gilder, *Autobiography of a Tomboy*, p. 246; Mary Esther Mulford Miller, *An East Hampton Childhood*, told to Abigail Fithian Halsey (East Hampton, Long Island, N.Y.: East Hampton Star Press, 1938), p. 15; Harriet M. Clos [Bonebright], *Reminiscences of Newcastle, Iowa, 1848: A History of the Founding of Webster City, Iowa, Narrated by Sarah Brewer-Bonebright, Written by Her Daughter* (Des Moines: Historical Department of Iowa, 1921), pp. 112–13.

44. On the meaning of slave children's games, see Joseph E. Ilick, *American Childhood* (Philadelphia: University of Pennsylvania Press, 2002), p. 41; and Mintz, *Huck's Raft*, p. 95.

45. "Harriet Miller," in Rawick, Suppl. 1, *Mississippi Narratives*, vol. 9, p. 1505; "Dempsey Pitts," in Rawick, Suppl. 1, *Mississippi Narratives*, vol. 9, p. 1716; "Charity Jones," in Rawick, Suppl. 1, *Mississippi Narratives*, vol. 8, p. 1195; "Randall Flagg," in Rawick, Suppl. 1, *Georgia Narratives*, vol. 3, p. 249.

46. "Abe McKlennan," in Rawick, Suppl. 1, *Mississippi Narratives*, vol. 9, p. 1409; "Westly Little," in Rawick, Suppl. 1, *Mississippi Narratives*, vol. 8, pp. 1320–21; "Joe Coney," in Rawick, Suppl. 1, *Mississippi Narratives*, vol. 7, p. 488.

47. Jean Temple and Rev. David Miles, eds., *Memoirs of a Circuit Rider: The Reverend William McKnight* (Elsie, Mich.: Sun, 1979), p. 5.

48. Harvey Newcombe, *How to Be a Man: A Book for Boys* (Boston: Gould, Kendall, and Lincoln, 1847), p. 11.

49. William Hoppin diary, cited in Graff, *Conflicting Paths*, pp. 174–75; Charles D. Drake, ed., *Pioneer Life in Kentucky: A Series of Reminiscential Letters from Daniel Drake, M.D., of Cincinnati, to His Children* (Cincinnati: Robert Clark,

1870), p. 110; George F. Hoar, *A Boy Sixty Years Ago* (Boston: Perry Mason, 1898), p. 14; Joseph Hodges Choate, *The Boyhood Youth of Joseph Hodges Choate* (New York: privately printed, 1917), pp. 54, 60; Sallie Hester, "As Far as the Eye Can Reach . . . Nothing but Wagons," in Josef Berger and Dorothy Berger, eds., *Small Voices* (New York: Paul S. Ericksson, 1966), pp. 67–74.

50. Mergen, *Play and Playthings*, p. 21; Mintz, *Huck's Raft*, pp. 83–85; Hale, *New England Boyhood*, p. 57.

51. Robert J. Lucid, ed., *The Journal of Richard Henry Dana, Jr.*, 2 vols. (Cambridge, Mass.: Harvard University Press, 1968), vol. 1, p. 5.

52. Thurston, "Journal," n.p.; Hale, *New England Boyhood*, p. 45; Orleana Ellery Pell, *Recollections of a Long Life* (London: W. P. Griffith, 1896), quoted in Graff, *Conflicting Paths*, p. 10; R. L. B. [Mrs. Harriet G. Doutney (Storer)], *An Autobiography: Being Passages from a Life and Progression in the City of Boston*, quoted in Graff, *Conflicting Paths*, p. 21.

53. John Muir, *The Story of My Boyhood and Youth* (Boston: Houghton Mifflin, 1913), pp. 24–25.

54. Mintz, *Huck's Raft*, p. 107.

55. "Orris Harris," in Rawick, Suppl. 1, *Mississippi Narratives*, vol. 7, p. 929; "Jim Martin," in Rawick, Suppl. 1, *Mississippi Narratives*, vol. 9, pp. 139–41; "Dora Franks," in Rawick, Suppl. 1, *Mississippi Narratives*, vol. 7, p. 790; "George Caulton," in Rawick, Suppl. 1, *Georgia Narratives*, vol. 3, p. 175; "Emmaline Sturgis," in Rawick, Suppl. 1, *Georgia Narratives*, vol. 4, p. 601; "Prince Johnson," in Rawick, Suppl. 1, *Mississippi Narratives*, vol. 7, p. 1169.

56. Muir, *Story of My Boyhood*, pp. 43, 48.

57. Wright, "Human Life," p. 137.

Notes to Chapter 3

1. Jacob Abbott, *Gentle Measures in the Management and Training of the Young* (New York: Harper and Brothers, 1871), pp. 11, 16, 32, 193.

2. Stephen Kline, *Out of the Garden: Toys, TV, and Children's Culture in the Age of Marketing* (London: Verso, 1993), pp. 151–52.

3. Karin Calvert, *Children in the House: The Material Culture of Early Childhood, 1600–1900* (Boston: Northeastern University Press, 1992), p. 118; George Ellsworth Johnson, "Education by Play and Games," *Pedagogical Seminary* 3 (October 1894), p. 98.

4. Maria Kraus-Bolte, quoted in Bernard Mergen, *Play and Playthings: A Reference Guide* (Westport, Conn.: Greenwood Press, 1982), p. 57; emphasis added. See also Joseph E. Illick, *American Childhood* (Philadelphia: University of Pennsylvania Press, 2002), p. 95; Gary Cross, *Kids' Stuff: Toys and the Changing World of American Childhood* (Cambridge, Mass.: Harvard University

Press, 1997), p. 37; Mary Lynn Stevens Heininger, "Children, Childhood, and Change in America, 1820–1920," in Heininger, ed., *A Century of Childhood, 1820–1920* (Rochester, N.Y.: Strong National Museum of Play, 1984), p. 13.

5. Kline, *Out of the Garden*, p. 151; Mergen, *Play and Playthings*, pp. 57, 69; Donald Mrozek, "The Natural Limits of Unstructured Play, 1880–1914," in Kathryn Grover, ed., *Hard at Play: Leisure in America, 1840–1940* (Amherst: University of Massachusetts Press, 1992), pp. 212–14; Amanda Dargan and Steven Zeitlin, *City Play* (New Brunswick, N.J.: Rutgers University Press, 1990), p. 183; Priscilla Ferguson Clement, *Growing Pains: Children in the Industrial Age, 1850–1890* (New York: Twayne, 1997), p. 160.

6. U.S. Census Bureau, *The Statistical History of the United States from Colonial Times to the Present* (Stamford, Conn.: Fairfield, 1965), pp. 8–11, 168; Steven Mintz, *Huck's Raft: A History of American Childhood* (Cambridge, Mass.: Harvard University Press, 2004), pp. 77–78.

7. Harvey Graff, *Conflicting Paths: Growing Up in America* (Cambridge, Mass.: Harvard University Press, 1995), p. 253; Gary Cross, *Kids' Stuff: Toys and the Changing World of American Childhood* (Cambridge, Mass.: Harvard University Press, 1997), p. 23.

8. Mintz, *Huck's Raft*, p. 135.

9. Howard P. Chudacoff, *How Old Are You? Age Consciousness in American Culture* (Princeton, N.J.: Princeton University Press, 1989), pp. 29–64.

10. Elliott West, "Children on the Plains Frontier," in Elliot West and Paula Petrik, eds., *Small World: Children and Adolescents in America, 1850–1950* (Lawrence: University Press of Kansas, 1992), pp. 28–32, 37; Clement, *Growing Pains*, pp. 63–65, 178; Mergen, *Play and Playthings*, p. 53.

11. Mintz, *Huck's Raft*, pp. 170–71.

12. One of the most insightful summaries of G. Stanley Hall's and Luther Halsey Gulick's beliefs is found in Mrozek, "Natural Limits of Unstructured Play," pp. 213–21. See also Mintz, *Huck's Raft*, pp. 178–80.

13. Mrozek, "Natural Limits of Unstructured Play."

14. William Wells Newell, *Games and Songs of American Children* (New York: Dover, 1963). This is a reprint of the 2nd edition from 1903; first published in 1883.

15. Mergen, *Play and Playthings*, pp. 60, 67; Dargan and Zeitlin, *City Play*, pp. 180–81.

16. Ilick, *American Childhood*, p. 95; Dargan and Zeitlin, *City Play*, p. 185; Joe L. Frost and Irma C. Woods, "Perspectives on Play in Playgrounds," in Doris P. Fromberg and Doris Bergen, eds., *Play from Birth to Twelve and Beyond* (New York: Garland, 1998), pp. 232–33.

17. Cross, *Kids' Stuff*, p. 87; Kline, *Out of the Garden*, pp. 151–52; Mergen, *Play and Playthings*, p. 69; Kathleen W. Jones, *Taming the Troublesome Child: American Families, Child Guidance, and the Limits of Psychiatric Authority* (Cam-

bridge, Mass.: Harvard University Press, 1999); Neil Postman, *The Disappearance of Childhood* (New York: Delacorte, 1962), p. 67.

18. Kline, *Out of the Garden*, p. 152; Bernard Mergen, "The Discovery of Children's Play," *American Quarterly* 27 (October 1975), pp. 399–420; Cross, *Kids' Stuff*, pp. 35–36; Heininger, "Children, Childhood, and Change in America," pp. 13–14; Mergen, "Discovery of Children's Play," pp. 408–9; T. Benjamin Atkins, *Out of the Cradle into the World of Self Education through Play* (Columbus, Ohio: Sterling, 1895).

19. Cross, *Kids' Stuff*, pp. 18–31; Mergen, *Play and Playthings*, pp. 106–8; Heininger, "Children, Childhood, and Change in America," pp. 16–17; Bernard Mergen, "Made, Bought, and Stolen: Toys and the Culture of Childhood," in Elliott West and Paula Petrik, eds., *Small World: Children and Adolescents in America, 1850–1950* (Lawrence: University Press of Kansas, 1992), p. 83.

20. Heininger, "Children, Childhood, and Change in America," pp. 16–17; Bernard Barenhoz and Inez McClintock, *American Antique Toys, 1830–1900* (New York: Harry N. Abrams, 1980), n.d.; Cross, *Kids' Stuff*, pp. 26–30; Mergen, *Play and Playthings*, p. 32; Mergen, "Made, Bought, and Stolen," pp. 83–84; Birgitta Almqvist, "Educational Toys, Creative Toys," in Jeffrey H. Goldstein, ed., *Toys, Play, and Child Development* (Cambridge, N.Y.: Cambridge University Press, 1994), p. 48.

21. These books are discussed in Mergen, "Made, Bought, and Stolen," pp. 96–97.

22. Kline, *Out of the Garden*, pp. 81–95; Cross, *Kids' Stuff*, p. 35; Daniel T. Rodgers, *The Work Ethic in Industrial America* (Chicago: University of Chicago Press, 1974), pp. 132–34.

23. Rodgers, *Work Ethic*, pp. 133–34.

24. Frank Luther Mott, *A History of American Magazines, 1741–1930*, 5 vols. (New York: D. Appleton, 1930–1968), vol. 2: *1850–1865*, pp. 267–74; vol. 3: *1865–1885*, pp. 174–80. Mott does not identify how he knew that readers passed over the introduction to *Youth's Companion* anecdotes, but, given diary and autobiographical evidence about children's independent activities, his assertion seems credible.

25. Asa Bullard, comp., *Aunt Lizzie's Stories* (Boston: Lee and Shepard, 1863); Francis Woodworth, *The Girl's Story Book* (New York: Clark, Austin, and Smith, 1855), p. 8.

26. Theodore Dreiser, *Dawn* (New York: Horace Liveright, 1931), p. 125.

27. Rodgers, *Work Ethic*, pp. 127–28.

28. David I. Macleod, *The Age of the Child: Children in America, 1890–1920* (New York: Twayne, 1998), p. 65. See also Dargan and Zeitlin, *City Play*, p. 2.

29. R. L. Duffus, *Williamstown Branch: Impersonal Memories of a Vermont Boyhood* (New York: W. W. Norton, 1958), p. 45; Isabel Bolton, *Under Gemini*

(New York: Harcourt, Brace and World, 1966), pp. 13, 76; Della T. Lutes, *Home Grown* (Boston: Little, Brown, 1937), p. 132.

30. Luther Standing Bear, *My Indian Boyhood* (Lincoln: University of Nebraska Press, 1959; reprint of 1931 edition), pp. 12, 131–43; Aubrey Lee Brooks, *A Southern Lawyer* (Chapel Hill: University of North Carolina Press, 1950), p. 6; Ralph Blumenthal, *Home Town: Story of a Dream That Came True* (New York: Hutchinson, 1948), pp. 29, 59; Roger Kahn, *A Flame of Pure Fire: Jack Dempsey and the Roaring '20s* (New York: Harcourt Brace, 1999), p. 182; Edna Ferber, *A Peculiar Treasure* (Garden City, N.Y.: Doubleday, 1960), p. 73; Sarah Bixby Smith, *Adobe Days* (Fresno, Calif.: Valley Publishers, 1974), p. 81.

31. Bixby Smith, *Adobe Days*, p. 94; Henry Seidel Canby, *The Age of Confidence: Life in the Nineties* (New York: Farrar and Rinehart, 1934), p. 35; Catharine Brody, "A New York Childhood," *American Mercury* 14 (1928), pp. 58, 60, quoted in Graff, *Conflicting Paths*, pp. 273–74.

32. Canby, *Age of Confidence*, p. 35; Bixby Smith, *Adobe Days*, p. 94; Stewart Culin, "Street Games of Boys in Brooklyn," *Journal of American Folklore* 4 (1891), p. 230, as quoted in Mergen, *Play and Playthings*, pp. 60–61.

33. Mergen, *Play and Playthings*, p. 82; Cross, *Kids' Stuff*, pp. 34–35; David P. Handlin, *The American Home: Architecture and Society, 1815–1915* (Boston: Little, Brown, 1979); Joseph C. Bigott, *From Cottage to Bungalow: Houses and the Working Class in Metropolitan Chicago, 1869–1929* (Chicago: University of Chicago Press, 2000).

34. Eleanor Hallowell Abbot, *Being Little in Cambridge (When Everyone Else Was Big)* (New York: Appleton Century, 1936), p. 114; Canby, *Age of Confidence*, p. 46.

35. Miriam Formanek-Brunell, *Made to Play House: Dolls and the Commercialization of American Girlhood, 1830–1930* (New Haven, Conn.: Yale University Press, 1993), pp. 1–4, 36–62; Mary Scarborough Paxson, "I Am Tired of Only Me to Play With," in Josef Berger and Mary Berger, eds., *Small Voices* (New York: Paul S. Ericksson, 1966), pp. 14–15.

36. Duffus, *Williamstown Branch*, pp. 24, 122.

37. James Langdon Hill, *My First Years as a Boy* (Andover, Mass.: Andover Press, 1928), p. 168; Harvey Fergusson, *Home in the West* (New York: Duell, Sloan and Pearce, 1945), p. 88; Mergen, "Made, Bought, and Stolen," p. 94.

38. Mergen, *Play and Playthings*, p. 106; Cross, *Kids' Stuff*, pp. 67–68; Barenhoz and McClintock, *American Antique Toys*, pp. 53–98, 120–39; Mergen, "Made, Bought, and Stolen," p. 88; Kate Douglas Wiggins, quoted in Calvert, *Children in the House*, p. 119.

39. Abbot, *Being Little in Cambridge*, p. 54; Hill, *My First Years as a Boy*, p. 110; Pierrepont Burt Noyes, *My Father's House: An Oneida Boyhood* (New York: Farrar and Rinehart, 1937), p. 97.

40. Lizette Woodworth Reese, *A Victorian Village: Reminiscences of Other Days* (New York: Farrar and Rinehart, 1929), p. 46.

41. John Albee, *Confessions of Boyhood* (Boston: Richard G. Badger, 1910), pp. 42–43.

42. William Allen White, *The Autobiography of William Allen White,* as quoted in Mergen, "Made, Bought, and Stolen," p. 95; Taylor Gordon, *Born to Be* (Lincoln: University of Nebraska Press, 1995), p. 7; Bellamy Partridge, *Big Family* (New York: Whittlesey House, 1941), p. 86.

43. Mergen, "Made, Bought, and Stolen," p. 91; West and Petrik, "Introduction," p. 5; Partridge, *Big Family,* p. 86.

44. Walter Brooks, quoted in Mergen, "Made, Bought, and Stolen," p. 91; Mergen, *Play and Playthings,* pp. 106–8.

45. Asa Bullard, ed., *Going to School: A Sunnybrook Stories Book* (Boston: Lee and Shepard, 1863), p. 27; Ethel Spencer, quoted in Michael P. Weber and Peter N. Stearns, eds., *The Spencers of Amberson Avenue* (Pittsburgh: University of Pittsburgh Press, 1983), p. 58. On the rise of peer groups, see Chudacoff, *How Old Are You,* pp. 92–116.

46. Mary Church Terrell, *A Colored Woman in a White World* (Washington, D.C.: Randsdell, 1940), p. 26.

47. Lincoln Steffens, *The Autobiography of Lincoln Steffens* (New York: Harcourt, Brace and World, 1931), vol. 1, p. 9.

48. Dreiser, *Dawn,* p. 81.

49. Hill, *My First Years as a Boy,* pp. 159–60, 219–20.

50. Charles A. Eastman (Ohiyesa), *Indian Boyhood* (New York: McClure, Phillips, 1902), pp. 65–67; Gordon, *Born to Be,* p. 38.

51. Charles Nagel, *A Boy's Civil War Story* (St. Louis: Eden Publishing, 1934), p. 114; Francis Bennett Jr., "Diary, 1852–54," manuscript collections of the American Antiquarian Society, Worcester, Massachusetts; George F. Hoar, *A Boy Sixty Years Ago* (Boston: Perry Mason1898), p. 20.

52. Isabel Bolton, *Under Gemini* (New York: Harcourt, Brace and World, 1966), p. 15; Zona Gale, *When I Was a Little Girl* (1925), quoted in Mergen, "Made, Bought, and Stolen," p. 96; Frances Parkinson Keyes, *Roses in December* (New York: Liveright, 1960), p. 48; Paxson, "I Am Tired of Only Me to Play With," pp. 13–15.

53. Loretta Berner, "Sketches from 'Way Back," *Los Fierros* 7 (Spring 1970), p. 2, quoted in Victoria Bissell Brown, "Golden Girls: Female Socialization among the Middle Class of Los Angeles, 1880–1910," in Elliott West and Paula Petrik, eds., *Small World: Children and Adolescents in America, 1850–1950* (Lawrence: University Press of Kansas, 1992), p. 254; Abbot, *Being Little in Cambridge,* p. 146; Edna Ferber, *A Peculiar Treasure* (Garden City, N.Y.: Doubleday, 1960), p. 62.

54. Formanek-Brunell, *Made to Play House*, pp. 31–32.

55. William E. Cox, *Southern Sidelights: A Record of Personal Experience* (Raleigh, N.C.: Edwards and Broughton, 1942), p. 4; Bixby Smith, as noted in Brown, "Golden Girls," p. 245; Kroll, as noted in Brown, "Golden Girls," p. 247.

56. Reese, *Victorian Village*, pp. 155, 157; Abbot, *Being Little in Cambridge*, pp. 74, 78; Fergusson, *Home in the West*, p. 113.

57. Keyes, *Roses in December*, pp. 145–48; Canby, *Age of Confidence*, pp. 37–38; Irving Bacheller, *Coming Up the Road: Memories of a North Country Boyhood* (Indianapolis: Bobbs-Merrill, 1928), pp. 24, 42.

58. Keyes, *Roses in December*, p. 132; Noyes, *My Father's House*, pp. 52, 107.

59. Dargan and Zeitlin, *City Play*, p. 17; Abbot, *Being Little in Cambridge*, p. 166.

60. "Stephen F. Littlefield, Diaries, 1888–1891," manuscript collections of the American Antiquarian Society, Worcester, Massachusetts.

61. Mergen, *Play and Playthings*, p. 58; Culin, "Street Games of Boys in Brooklyn," pp. 221–35; Mergen, *Play and Playthings*, p. 405; T. R. Crosswell, "Amusements of Worcester Schoolchildren," *Pedagogical Seminary* 6 (September 1899), quoted in Mergen, *Play and Playthings*, p. 66.

62. Figures derived from Crosswell, "Amusements of Worcester Schoolchildren," and from Zachariah McGhee, "A Study of the Play Life of Some South Carolina Children," *Pedagogical Seminary* 7 (1900), pp. 459–78, both cited in Mergen, *Play and Playthings*, pp. 69, 106–8.

63. Canby, *Age of Confidence*, p. 36; Albee, *Confessions of Boyhood*, p. 135; Noyes, *My Father's House*, p. 88; Ervin King, quoted in Brown, "Golden Girls," pp. 250–51.

64. Paxson, "I Am Tired of Only Me to Play With," p. 15.

65. Rufus Matthew Jones, *A Small Town Boy* (New York: Macmillan, 1941), pp. 108, 110.

66. Ferber, *Peculiar Treasure*, p. 74; Albee, *Confessions of Boyhood*, p. 170.

67. Aline Bernstein, *An Actor's Daughter* (Athens: Ohio University Press, 1941), p. 48.

68. Albee, *Confessions of Boyhood*, p. 129.

69. Granville Howland Norcross diary, cited in Graff, *Conflicting Paths*, p. 283.

70. Adeline Atwater, "The Autobiography of an Extrovert: One Woman's Story [by the late Mrs. Henry C. Pynchon]," Atwater Papers, Newberry Library, Chicago, Illinois, p. 15.

71. William Wells Newell, *Games and Songs of American Children* (New York: Dover, 1963), p. 12. This is a reprint of the 2nd edition from 1903; first published in 1883.

72. Bullard, *Aunt Lizzie's Stories*, pp. 53–54.

Notes to Chapter 4

1. White House Conference on Child Health and Protection, quoted in Judith Sealander, *The Failed Century of the Child: Governing America's Young in the Twentieth Century* (Cambridge, Mass.: Cambridge University Press, 2003), p. 137.

2. B. F. Boller, "Physical Training," *Mind and Body* 7 (April 1900), p. 26. See also Donald J. Mrozek, *Sport and American Mentality, 1880–1910* (Knoxville: University of Tennessee Press, 1983), p. 39.

3. Harvey C. Lehman and Paul A. Witty, *The Psychology of Play Activities* (New York: A. S. Barnes, 1927), p. 51. See also Bernard Mergen, "The Discovery of Children's Play," *American Quarterly* 27 (October 1975), pp. 415–16.

4. Robert Paul Smith, *"Where Did You Go?" "Out" "What Did You Do?" "Nothing"* (New York: W. W. Norton, 1957), pp. 40–41.

5. Miriam Formanek-Brunell, *Made to Play House: Dolls and the Commercialization of American Girlhood, 1830–1930* (New Haven, Conn.: Yale University Press, 1993), p. 168.

6. The two models of childhood have been described by David I. Macleod, *The Age of the Child: Children in America, 1890–1920* (New York: Twayne, 1998), pp. xi–xii. Steven Mintz, in *Huck's Raft: A History of American Childhood* (Cambridge, Mass.: Harvard University Press, 2004), pp. 75–76, identifies the emergence of the sheltered model with the rise of the middle class in the mid-nineteenth century. While accepting Mintz's interpretation, I believe with Macleod that the sheltered model did not become widespread until the twentieth century.

7. Smith, *"Where Did You Go?"* pp. 22–23.

8. U.S. Census Bureau, *The Statistical History of the United States from Colonial Times to the Present* (Stamford, Conn.: Fairfield, 1965), pp. 8–11.

9. Summaries of these changes are in Mintz, *Huck's Raft,* pp. 191–96; Harvey Graff, *Conflicting Paths: Growing Up in America* (Cambridge, Mass.: Harvard University Press, 1995), pp. 302–5; and Howard P. Chudacoff, *How Old Are You? Age Consciousness in American Culture* (Princeton, N.J.: Princeton University Press, 1989), pp. 65–91.

10. Elliott West and Paula Petrik, eds., "Introduction," *Small World: Children and Adolescence in America, 1850–1950* (Lawrence: University Press of Kansas, 1992), p. 5; David Nasaw, *Children of the City: At Work and at Play* (Garden City, N.Y.: Anchor/Doubleday, 1985), pp. 117–20; Lisa Jacobson, *Raising Consumers: Children and the American Mass Market in the Early Twentieth Century* (New York: Columbia University Press, 2004), pp. 16–159.

11. Neil Postman, *The Disappearance of Childhood* (New York: Delacorte, 1982), pp. 52–64.

12. Macleod, *Age of the Child,* pp. 24–25; Donald Mrozek, "The Natural

Limits of Unstructured Play, 1880–1914," in Kathryn Glover, ed., *Hard at Play: Leisure in America, 1840–1940* (Amherst: University of Massachusetts Press, 9192), p. 222; Mergen, "Discovery of Children's Play," p. 402.

13. Graff, *Conflicting Paths*, p. 302; Mintz, *Huck's Raft*, p. 191; L. Emmett Holt, *The Diseases of Infancy and Childhood*, 6th ed. (New York: D. Appleton, 1914), pp. 15–21.

14. Sealander, *Failed Century of the Child*, p. 137; Viviana A. Zelizer, *Pricing the Priceless Child: The Changing Social Value of Children* (New York: Basic, 1985), pp. 56–60.

15. John Dewey, *Democracy and Education: An Introduction to the Philosophy of Education* (New York: Macmillan, 1916), p. 241; Luther Gulick, *The Philosophy of Play* (New York: Scribner's, 1920), p. 71. See also Gary Cross, *The Cute and the Cool: Wondrous Innocence and Modern American Children's Culture* (New York: Oxford University Press, 2004), p. 36; Cross, *Kids' Stuff: Toys and the Changing World of American Childhood* (Cambridge, Mass.: Harvard University Press, 1997), pp. 125–26; Sealander, *Failed Century of the Child*, p. 298; Mrozek, "Natural Limits of Unstructured Play," pp. 212–14; Macleod, *Age of the Child*, p. 23; Jacobson, *Raising Consumers*, pp. 160–62.

16. Lehman and Witty, *Psychology of Play Activities*, pp. iv, 224–26.

17. In 1914, Congress passed a joint resolution recognizing Mother's Day. In 1926, the same year that the Childhood League recommended establishment of a Children's Day, a National Father's Day committee was organized in New York City, though a Congressional Resolution did not formalize a national holiday until 1956.

18. Formanek-Brunell, *Made to Play House*, pp. 170–74.

19. U.S. Census Bureau, *Statistical History of the United States: Colonial Times to 1957* (Washington, D.C.: Government Printing Office, 1960), p. 14.

20. Quoted in Amanda Dargan and Steven Zeitlin, *City Play* (New Brunswick, N.J.: Rutgers University Press, 1990), p. 181. See also Peter C. Baldwin, *Domesticating the Street: The Reform of Public Space in Hartford, 1850–1930* (Columbus: Ohio State University Press, 1999), pp. 148, 156.

21. Formanek-Brunell, *Made to Play House*, p. 174; Dargan and Zeitlin, *City Play*, pp. 151–52; Baldwin, *Domesticating the Street*, pp. 172–73; Mary Stevenson Calcott, *Child Labor Legislation in New York* (New York: Macmillan, 1931), pp. 29–32.

22. Baldwin, *Domesticating the Street*, pp. 154, 148; Dargan and Zeitlin, *City Play*, p. 155; Mergen, *Play and Playthings*, p. 86; Colin Ward, *The Child in the City* (New York: Pantheon, 1970), p. 86.

23. Cohen, quoted in Baldwin, *Domesticating the Street*, p. 152. See also Alexander S. Outman, "East Side, Street Wise: The Children and Streets of Manhattan's Lower East Side, 1890–1910," honors thesis, Department of History, Brown University, 1996, pp. 77–78.

24. Bernard Mergen, "Made, Bought, and Stolen: Toys and the Culture of Childhood," in Elliott West and Paula Petrik, eds., *Small World: Children and Adolescents in America, 1850–1950* (Lawrence: University Press of Kansas, 1992), p. 101; George Ellsworth Johnson, *Education through Play and Games* (Boston: Ginn, 1907), as cited in Mergen, *Play and Playthings: A Reference Guide* (Westport, Conn.: Greenwood, 1982), pp. 64–70, 80. See also Cary Goodman, *Choosing Sides: Playground and Street Life on the Lower East Side* (New York: Schocken, 1979), p. 17; Macleod, *Age of the Child*, p. 125 .

25. Wilbur P. Bowen, *The Theory of Organized Play: Its Nature and Significance* (New York: Century, 1923), p. 57.

26. Katherine Glover and Evelyn Dewey, *Children of the New Day* (New York: Appleton-Century, 1934), p. 241.

27. Joe L. Frost and Irma C. Woods, "Perspectives on Play in Playgrounds," in Doris Fromberg and Doris Bergen, eds., *Play from Birth to Twelve and Beyond* (New York: Garland, 1998), p. 233; Mergen, *Play and Playthings*, pp. 87–92; Macleod, *Age of the Child*, p. 65; Sealander, *Failed Century of the Child*, p. 298.

28. Bernard Mergen, "Playgrounds and Playground Equipment, 1885–1925: Defining Play in Urban America," in Helen Schwartzman, ed., *Play and Culture* (West Point, N.Y.: Leisure Press, 1980), p. 199.

29. Henry S. Curtis, "Playground Progress and Tendencies of the Year," *Proceedings of the First Annual Playground Congress* (Chicago: National Recreation Congress, 1907), p. 27.

30. Mergen, "Playgrounds and Playground Equipment," pp. 198, 202; Mergen, *Play and Playthings*, p. 95.

31. Baldwin, *Domesticating the Street*, p. 166; Mergen, *Play and Playthings*, p. 92.

32. Henry S. Curtis, *The Reorganized School Playground*, U.S. Bureau of Education Bulletin, no. 40 (Washington, D.C.: Government Printing Office, 1913), p. 16; Brian Sutton-Smith, "The Play of Girls," in Claire B. Kopp, ed., *Becoming Female: Perspectives on Development* (New York: Plenum, 1973), p. 232; Formanek-Brunell, *Made to Play House*, p. 170.

33. Clarence Rainwater, *The Play Movement in the United States: A Study of Community Recreation* (Chicago: University of Chicago Press, 1922); Frost and Woods, "Perspectives on Play in Playgrounds," p. 233; Sealander, *Failed Century of the Child*, pp. 298–301; Macleod, *Age of the Child*, pp. 60, 127; George Parker, quoted in Baldwin, *Domesticating the Street*, p. 170; Worcester child, quoted in Roy Rosenzweig, *Eight Hours for What We Will: Workers and Leisure in an Industrial City, 1870–1920* (Cambridge: Cambridge University Press, 1983), p. 151.

34. Jacobson, *Raising Consumers*, pp. 165–75.

35. Cross, *Kids' Stuff*, p. 128; Natt Hoyes Dodge, "Come Out and Play!"

Parents' Magazine 9 (June 1934), p. 31, quoted in Jacobson, *Raising Consumers,* p. 178.

36. Sealander, *Failed Century of the Child,* p. 300.

37. "The Mission of Little League," *Little League Online,* 2003, www.little league.org/about/mission.asp (accessed September 2004). See also Brian Sutton-Smith, *Toys as Culture* (New York: Gardner, 1986), p. 229.

38. Cross, *Kids' Stuff,* pp. 79–85; Mintz, *Huck's Raft,* p. 217; Stephen Kline, *Out of the Garden: Toys, TV, and Children's Culture in the Age of Marketing* (London: Verso, 1993), p. 145.

39. Cross, *Kids' Stuff,* pp. 79–80; Kline, *Out of the Garden,* p. 189.

40. Quoted in Mergen, *Play and Playthings,* p. 109; Kline, *Out of the Garden,* pp. 149–53; Cross, *Kids' Stuff,* p. 129; Joseph Ilick, *American Childhood* (Philadelphia: University of Pennsylvania Press, 2002), p. 107; William Leach, *Land of Desire: Merchants, Power, and the Rise of a New American Culture* (New York: Vintage, 1993), p. 329.

41. Birgitta Almqvist, "Educational Toys, Creative Toys," in Jeffrey H. Goldstein, ed., *Toys, Play, and Child Development* (Cambridge: Cambridge University Press, 1994), pp. 46–49; Ilick, *American Childhood,* p. 107; Cross, *Kids' Stuff,* pp. 82–83, 91–92; Macleod, *Age of the Child,* p. 67.

42. The analysis of the Strong National Museum of Play oral histories of doll playing in Chapter 6 explores this activity.

43. Cross, *Kids' Stuff,* pp. 77–88, 116–17; Mintz, *Huck's Raft,* p. 217.

44. Cross, *Kids' Stuff,* pp. 88, 115–16; Sutton-Smith, "Play of Girls," p. 232.

45. Macleod, *Age of the Child,* pp. 129–30; Kline, *Out of the Garden,* pp. 96–97.

46. Kline, *Out of the Garden,* pp. 99–103; Cross, *Cute and the Cool,* pp. 124–42; Nasaw, *Children of the City,* pp. 125–26; Glover and Dewey, *Children of the New Day,* pp. 242–44.

47. Mintz, *Huck's Raft,* p. 217; Kline, *Out of the Garden,* p. 157, Cross, *Kids' Stuff,* pp. 65–66;.

48. Cross, *Kids' Stuff,* pp. 99–100; Kline, *Out of the Garden,* pp. 145, 189; Mergen, *Play and Playthings,* p. 82.

49. Jacobson, *Raising Consumers,* pp. 58–69

50. Cross, *Cute and the Cool,* pp. 124–42; Kline, *Out of the Garden,* pp. 96–99.

51. Glover and Dewey, *Children of the New Day,* p. 230.

52. Ibid., p. 251.

53. Cross, *Kids' Stuff,* p. 124.

54. Lehman and Witty, *Psychology of Play Activities,* pp. 87–93, 123–56, 222.

55. Cross, *Kids' Stuff,* pp. 116–17.

56. Kline, *Out of the Garden,* p. 118.

Notes to Chapter 5

1. S. N. Behrman, *The Worcester Account* (New York: Random House, 1954), p. 8.

2. Ruby Berkley Goodwin, *It's Good to Be Black* (Garden City, N.Y.: Doubleday, 1953), pp. 194–95.

3. Doll Oral History Collection, Strong National Museum of Play, Rochester, New York.

4. Janet Gillespie, *With a Merry Heart* (New York: Harper and Row, 1976), pp. 16–17.

5. Robert Paul Smith, *"Where Did You Go?" "Out" "What Did You Do?" "Nothing"* (New York: W. W. Norton, 1957), p. 46.

6. John Gould, *And One to Grow On* (New York: William Morrow, 1949), p. 31; Richard Wright, *Black Boy* (New York: Harper, 1945), p. 38; Dorothy Howard, as described in David I. Macleod, *The Age of the Child: Children in America, 1890–1920* (New York: Twayne, 1998), p. 65; Hal Glen Borland, *Country Editor's Boy* (Philadelphia: J. B. Lippincott, 1970), p. 52.

7. Louise Dickinson Rich, *Innocence under the Elms* (London: Robert Hale, 1935), p. 106; Opal Whiteley, "I Did Have Joy Feels All Over," in Josef Berger and Dorothy Berger, eds., *Small Voices* (New York: Paul S. Ericksson, 1966), pp. 34–52; Frank Conroy, *Stop Time* (New York: Penguin, 1977), p. 24.

8. Samuel Hynes, *The Growing Season: An American Boyhood before the War* (New York: Viking, 2003), pp. 36, 73.

9. Kate Simon, *Bronx Primitive: Portraits in a Childhood* (New York: Viking, 1982), p. 83.

10. Catharine Brody, "A New York Childhood," *American Mercury* 14 (1928), pp. 57–58, quoted in Harvey Graff, *Conflicting Paths: Growing Up in America* (Cambridge, Mass.: Harvard University Press, 1995), pp. 273–74.

11. Sophie Ruskay, *Horsecars and Cobblestones* (New York: A. S. Barnes, 1948), p. 38. See also David Nasaw, *Children of the City: At Work and at Play* (Garden City, N.Y.: Anchor / Doubleday, 1985), p. 24.

12. George Burns, quoted in Amanda Dargan and Steven Zeitlin, *City Play* (New Brunswick, N.J.: Rutgers University Press, 1990), p. 40.

13. Emily Kimbrough, *How Dear to My Heart* (New York: Dodd, Mead, 1944), p. 173.

14. Smith, *"Where Did You Go?"* pp. 60, 62–68; Simon, *Bronx Primitive*, p. 2; Michael Gold, *Jews without Money* (New York: H. Liveright, 1930), p. 46.

15. Henry F. May, *Coming to Terms: A Study in Memory and History* (Berkeley: University of California Press, 1987), p. 4; Smith, *"Where Did You Go?"* pp. 68–70; Zachary Summers, quoted in Dargan and Zeitlin, *City Play*, p. 20.

16. Kyra Gaunt, "The Games Black Girls Play," Ph.D. diss., University of

Michigan, 1997, pp. 161, 167, and elsewhere; Altona Trent-Johns, *Play Songs of the Deep South* (Washington, D.C.: Associated Publishers, 1944), p. 26.

17. Gaunt, "Games Black Girls Play," pp. 205–6.

18. Ruskay, *Horsecars and Cobblestones,* p. 42; Peter C. Baldwin, *Domesticating the Street: The Reform of Public Space in Hartford, 1850–1930* (Columbus: Ohio State University Press, 1999), pp. 172–73; Dargan and Zeitlin, *City Play,* pp. 151–52, 155.

19. Hynes, *Growing Season,* p. 114; Edwin Way Teale, *Dune Boy: The Early Years of a Naturalist* (New York: Dodd, Mead, 1943), p. 186; Flannery Lewis, *Brooks Too Broad for Learning* (New York: Macmillan, 1938), pp. 121–22. See also Bernard Mergen, *Play and Playthings: A Reference Guide* (Westport, Conn.: Greenwood, 1982), pp. 83–86.

20. Susan Brown, quoted in Dargan and Zeitlin, *City Play,* p. 138; Wright, *Black Boy,* p. 37; Jade Snow Wong, *Fifth Chinese Daughter* (New York: Harper, 1945), p. 4,

21. Rich, *Innocence under the Elms,* p. 84; Elizabeth Laura Adams, *Dark Symphony and Other Works* (New York: G. K. Hall, 1997; reprint of 1942 edition), p. 31.

22. Hynes, *Growing Season,* p. 130.

23. Helen Smith Bevington, *Charley Smith's Girl: A Memoir* (New York: Simon and Schuster, 1965), p. 129.

24. Nancy Hale, *A New England Girlhood* (Boston: Little, Brown, 1958), pp. 28–29.

25. Barbara Jordan and Shelby Hearon, *Barbara Jordan: A Self-Portrait* (Garden City, N.Y.: Doubleday, 1979), p. 7; Estha Briscoe (Stowe), *Oil Field Child* (Fort Worth: Texas Christian University Press, 1989), p. 94; Simon, *Bronx Primitive,* p. 61; Mary E. Mebane, *Mary* (New York: Viking, 1981), p. 10.

26. Bruce Catton, *Waiting for the Morning Train: An American Boyhood* (Garden City, N.Y.: Doubleday, 1972), p. 41.

27. Sam Levenson, *Everything but Money* (New York: Pocket Books, 1967), p. 83.

28. John Cammonelli, quoted in Dargan and Zeitlin, *City Play,* p. 27.

29. Anne Jackson, *Early Stages* (Boston: Little, Brown, 1979), p. 142; Caryl Rivers, *Aphrodite at Mid-Century: Growing Up Catholic and Female in Postwar America* (Garden City, N.Y.: Doubleday, 1977), pp. 23, 25.

30. Ruskay, *Horsecars and Cobblestones,* p. 42.

31. Established in 1968, the Strong National Museum of Play originally was intended to display the extensive collection of dolls, dollhouses, and other doll accoutrements that Margaret Woodbury Strong had accumulated over the years, though it now specializes in the artifacts of play. Transcripts of the oral histories are housed in the museum library and archives. Henceforth listed as DOHC (Doll Oral History Collection).

32. The most thorough and sophisticated history of dolls and doll play in the United States is Miriam Formanek-Brunell, *Made to Play House: Dolls and the Commercialization of American Girlhood, 1830–1930* (New Haven, Conn.: Yale University Press, 1993); see esp. pp. 68–72.

33. Ann Klos, Francis Fancy, Saleta W. Smith, Helen Skoland, Joanne Wasenska, and others, DOHC.

34. Alice Wolpert, Phoebe Watts, Barbara Beard, Gerogianna Apolant, and others, DOHC.

35. Ann Reebok, Rita Blum, Lois Greene-Stone, and others, DOHC.

36. Judy M. Johnson, "History of Paper Dolls," 1999, updated December 2005, www.opdag.com/History.html (accessed August 2004); from an article that originally appeared in *The Doll Sourcebook* by Betterway Books, Cincinnati, Ohio.

37. Alice Clifford, Norma Tetamore, Shirley Cohen Fagenbaum, Jane Yuile, Phoebe Watts, Margaret Rohack, Virginia Littman, Lois Green-Stone, Roberta Rugg, Saleta W. Smith, Mrs. James Kern, DOHC.

38. Mary Kinsella, Mary Weber, Helen Becker, Jeanne Wenrich, DOHC.

39. Kimbrough, *How Dear to My Heart*, p. 179; Teale, *Dune Boy*, pp. 133–44; Gary Cross, *The Cute and the Cool: Wondrous Innocence and Modern American Children's Culture* (New York: Oxford University Press, 2004), p. 131.

40. Conroy, *Stop Time*, pp. 114–15.

41. Brian Sutton-Smith, "The Play of Girls," in Claire B. Kopp, ed., *Becoming Female: Perspectives on Development* (New York: Plenum, 1979), p. 232; Hynes, *Growing Season*, p. 88.

42. Ruskay, *Horsecars and Cobblestones*, p. 38; Wright, *Black Boy*, p. 78; Sylvia McNeely, "All Boys Are Nuts as Usual," in Josef Berger and Dorothy Berger, eds., *Small Voices* (New York: Paul S. Ericksson, 1966), pp. 114, 115; Rich, *Innocence under the Elms*, p. 77.

43. E. Anthony Rotundo, "Boy Culture," in Henry Jenkins, ed., *The Children's Culture Reader* (New York: New York University Press, 1998), pp. 337–62.

44. Dore Schary, quoted in MacLeod, *Age of the Child*, p. 127.

45. Catton, *Waiting for the Morning Train*, pp. 46–48; Hynes, *Growing Season*, p. 108; Albert Halper, *On the Shore* (New York: Viking, 1934).

46. Rich, *Innocence under the Elms*, pp. 131, 138; Ellen Tarry, *The Third Door: The Autobiography of an American Negro Woman* (New York: David McKay, 1955), p. 8; Rivers, *Aphrodite at Mid-Century*, pp. 20–21.

47. Sally Carrighar, *Home to the Wilderness* (Boston: Houghton Mifflin, 1973), p. 46; Goodwin, *It's Good to Be Black*, pp. 199–200; McNeely, "All Boys Are Nuts as Usual," p. 115; Jackson, *Early Stages*, p. 110.

48. McNeely, "All Boys Are Nuts as Usual," p. 115; Simon, *Bronx Primitive*, p. 87; Kimbrough, *How Dear to My Heart*, p. 130.

49. Rich, *Innocence under the Elms*, p. 136; Mebane, *Mary*, pp. 45–46.

50. Simon, *Bronx Primitive*, p. 89.

51. Wong, *Fifth Chinese Daughter*, pp. 13–19; Benjamin E. Mays, *Born to Rebel* (New York: Scribner's, 1971), p. 23.

52. Ely Green, *Ely: An Autobiography* (New York: Seabury, 1966), p. 18.

53. Mays, *Born to Rebel*, p. 26.

54. Nancy Hale, *A New England Girlhood* (Boston: Little, Brown, 1958), pp. 15–17; Patricia Ziegfeld, *The Ziegfeld's Girl: Confessions of an Abnormally Happy Childhood* (Boston: Little, Brown, 1964), p. 49; Teale, *Dune Boy*, pp. 27–33; Chester B. Himes, *The Quality of Hurt: The Autobiography of Chester Himes* (Garden City, N.Y.: Doubleday, 1972), vol. 1, p. 13.

55. Quoted in MacLeod, *Age of the Child*, p. 120.

56. Ben Swerdowsky, quoted in Dargan and Zeitlin, *City Play*, p. 25; Bernard Mergen, "Made, Bought, and Stolen: Toys and the Culture of Children," in Elliott West and Paula Petrik, eds., *Small World: Children and Adolescents in America, 1850–1950* (Lawrence: University Press of Kansas, 1992), pp. 97–98.

57. Brown, in Dargan and Zeitlin, *City Play*, p. 138; Rivers, *Aphrodite at Mid-Century*, pp. 21–22; Wright, *Black Boy*, p. 78.

58. Cross, *Cute and the Cool*, p. 36; Cross, *Kids' Stuff*, p. 133; Donald Mrozek, "The Natural Limits of Unstructured Play, 1880–1914," in Kathryn Grover, ed., *Hard at Play: Leisure in America, 1840–1940* (Amherst: University of Massachusetts Press, 1992), pp. 212–14. Early examples of Gulick's and Hall's ideas can be found in Luther Gulick, *The Philosophy of Play* (New York: Scribner's, 1920), pp. 12, 71; and G. Stanley Hall, "A Story of Sand Play," *Scribner's* 3 (June 1888), pp. 690–96.

59. Ruskay, *Horsecars and Cobblestones*, p. 11.

60. Quoted in Alexander S. Outman, "East Side, Street Wise: The Children and Streets of Manhattan's Lower East Side, 1890–1919," honors thesis, Brown University, 1996, p. 97.

61. Jordan and Hearon, *Barbara Jordan*, p. 8; Arthur Goldhaft, *The Golden Egg* (New York: Horizon, 1957), p. 122; Louis Green, quoted in Irving Howe, *World of Our Fathers* (New York: Harcourt Brace Jovanovich, 1975), p. 259; Smith, *"Where Did You Go?"* pp. 40–41.

62. Hynes, *Growing Season*, p. 69; Jackson, *Early Stages*, p. 93; Gold, *Jews without Money*, pp. 16, 260.

63. Gold, *Jews without Money*, p. 16; Harpo Marx and Barbara Rowland, *Harpo Speaks* (New York: Geis, 1974), p. 36; Jackson, *Early Stages*, p. 93; Rivers, *Aphrodite at Mid-Century*, p. 21.

64. Hynes, *Growing Season*, p. 93.

65. Emily Wortis, "In Speling [sic] I Got 100%," in Josef Berger and Dorothy Berger, eds., *Small Voices* (New York: Paul S. Ericksson, 1966), p. 27–29.

Notes to Chapter 6

1. Quoted in Jerry Bowles, *Forever Hold Your Banner High: The Story of the Mickey Mouse Club and What Happened to the Mouseketeers* (New York: Doubleday, 1976), p. 14. See also Kirse Granat May, *Golden State, Golden Youth: The California Image in Popular Culture, 1955–1966* (Chapel Hill: University of North Carolina Press, 2002), pp. 49–50; Stephen Kline, *Out of the Garden: Toys and Children's Culture in the Age of TV Marketing* (London: Verso, 1993), pp. 166–67.

2. Gary Cross, *Kids' Stuff: Toys and the Changing World of American Childhood* (Cambridge, Mass.: Harvard University Press, 1997), pp. 150–51; M. G. Lord, *Forever Barbie: The Unauthorized Biography of a Real Doll* (New York: Avon, 1994), pp. 21–22.

3. Kline, *Out of the Garden,* pp. 167–68; Cy Schneider, *Children's Television: The Art, the Business, and How It Works* (Chicago: NTC Business Books, 1993), p. 90.

4. Quoted in Peter Fancese, *American Demographic Trends and Opportunities in the Children's Market* (Ithaca, N.Y.: Cornell University Press, 1985).

5. Ruth Handler, quoted in Lord, *Forever Barbie,* p. 30.

6. Ibid., pp. 29–32; Cross, *Kids' Stuff,* p. 172; "The History of Barbie," 2005, http://groups.msn.com/BarbiesSecret/thehistoryofbarbie.msnw (accessed March 2005).

7. Sydney Landensohn Stern and Ted Schoenbaum, *Toyland: The High-Stakes Game of the Toy Industry* (New York: Contemporary, 1990), p. 55.

8. U.S. Census Bureau, *Historical Statistics of the United States, Colonial Times to 1970* (Washington, D.C.: Government Printing Office, 1975), p. 15; U.S. Census Bureau, *Statistical Abstract of the United States, 2004–2005* (Washington, D.C.: Government Printing Office, 2005), pp. 12, 16, 60; Steven Mintz, *Huck's Raft: A History of American Childhood* (Cambridge, Mass.: Harvard University Press, 2005), pp. 276–77.

9. James T. Patterson, *Restless Giant: The United States from Watergate to Bush v. Gore* (New York: Oxford University Press, 2005), pp. 271–72.

10. Amara Bachu, "Fertility of American Women: June 1994" (Washington, D.C.: Bureau of the Census, September 1995), xix, table K.

11. Jay D. Teachman, "The Childhood Living Arrangements of Children and the Characteristics of Their Marriages," *Journal of Family Issues* 25 (January 2004), 86–111; Dan Hurley, "The Divorce Rate: It's Not as High as You Think," *New York Times,* April 19, 2005; Mintz, *Huck's Raft,* p. 342.

12. Landon Jones, *Great Expectations: America and the Baby Boom Generation* (New York: Ballantine, 1981), pp. 32–33.

13. Kline, *Out of the Garden,* pp. 179–80.

14. Frances Kemper Alston, "Latch Key Children," New York University Child Study Center, 1999–2006, http://www.aboutourkids.org/aboutour/articles/latchkey.html (accessed January 2005).

15. See, for example, the cover of *Child,* September 2005. The magazine's slogan, printed above the title, states "Raising kids with smarts and style."

16. Juliet B. Schor, *Born to Buy: The Commercialized Child and the New Consumer Culture* (New York: Scribner, 2004), p. 9.

17. Sandford Brown, "The World of Play," *Saturday Evening Post* 19 (December 1964), p. 17.

18. Kline, *Out of the Garden,* pp. 171–2; Schor, *Born to Buy,* p. 23.

19. Benjamin Spock, *Common Sense Guide to Baby and Child Care,* 4th ed. (New York: Meredith, 1968), p. 389; Mintz, *Huck's Raft,* pp. 279–80.

20. Robert O. Blood Jr., "Consequences of Permissiveness for Parents of Young Children," *Marriage and Family Living* 15 (August 1953), 209; Spock, *Baby and Child Care,* p. 390.

21. "Safety Out and About," University of Michigan Health System, updated June 2006, http://www.med.umich.edu/1libr/yourchild/outabout.htm (accessed October 2006).

22. Spock, *Baby and Child Care,* p. 308.

23. Rudolph Wittenberg, "Getting at the Fundamentals of Group Discipline," *Recreation* (1955), p. 148.

24. Dorothy Barclay, "Free Play in Child's Play," *New York Times Magazine* (July 30, 1961), p. 41.

25. Katherine Fishman, "Danger: Children at Play," *New York Times,* September 25, 1966, p. 286.

26. Brian Sutton-Smith, "Does Play Prepare the Future?" in Jeffrey H. Goldstein, ed., *Toys, Play, and Child Development* (Cambridge: Cambridge University Press, 1994), p. 137; Joe L. Frost and Irma C. Woods, "Perspectives on Play in Playgrounds," in Doris P. Fromberg and Doris Berger, eds., *Play from Birth to Twelve and Beyond* (New York: Garland, 1998), pp. 234–35; Judith Sealander, *The Failed Century of the Child: Governing America's Young in the Twentieth Century* (Cambridge: Cambridge University Press, 2003), pp. 311–12.

27. Mintz, *Huck's Raft,* p. 343; Eli Bower, "Play's the Thing," *Today's Education* 57 (September 1968), p. 12.

28. Mintz, *Huck's Raft,* p. 343; Gary Alan Fine, *With the Boys: Little League Baseball and Preadolescent Culture* (Chicago: University of Chicago Press, 1987), p. 27; Dargan and Zeitlin, *City Play,* p. 4; Joe Cranston, "Youth's Number 1 Need," *Recreation* (1960), p. 19; Marcy Guddemi, Tom Jambor, and Robin Moore, "Advocacy for the Child's Right to Play," in Doris P. Fromberg and Doris Berger, eds., *Play from Birth to Twelve and Beyond* (New York: Garland, 1998), p. 520; Tom Jambor, "Challenge and Risk-Taking in Play," in Doris P. Fromberg and Doris Berger, eds., *Play from Birth to Twelve and Beyond* (New

York: Garland, 1998), pp. 322–23; Rev. Nicholas Wegner, "The Significance of Play," *Recreation* (October 1955), p. 358.

29. Wilbur Schramm, Jack Lyle, and Edwin B. Parker, *Television in the Lives of Our Children* (Stanford, Calif.: Stanford University Press, 1961).

30. Kline, *Out of the Garden*, p. 124; Mintz, *Huck's Raft*, p. 198; Neil Postman, *The Disappearance of Childhood* (New York: Delacorte, 1982), p. 97.

31. For example, Kline, *Out of the Garden*, pp. 316–33.

32. Ibid., pp. 210–14.

33. Television Bureau of Advertising, "Target Selling the Children's Market," quoted in Kline, *Out of the Garden*, p. 18.

34. Ibid.; see also Schor, *Born to Buy*, pp. 24–25.

35. Discussed in Susan Linn, *Consuming Kids: Protecting Our Children from the Onslaught of Marketing and Advertising* (New York: Anchor, 2005), p. 197.

36. Kline, *Out of the Garden*, p. 147; Cross, *Kids' Stuff*, pp. 5–9, 188; Birgitta Almqvist, "Educational Toys, Creative Toys," in Jeffrey H. Goldstein, ed., *Toys, Play, and Child Development* (Cambridge: Cambridge University Press, 1994), p. 51; Schor, *Born to Buy*, p. 40; Susan Linn, *Consuming Kids: The Hostile Takeover of Childhood* (New York: New Press, 2004), p. 34. For more on the topic of "pestering," see Chapter 8.

37. Helen Boehm, "Toys and Games to Learn By," *Psychology Today* 23 (September 1989), p. 62.

38. Cross, *Kids' Stuff*, pp. 149–58; Linn, *Consuming Kids*, p. 39, 71; Kline, *Out of the Garden*, p. 170.

39. Cross, *Kids' Stuff*, p. 189.

40. Kline, *Out of the Garden*, pp. 265–70; Ilick, *American Childhood*, p. 120; Cross, *Kids' Stuff*, pp. 4, 171, 203; Bernard Mergen, "Made, Bought, and Stolen: Toys and the Culture of Childhood," in Elliott West and Paula Petrik, eds., *Small World: Children and Adolescence in America, 1850–1950* (Lawrence: University Press of Kansas, 1993), pp. 105–6.

41. Kline, *Out of the Garden*, p. 219.

42. Linn, *Consuming Kids*, p. 62.

43. Kline, *Out of the Garden*, pp. 253, 340–42; Almqvist, "Educational Toys, Creative Toys," p. 62; Bernard Mergen, *Play and Playthings: A Reference Guide* (Westport, Conn.: Greenwood, 1982), p. 106; Schor, *Born to Buy*, p. 44.

44. Kline, *Out of the Garden*, pp. 148, 280, 333–34. For more on unscripted styles of play, see Chapter 8.

45. W. D. Marbach, "A New Galaxy of Video Games," *Newsweek*, October 25, 1982, 123; Nancy Gibbs, "You Call These Toys?" *Time*, December 7, 1987, pp. 42–43; Cross, *Kids' Stuff*, p. 221; Eugene Provenzo Jr., "Electronically Mediated Playscapes," in Doris P. Fromberg and Doris Berger, eds., *Play from Birth to Twelve and Beyond* (New York: Garland, 1998), p. 515.

46. Provenzo, "Electronically Mediated Playscapes," p. 516.

47. Sherry Turkle, quoted in ibid., pp. 515–17.

48. Lynn Langway, "Video Games," *Newsweek,* August 9, 1976, p. 61; Steven Johnson, *Everything Bad Is Good for You: How Today's Popular Culture Is Actually Making Us Smarter* (New York: Riverside, 2005), pp. 42–47.

49. Quoted in Johnson, *Everything Bad Is Good for You,* p. 17.

50. Schor, *Born to Buy,* p. 138; Linn, *Consuming Kids,* p. 105.

51. Jean Armour Polly, review of "Stardoll.com (Paperdollheaven.com)," Family Website Reviews, Commonsense Media, 2006, http://www.common sensemedia.org/website-reviews/PaperdollHeaven.html (accessed March 2005).

52. Posted by aecdoglover, April 8, 2006, http://www.commonsense media.org/website-reviews/Neopets.html?show=adult (accessed March 2005).

53. "Background Information," document provided by American Girl, Middleton, Wisconsin; Alex Kuczynski, "A Dress-Up Doll for Retro Girls (Scram Barbie)," *New York Times,* December 20, 2005, p. E4.

54. "Background Information," American Girl.

55. Ibid.

56. Pleasant Rowland and Julie Sloane, "A New Twist on Timeless Toys," *Fortune Small Business,* October 1, 2002, http://money.cnn.com/magazines/fsb/fsb_archive/2002/10/01/330574/index.htm (accessed March 2005).

57. "Background Information," American Girl.

58. Letters published in *American Girl,* March/April 2005 and May/June 2005.

59. Private communication, December 4, 2005.

60. "FY99 Recalls and Corrective Actions for Toys and Children's Products," U.S. Consumer Product Safety Commission, Washington, D.C., November 18, 1999, http://www.cpsc.gov/BUSINFO/tcprec.pdf (accessed April 2005).

61. Brian Sutton-Smith, *Toys as Culture* (New York: Gardner, 1986), pp. 8–9.

62. Ibid., p. 9.

63. Linn, *Consuming Kids,* pp. 70–71.

64. Eda LeShan, "Are We Making Their Lives Too Full?" *New York Times,* August 7, 1960, p. 1.

65. Dixie Oliver, "Forget TV, Children, Let's Play," *Life* (September 1, 1967), p. 11.

66. Roland Barthes, *Mythologies* (London: Paladin, 1957), pp. 53–54.

67. Schor, *Born to Buy,* p. 173.

68. Lisa Morgan, quoted in Linn, *Consuming Kids,* pp. 64–65.

Notes to Chapter 7

1. Sydney Landensohn Stern and Ted Schoenbaum, *Toyland: The High Stakes Game of the Toy Industry* (New York: Contemporary Books, 1990), p. 23.

2. Quoted in Stephen Kline, *Out of the Garden: Toys, TV, and Children's Culture in the Age of Marketing* (London: Verso, 1993), p. 185.

3. Ibid., p. 172.

4. Annie Dillard, *An American Childhood* (New York: Harper and Row, 1987), p. 149.

5. For example, Helen B. Schwartzman, "Child-Structured Play," in Franklin E. Manning, *The World of Play* (New York: Leisure Press, 1983), p. 210; Gary Alan Fine, *With the Boys: Little League Baseball and Preadolescent Culture* (Chicago: University of Chicago Press, 1987), p. 60.

6. Bernard Mergen, *Play and Playthings: A Reference Guide* (Westport, Conn.: Greenwood, 1982), p. 98.

7. Laurence H. Reece, "The Play Needs of Children Aged 6 to 12," *Marriage and Family Living* 16 (May 1954), p. 131.

8. Amanda Dargan and Steven Zeitlin, "City Play," in Doris Fromberg and Doris Bergen, eds., *Play from Birth to Twelve and Beyond* (New York: Garland, 1998), p. 222.

9. Amanda Dargan and Steven Zeitlin, *City Play* (New Brunswick, N.J.: Rutgers University Press, 1990), p. 120.

10. Kate Simon, *Bronx Primitive: Portraits in a Childhood* (New York: Viking, 1982).

11. Dillard, *American Childhood*, pp. 123–24.

12. Don Fellman, quoted in Dargan and Zeitlin, *City Play*, pp. 81–82.

13. "The Games: Hit the Stick," Streetplay.com, 2006, http://www.streetplay.com/thegames/hitstick.htm (accessed April 2005).

14. Marcy Guddemi, Tom Jambor, and Robin Moore, "Advocacy for the Child's Right to Play," in Doris Fromberg and Doris Bergen, eds., *Play from Birth to Twelve and Beyond* (New York: Garland, 1998), p. 522.

15. Ibid., p. 521; Joe L. Frost and Irma C. Woods, "Perspectives on Play in Playgrounds," in Doris P. Fromberg and Doris Berger, eds., *Play from Birth to Twelve and Beyond* (New York: Garland, 1998), pp. 234–35.

16. Frost and Woods, "Perspectives on Play in Playgrounds," pp. 234–35.

17. Brian Sutton-Smith, "Does Play Prepare the Future?" in Jeffrey H. Goldstein, ed., *Toys, Play, and Child Development* (Cambridge: Cambridge University Press, 1994), p. 139.

18. Brian Sutton-Smith, *A History of Children's Play: New Zealand, 1940–1950* (Philadelphia: University of Pennsylvania Press, 1982), p. 288.

19. Sandra L. Hofferth and John F. Sandberg, "How American Children Spend Their Time," *Journal of Marriage and the Family* 63 (May 2001), p. 301. Hofferth and Sandberg found that older children watched more TV than did younger children. Those aged nine to twelve, they found, watched, on average, thirteen and a half hours of TV per week. Other researchers, however,

have suggested that preteen kids watch TV many more hours than what Hofferth and Sandberg identified.

20. Dargan and Zeitlin, *City Play*, pp. 169–70.

21. Brian Sutton-Smith, *Toys as Culture* (New York: Gardner, 1986), p. 11.

22. This viewpoint has been forcefully expressed by Kline, *Out of the Garden*, pp. 103–4.

23. Reinhold Reitberger and Wolfgang Fuchs, *Comics, Anatomy of a Mass Medium* (London: Studio Vista, 1972), cited in Kline, *Out of the Garden*, p. 100.

24. Kline, *Out of the Garden*, pp. 100–103.

25. Frederick Wertham, *The Seduction of the Innocent* (New York: Rinehart, 1953). See also James B. Gilbert, *A Cycle of Outrage: America's Reaction to the Juvenile Delinquent in the 1950s* (New York: Oxford University Press, 1986), p. 97; Mintz, *Huck's Raft*, p. 292.

26. For a concise history of comic books, see "The Comic Page," 1995–1998, http://www.dereksantos.com/comicpage/comicpage.html (accessed February 2005).

27. Kline, *Out of the Garden*, pp. 184–86; Juliet Schor, *Born to Buy: The Commercialized Child and the New Consumer Culture* (New York: Scribner, 2004), pp. 50, 69, 106–12.

28. Quoted in Kline, *Out of the Garden*, p. 184; see also pp. 170–74, and Penelope Leach, "Introduction," in Susan Linn, *Consuming Kids: The Hostile Takeover of Childhood* (New York: New Press, 2004), p. x.

29. *Discount Store News*, September 20, 1999.

30. Cheryl Idell, "MarketResearch: C'mon, Mom! Kids Nag Parents to Chuck E. Cheese's," *Selling to Kids*, May 12, 1999, http://www.findarticles.com/p/articles/mi_m0FVE/is_9_4/ai_54631243 (accessed July 2005).

31. Discussed in Schor, *Born to Buy*, p. 54.

32. Kline, *Out of the Garden*, pp. 182–83.

33. James U. McNeal, "Tapping the Three Kids' Markets," *American Demographics* 20 (1998), pp. 37–41.

34. Gary Cross, *Kids' Stuff: Toys and the Changing World of American Childhood* (Cambridge, Mass.: Harvard University Press, 1997), pp. 171, 238. See also Cross, *The Cute and the Cool: Wondrous Innocence and Modern American Children's Culture* (New York: Oxford University Press, 2004), pp. 154–55; Kline, *Out of the Garden*, p. 99.

35. Mergen, *Play and Playthings*, p. 119; Mergen, "Made, Bought, and Stolen: Toys and the Culture of Childhood," in Elliott West and Paula Petrik, eds., *Small World: Children and Adolescents in America, 1850–1950* (Lawrence: University Press of Kansas, 1992), p. 89.

36. Janice Beran, "Attitudes of Iowa Children toward Play," in Helen Schwartzman, ed., *Play and Culture* (West Point, N.Y.: Leisure Press, 1980), 187–98.

37. Miriam Formanek-Brunell, *Made to Play House: Dolls and the Commercialization of American Girlhood, 1830–1930* (New Haven, Conn.: Yale University Press, 1993), p. 188; Alex Kuczynski, "A Dress-up Doll for Retro Girls (Scram, Barbie)," *New York Times*, December 29, 2005, p. E4.

38. Sutton-Smith, *Toys as Culture*, p. 189; Kline, *Out of the Garden*, pp. 210, 326; Jerome L. Singer and Dorothy G. Singer, *Television, Imagination, and Aggression: A Study of Preschoolers* (Hillsdale, N.J.: Erlbaum, 1981), p. 37.

39. John Skow, "Those Beeping, Thinking Toys," *Time*, December 10, 1979, pp. 86–88.

40. Gary Selnow, "The Fall and Rise of Video Games," *Journal of Popular Culture* 21 (1988), pp. 53–60; Cross, *Cute and the Cool*, p. 177; Jeffrey H. Goldstein, "Sex Differences in Toy Play and Use of Video Games," in Jeffrey H. Goldstein, ed., *Toys, Play, and Child Development* (Cambridge: Cambridge University Press, 1994), pp. 117–22.

41. Steven Johnson, *Everything Bad Is Good for You: How Today's Popular Culture Is Actually Making Us Smarter* (New York: Riverside Books, 2005), p. 41.

42. Goldstein, "Sex Differences in Toy Play," pp. 119–22.

43. Sutton-Smith, *Toys as Culture*, pp. 11, 252,

44. Susan Robben, "We Made Blood Sisters," in Josef Berger and Dorothy Berger, eds., *Small Voices* (New York: Paul S. Ericksson, 1966), p. 202.

45. Brian Sullivan, described in "It's Scary Sometimes, but a Lot of Fun," *Life* (November 17, 1972), pp. 74–75.

46. Hofferth and Sandberg, "How American Children Spend Their Time," p. 301 and table 1.

47. Schwartzman, "Child-Structured Play," pp. 206–7; Leona Tyler, "The Development of 'Vocational Interests': I. The Organization of Likes and Dislikes in Ten-Year-Old Children," *Journal of Genetic Psychology* 86 (1955), pp. 33–44; Simon, *Bronx Primitive*, p. 50; Maria Cuca, "Some Day We Shall Conquer War and Sadness," in Josef Berger and Dorothy Berger, eds., *Small Voices* (New York: Paul S. Ericksson, 1966), p. 87; Dillard, *American Childhood*, p. 90.

48. Linda Wharton-Boyd, "The Significance of Black American Children's Singing Games in an Educational Setting," *Journal of Negro Education* 52 (Winter 1983), p. 46; Brian Sutton-Smith, "The Play of Girls," in Claire B. Kopp, ed., *Becoming Female: Perspectives on Development* (New York: Plenum, 1979), pp. 249–50; Dargan and Zeitlin, *City Play*, p. 221.

49. Rick Telander, *Heaven Is a Playground* (Lincoln: University of Nebraska Press, 1995); Peter Alfano, "Two Students of the City Game," *New York Times*, March 3, 1983, p. B15; Steve Popper, "Raves at a Rucker Tournament Are Reserved for Boy Wonders," *New York Times*, August 6, 2001, p. D5.

50. For more on paperdollheaven.com and the other websites, see Chapter 7.

51. Kline, *Out of the Garden*, pp. 192, 246–47. See also Vivian Gussin Paley, "Superheroes in the Dollhouse," *Natural History* (March 1985), pp. 20–25.

52. Simon, *Bronx Primitive*, pp. 152–54.

53. Dillard, *American Childhood*, pp. 45, 97.

54. B. G. Rosenberg and Brian Sutton-Smith, "A Revised Conception of Masculine-Feminine Differences in Play Activities," *Journal of Genetic Psychology* 96 (1960), pp. 165–70.

55. Sutton-Smith, "Play of Girls," pp. 233, 250–51.

56. Brian Sutton-Smith, "Ambivalence in Toyland," *Natural History* (December 1985), p. 8.

57. On Piaget and others, see Anthony D. Pellegrini and Ithel Jones, "Play, Toys, and Language," in Jeffrey H. Goldstein, ed., *Toys, Play, and Child Development* (Cambridge: Cambridge University Press, 1994), pp. 38–39.

58. Sutton-Smith, "Ambivalence in Toyland," p. 8.

59. Ann Hulbert, "Tweens 'R' Us," *New York Times Magazine*, November 28, 2004, pp. 31–32.

60. Frances Horwich, "Don't Rob Them of Their Childhood," *Today's Education* 54 (February 1954), pp. 14–15.

61. Dorothy Barclay, "Children's Hour—Adults Keep Out," *New York Times Magazine*, September 17, 1961, p. 86.

62. Bernard Mergen, "The Discovery of Children's Play," *American Quarterly* 27 (October 1975), p. 418.

63. Peter Opie and Ilona Opie, *Children's Games in Street and Playground: Chasing, Catching, Seeking, Hunting, Racing, Duelling, Exerting, Daring, Guessing, Acting, Pretending* (Oxford: Clarendon, 1969), p. 16.

64. Eli Bower, "Play's the Thing," *Today's Education* 57 (September 1968), p. 10.

65. Sylvia Knopp Polgar, "The Social Context of Games: Or When Is Play Not Play?" *Sociology of Education* 49 (October 1976), pp. 265–71.

66. Alvin Schwartz, "Play Is Child's Work," *Parent's Magazine* (November 1963), pp. 74–75.

67. National Center for Education Statistics, *Digest of Education Statistics, 2003* (Washington, D.C.: NCES, 2004), p. 205, table 167.

68. Ibid.

69. U.S. Census Bureau, *Statistical Abstract of the United States, 2004–2005* (Washington, D.C.: Government Printing Office, 2005), p. 147, table 224.

70. Ibid., p. 135, table 202.

71. Ibid., p. 151, table 229.

72. Robben, "We Made Blood Sisters," p. 203.

73. Dargan and Zeitlin, *City Play*, p. 162; Opie and Opie, *Children's Games in Street and Playground*, p. 11; "It's Scary Sometimes, but a Lot of Fun," pp. 74–75.

74. Simon, *Bronx Primitive*, pp. 4–5.

75. Dillard, *American Childhood*, p. 43.

76. An overview of "illicit" play in the school setting can be found in Greta C. Fein and Nancy W. Wiltz, "Play as Children See It," in Doris Fromberg and Doris Bergen, eds., *Play from Birth to Twelve and Beyond* (New York: Garland, 1998), p. 43.

77. Marilyn Bell, "Have I Been Busy This Year! Whew!," in Josef Berger and Dorothy Berger, eds., *Small Voices* (New York: Paul S. Ericksson, 1966), p. 236.

78. Tom Jambor, "Challenge and Risk-Taking in Play," in Doris Fromberg and Doris Bergen, eds., *Play from Birth to Twelve and Beyond* (New York: Garland, 1998), p. 322; Guddemi, Jambor, and Moore, "Advocacy for the Child's Right to Play," p. 322.

79. Guddemi, Jambor, and Moore, "Advocacy for the Child's Right to Play," p. 319.

80. National Association of Early Childhood, "Recess and the Importance of Play: A Position Paper on Young Children and Recess," 2002, http://naecs .crc.uiuc.edu/position/recessplay.html (accessed March 2005).

81. Guddemi, Jambor, and Moore, "Advocacy for the Child's Right to Play," pp. 521–22.

82. Sutton-Smith, "Does Play Prepare the Future?" p. 146.

83. "About Us," Kid Power Xchange, 2006, http://www.iqpc.com/cgi-bin/templates/document.html?topic=445&document=33098 (accessed April 2005).

84. Chris McKee, quoted in Jon Gertner, "Hey, Mom, Is It OK if These Guys Market Stuff to Me?" *New York Times Magazine*, November 28, 2004, p. 103. See also Lisa Jacobson, *Raising Consumers: Children and the American Mass Market in the Early Twentieth Century* (New York: Columbia University Press, 2005).

85. Cross, *Cute and the Cool*, p. 177.

86. Among the most recent critiques of the commercialization of children's culture are Schor, *Born to Buy*, and Linn, *Consuming Kids*. See also Kline, *Out of the Garden*, p. 327, and Sutton-Smith, *Toys as Culture*.

87. Cross, *Kids' Stuff*, p. 235; Kline, *Out of the Garden*, p. 44.

88. Isabel Alvarez, quoted in Dargan and Zeitlin, *City Play,*, p. 121.

Notes to the Conclusion

1. "Figure 1, Prevalence of Overweight Among Children and Adolescents Ages 6 to 19 Years," CDC/NCH3, NHES, and NHANES, n.d., http://www .cdc.gov/nchs/products/pubs/pubd/hestats/overfig1.GIF (accessed October 2006). See also National Association of School Nurses, "Position Statement:

Overweight Children and Adolescents," adopted June 2002, http://www.nasn .org/Default.aspx?tabid=236 (accessed June 2005).

2. "Rediscovering Playtime," *Time*, June 6, 2005, pp. 56–57.

3. Peter Applebome, "How We Took the Child Out of Childhood," *New York Times*, January 8, 2006, p. I.21; Michael D. Lemonick, "America's Youth Are in Worse Shape Than Ever, but There's a Movement Afoot to Remedy That," *Time*, June 6, 2005, pp. 56–58.

4. For example, Neil Postman, *The Disappearance of Childhood* (New York: Delacorte, 1982).

5. See Chapters 3 and 4.

6. See Chapters 5 and 7.

7. Gary Cross, *Kids' Stuff: Toys and the Changing World of American Childhood* (Cambridge, Mass.: Harvard University Press, 1997), p. vi.

8. Juliet Schor, *Born to Buy: The Commercialized Child and the New Consumer Culture* (New York: Scribner, 2004), p. 56.

9. Susan Linn, *Consuming Kids: The Hostile Takeover of Childhood* (New York: Free Press, 2004), pp. 111, 132.

10. Benedict Carey, "Babes in a Grown-up Toyland," *New York Times*, November 28, 2004.

11. See Chapters 3 and 4.

12. Applebome, "How We Took the Child Out of Childhood." See Chapter 5.

13. See Chapter 6.

14. Sandra L. Hofferth and John F. Sandberg, "How American Children Spend Their Time," *Journal of Marriage and the Family* 63 (May 2001), pp. 295–308.

15. See Chapter 3.

16. John Updike, "Mixed Messages," *New Yorker*, March 14, 2005, p. 138.

17. See Chapter 6.

18. See Chapters 3, 4, and 6.

19. Robert Paul Smith, *"Where Did You Go?" "Out" "What Did You Do?" "Nothing"* (New York: W. W. Norton, 1957), pp. 40–41. See Chapter 4.

20. See Chapter 8.

21. See Chapters 7 and 8.

22. See Chapter 3.

23. See Chapter 4.

24. See Chapter 6.

25. Neil Postman, *The Disappearance of Childhood* (New York: Delacorte, 1982); Susan Recchia, quoted in Julian E. Barnes, "Where Did You Go, Raggedy Ann? Toys in the Age of Electronics," *New York Times*, February 10, 2001, pp. C1–2.

26. Recchia, quoted in Barnes, "Where Did You Go, Raggedy Ann?," p. C1.

27. Marie Winn, *The Plug-in Drug* (New York: Viking, 1985), quoted in Stephen Kline, *Out of the Garden: Toys and Children's Culture in the Age of TV Marketing* (London: Verso, 1993), p. 79.

28. Melissa Fay Greene, "Sandlot Summer: Hyperscheduled, Overachieving Children Learn How to Play," *New York Times Magazine*, November 28, 2004, p. 40.

29. Marcy Guddemi, Tom Jambor, and Robin Moore, "Advocacy for the Child's Right to Play," in Doris Fromberg and Doris Bergen, eds., *Play from Birth to Twelve and Beyond* (New York: Garland, 1998), p. 520.

30. Gary Cross, *The Cute and the Cool: Wondrous Innocence and Modern American Children's Culture* (New York: Oxford University Press, 2004), p. 203; Linn, *Consuming Kids*, p. 15.

31. Bruce Weber, "A Fierce Investment, in Skates and Family Time," *New York Times*, January 16, 2005, p. 1.1.

32. Smith, *"Where Did You Go?"* pp. 1213–24.

Index

(page number)

28, 31, 32, 35, 38, 43, 52–53, 57, 59, 62, 71, 80, 87–88

Jambor, Tom, 209–10
Johnson, George Ellsworth, 68, 109–10
Johnson, Steven, 197

"Kid Power," 211–12
Kids Sports Network, 2
Kline, Stephen, xiv, 167, 170, 171, 191, 192, 195, 203
Kraus-Boelte, Maria, 68, 218

Lee, Joseph, 112
Lehman, Harvey C., 98, 106, 123
Linn, Susan, 169, 179
Little League baseball, 2, 15, 115–16, 164, 206, 215
Little Orphan Annie, 190
Locke, John, 26–27, 34, 40, 67, 103
Louis Marx and Company, 155

Macleod, David, 119
Main, Gloria, 23
Mann, Horace, 45
Mather, Cotton, 22, 24–25, 165
Mattel Toy Company, 155–58, 162, 168, 169, 177
McGhee, Zacharia, 92–93
McKee, Chris, 211
McNeal, James U., 195
Media, mass, 8, 158, 168, 171–72, 195, 217, 221
Mergen, Bernard, xiv
Methodist Church of America, 26
Mickey Mouse, 120, 124
Mickey Mouse Club, 154–55
Mid-Atlantic region, 20, 23, 27
millsberry.com, 176, 201–2
Milton Bradley Company, 117, 183
Mintz, Steven, xiv, 64, 165
Mischief, 93–95, 127, 152, 208
Moore, Robin, 210
Mott, Frank Luther, 76, 77
Movies, 102, 170–72, 173, 181, 190
myspace.com, 200

Neopets, 175–76
New England, 19, 20–21, 24, 94
Newell, William Wells, 15–16, 73, 92, 95

Newspapers, children's amateur, 56
Newton, Douglas, 11
Nickelodeon, 167
Nintendo, 173, 195

Obesity, childhood, 214
Opie, Ilona and Peter, 16–17, 205–6, 208
Optic, Oliver. *See* Adams, William Taylor

paperdollheaven.com, 175, 202
Parker Brothers, 117
Peers, 6, 11, 14, 15, 35, 58–59, 69, 70–71, 73, 86–90, 93–95, 100, 147–50, 161–62, 189, 195, 198–99, 204
Perlstein, Linda, xv
"Pester power," 169, 183, 194
Peter Pan, 124, 154
Piaget, Jean, 14, 204, 212
Play: boys', 9–10, 11–12, 24, 28, 30, 31, 33, 35, 37–38, 46, 52–53, 53–54, 55, 59, 64, 80, 83, 87–88, 92–93, 108–9, 113, 117–19, 124, 137–38, 143–46, 170, 171–72, 174–75, 200–204; conflict with adults over, 5–6, 13–17, 19, 28, 37, 38, 39, 40–41, 61–66, 69, 96–97, 99, 100–101, 108–11, 133–34, 143–44, 151–53, 207–9; definitions of, xii, 1–3; environment, 3, 4–6, 28–32, 49–54, 73, 78–82, 107–11, 128–35, 184–89, 199, 210, 215–16; gender-integrated, 59, 60, 89–90, 145–46, 203; girls', 9–10, 11–12, 24, 28, 30, 33, 35, 37–38, 46, 53, 55, 59, 80, 83, 88–89, 92–93, 113, 117–18, 124, 132–33, 136–37, 138–42, 143, 146–47, 170–72, 175–79, 200–204; indoor, 29, 31–32, 49–50, 52, 81–82, 118–19, 134–35, 142, 171, 185, 188–89, 218, 222; organized, 46, 48, 57–58, 61, 68, 74, 98, 100, 106, 110–16, 164–65, 189, 199, 205–7, 212, 218, 223; outdoor, 29–31, 50–54, 78–81, 128–34, 173, 185–88, 189; "parallel," 202; racially integrated, 60, 64–65, 148; solitary, 11, 50, 57, 79, 86–87, 106, 118–20, 123, 129, 148–49, 160–61, 199–200, 204; unstructured, improvised, 2, 13–18, 19, 26, 27, 32, 49–55, 63–65, 69, 72, 84–85, 92–95, 96–97, 99, 126–53, 185–87, 189, 199, 205–11
"Play value," 182–83, 189–98
Playground Association of America, 112, 114

About the Author

HOWARD P. CHUDACOFF is George L. Littlefield Professor of American History and Professor of Urban Studies at Brown University, Providence, Rhode Island. His recent books include *How Old Are You? Age Consciousness in American Culture* and *The Age of the Bachelor: Creating an American Subculture.*